The Garden of the Soul

Soul

lessons from four flowers That Unearth the Self

LYNN SERAFINN

Give-Receive-Become-Be Publications
www.give-receive-become-be.com

April 2009

Dear Lindy —

May your garden be always full of beautiful flowers

Warm Wishes

Lynn

P.S. Thanks for the healing! xxx

A Bright Pen Book

Copyright Lynn Serafinn © 2009

Cover mandala painted by special commission by Kristina Berglund
www.principlesofvedicart.wordpress.com

Flower drawings by Christine Brown

Author's photograph by Andy Adams
www.andyadamsphotography.com

ISBN 978 0 7552 1126 5

Bright Pen is an imprint of
Authors On Line Ltd.
19 The Cinques
Gamlingay, Sandy
Bedfordshire SG19 3NU
England

Bright Pen

This book is also available in e-book format, details of which are available at www.authorsonline.co.uk

Praise for The Garden of the Soul

'Lynn beautifully weaves together fable and poetry with her personal journey of self-discovery. Through her lyrical style and brilliant imagination, she leads the reader on a magical adventure toward deeper understanding of the relationship between Self and the world.'
--Alan Seale, transformation coach
Author of *Soul Mission, Life Vision* and *The Manifestation Wheel*
Rochester, New York

'The Garden of the Soul is rich in teaching metaphors that speak to each of us...Lynn is a brilliant and creative out-of-the-box thinker. Her impact is powerful...and her magic comes through each page of this book...a message that is both simple and profound. Open up and receive her words and they will affect you in a most positive way.'
--Patrick Ryan, coach
Author of *The Eagle's Call*
Founder www.AwakenedWisdom.com
Vancouver, Canada

'As spiritual as the works of Deepak Chopra, and as magical as the novels of Paolo Coelho... Lynn is a master at beautifully and coherently weaving together prose and poetry, autobiography and fiction, fantasy and realism, drama and humour...This is a book I will be going back to again and again as a very powerful spiritual reference book that is infinitely entertaining, moving and engaging...I absolutely love it!'
--Lina Nahhas, social researcher
Founder of '1 Urban Humanity' for the Middle East
Dubai, UAE

'Wonderful! 10 out of 10! An epic journey...engaging, intimate, open and profound...Keep this book on your bookshelf right next to "Chicken Soup for the Soul".'
--Simon Ireland-Davies, executive coach

Director of ID Coaching Limited
Liverpool, England

'I was moved to tears—good ones—and put into a spiritual mood...It's a story I would love to retell and share! This book will help you discover your Soul has a voice...learn how to treasure and leverage your natural spirit...and be inspired to appreciate...the power of honouring your own nature.'
--Gail Sussman Miller, speaker, coach, teacher and writer
Inspired Choice, www.inspiredchoice.com
Chicago, Illinois, USA

'Lynn's gift for expressing herself through the written word is very clear. She has a fine sensibility for language...courageous and fascinating.... a considerable achievement.'
--Derek Hassack, coach, educational consultant and writer
LionHeart Coaching and Consulting
London, UK

'The Garden of the Soul helps you realise that you already have all the wisdom you need, and the answers to all your questions are to be found when you look inwards.'
--Fran Stockley, nutritional therapist and coach
Herfordshire, UK

'The Garden of the Soul provides compelling and sensitive insights about life, change and the beauty of the human spirit.'
--Susan Norton, CPCC
Designing Your Life Coaching
Massachusetts, USA

'Lynn has the gift of unfolding truths through the power and poetry of deceptively simple stories that resonate long after they are read.'
--Antony Parry, writing coach
Coach Words
London, UK

Table of Contents

Introduction:
Entering the Garden

ENTERING THE GARDEN

*Y*ou are already the hero of your own life. You did not earn this title. You did not have to. You were born the hero. It is your birthright. If you do not take up your birthright, no one else will do it for you. If you leave it unclaimed, the universe will remain bereft of something it passionately desires. The world will continue to long for that which only you can fulfil. It will dream of you again and again. It will call to you repeatedly. It will cry for you.

Then, one day, in this lifetime or the next, or the next after that, you will finally take up the path of least resistance to the Self, and simply become the person you were always meant to be. And on that day, ever so easily, you will see that you were always the hero of this story— your story—and that all you ever needed in order to be the hero, was to look within the simple stories of your own life.

This was the message I brought to a group of young entrepreneurs in South Africa when I delivered a workshop on the four principles 'Give-Receive-Become-Be' for the very first time. While I never stood up and read these exact words, throughout the course of the workshop, this message emerged organically. At the end of the workshop, several of the entrepreneurs came and told me and my co-leader that the four principles had enabled them to see just how powerful and important their lives already were. Some of the attendees even told us the experience had actually changed their lives. When I heard how profoundly this message had impacted them, I was astonished. The book was not even finished. This was the first time I had ever shared these principles with the public, and I had no idea whether I could translate my own spiritual model, which was still evolving, into something meaningful within a workshop setting. Of course, I was pleased that the principles themselves had blossomed so naturally and easily, months before the book was even published, but more than that, I began to realise how key this very process of natural unfolding has been to the writing of this book itself.

'Organically' is the word I would use to the way this book has grown since its inception. I didn't originally plan to write a book. I never sat down and decided I was going to define a set of spiritual principles. I never even thought I had a message to give to the world. All I knew was that I loved to write. I had written poetry since I was a teenager, but had lost connection with my poetic voice for many decades. Then, one day in 2003, a totally random comment a friend made sparked the entire story of 'The Very Good King,' which is now the prologue of this book and the foundation for all that follows. After years of poetic silence, I wrote that story in a single sitting. When that story came to me, it was more like 'listening' than writing. I 'heard' it and simply wrote it down, and just could not stop writing until the story itself decided to end. This, I discovered, was to become the primary method of my creative receptivity.

I found it extremely odd that 'The Very Good King' took the form of a fairytale. I had never written in such a style before. I knew, of course, that the story was full of metaphors that even I myself did not fully understand. I could sense that the Four Flowers in the story represented some lost parts of myself, but I couldn't quite put my finger on exactly what these parts were. I just knew that, taken together, these were the parts of me that longed to speak to the world, but I had no idea what they wanted to say. And this is what the story of 'The Very Good King' tells—the process of going from voicelessness to complete freedom of expression. And so, in a kind of lovely artistic irony, that story which itself is about finding one's voice, also began my own journey towards finding and claiming my authenticity.

But being able to 'hear' a whole story wasn't something that happened every day. Sometimes I would go for months without writing. But over time, the spirit to write came more and more frequently. I wrote dozens of short stories, all very different from each other with no seeming connection. At this point, I started to dream about what it would be like to have written a book, but still I could not imagine what I possibly had to say to the world. I went for four more years like this, and throughout that time, 'The Very Good King' seemed so unlike anything else I was writing, that I simply put it aside as a nice little piece that had no real purpose in the 'real world.' But my life was changing radically during those four years. I didn't realise that 'The Very Good King' had taken root in my Garden, and that the book was already growing, even without my awareness of it.

Just as we wake one day in early spring to find that our garden is sprouting new life without our intervention, as I lay asleep in bed one morning in March 2007, I suddenly 'heard' what my book was about. I sat up excitedly and shouted, 'Of course! That's it!' And in one flash of insight, vision or whatever you want to call it, I saw the Four Flowers and the Four Principles. I saw the attributes of the Four Principles. I saw how all the stories were linked. I saw how 'The Very Good King' was actually the seed of all the other ideas. I saw how it was all to be structured. Suddenly, I saw my book. But even though I now could see what the book would look like, I was still fairly clueless as to what the actual message of the book would be.

Fuelled by the vision of an actual book, I now began to write almost daily. I started writing longer and longer stories. The Flowers became more and more powerful, both within the book, and within my own life. Characters started to emerge, like Crow in 'Learning to Breathe.' That story began when an actual living crow did come to my window and wake me one morning that summer in 2007. His unexpected appearance sent me into a deep state of reverie in which I went on all the journeys in 'Learning to Breathe,' with Crow as my 'spirit guide.' As I started to write that story, Crow took on a complete character of his own, and I developed a magical relationship with him as I wrote.

Meeting Crow was a turning point in my writing because suddenly I was no longer just writing stories—I was having dialogues with the characters. This became the next phase for my creative process in writing this book, and it changed the book completely. Now, everything within the book, whether it was Crow, the Four Flowers or any number of other entities, all had their own voice. The metaphors popped out of the pages and spoke their own truths. They wove in and out of each other without my trying, just like climbing jasmine and passionflower. I learned how to sit down and let the *characters* direct the stories as I was writing them.

And these dialogues were just as organic as the Garden from which they sprang. I had no plan for them, and no control over their outcome. I simply spoke with the characters and wrote our conversations down. Sometimes the characters would ask me really challenging questions and I found myself wondering, *Now how the heck am I supposed to answer that?* Sometimes I had to stop writing when one of them asked me a particularly difficult question. I remember this happening when the Iris got me into a tight situation in a discussion about Time and Space. My first impulse was to tell her off saying, 'Who do you think I am—Einstein?' But instead of arguing with the Iris, instead of editing or deleting the question, as I might have done if I had been attached to being in control, I went away and meditated on the question instead, and came back later with my reply. This approach enabled me to take the reader into my own process of spiritual unfolding.

This method of dialogue, yet again another organically grown innovation, started to make the stories come alive in a way they had not been before. And the more alive the stories became, the more and more radically they began to depart from the original idea of the book. Eventually all of the original stories save two—'The Very Good King' and 'Message on the Bridge'—were deleted from the book altogether because they no longer matched the emerging tone, style, structure and theme. Just like seeds that break and dissolve away into the earth as the flowers start to reach for the sun, these old stories simply disappeared from the book, as they were no longer needed.

But still, even at that point, whenever people asked me to tell them something about the book—especially about its message—I frequently found myself at a total loss for words. Of course I found it quite ironic considering how much I love to use words. I fumbled over whether to call it a work of fiction or non-fiction. I fumbled over what genre it was or other kinds of books I might liken it to. I even fumbled over trying to describe what the book was all about.

But at last today, after setting aside all the fumbling, apologising and excuse making, I finally have an organically grown, free-range working description for the book you are about to read—

The Garden of the Soul is a story about becoming whole. It is a book that dances freely on both sides of the bridge between fiction and non-fiction, to illustrate the unearthing of the human spirit, using autobiography, dream work, poetry and metaphor. It is a journey on the 'path of least resistance to the Self' using the metaphor of Four Flowers that represent four spiritual principles that bring wholeness to the Self: 'Give' (the Rose), 'Receive' (the Iris), 'Become' (the Daffodil) and 'Be' (the Lily). It is an open invitation to readers to explore how they are already the heroes of their own lives.

And thus, the whole creative process of this book has been one of organic gardening, in which all living things were allowed to gestate, grow and blossom naturally, all in their own time.

I cannot stress the word 'metaphor' enough when speaking about this book. There is hardly a syllable of the book that is not metaphoric. **The Garden** is itself the primary metaphor, representing the Self, or the harmony of awareness between body, mind and spirit.

The Four Flowers—Rose, Iris, Daffodil and Lily—are four dynamic spiritual principles: Give, Receive, Become and Be. I say 'dynamic' because when these principles are allowed to manifest naturally, we feel fully alive. Life has meaning and purpose. Joy comes easily to us. We are balanced, fulfilled and 'in flow.'

The Four Principles themselves are also metaphoric in that they mean far more than the simple words might imply. **Giving** is the principle of all that comes from within us, and goes out

7

into the world. **Receiving** is the principle of all that comes from the world, and goes into us. There can be no giving without receiving. Life is a continual balance between the two. Our eating and our breathing are but two manifestations of the balance between the principles of Giving and Receiving. Even though it is commonly said, 'Tis better to give than to receive,' in actuality, there is no hierarchy between them. In their natural state, they are completely balanced and eternally interdependent. When we experience the natural balance between giving and receiving in our lives, we are in *harmony with the rest of the world.*

Similarly, we are simultaneously in a state of flow that is both becoming and being. **Becoming** is the principle of continuous change within us. **Being** is the principle of changelessness within us. Our 'Being' is immutable and continuous. We are always in a state of Being. But at the same time, we are at every moment evolving and growing, always born and reborn throughout our lives. Being and Becoming work together like a river. The river is always the river, but its waters are continuously shifting, swirling and gushing. Thus, it is always the same, but it is also always changing. You cannot say that one is more a part of the river's essence than the other. Both are equally present in its nature. In our own lives, we can see that without Being we have no sense of identity or Self; without Becoming we have no sense of aliveness or joy. Like Giving and Receiving, Being and Becoming are also eternally interdependent. When Being and Becoming are balanced, we are in *harmony within our own selves.*

Taken together, these Four Principles create a fluid model for spiritual balance and fulfilment in our lives. In the book, this is represented by the image of the **Mandala,** or meditational icon, comprised of many interwoven patterns of brilliant colours, representing the Four Principles, enclosed in a ring of vibrant green, representing the Garden itself—the Garden of the Soul.

At a deeper level, we can see the more subtle ways in which the principles work together. Two of the principles (Giving and

Becoming) are outward reaching and expansive, while the two others (Receiving and Being) are inward reaching and deepening. Two of the principles (Giving and Receiving) create a conduit for knowing the world, while the two others (Becoming and Being) create a conduit for knowing the Self. Two of the principles (Giving and Being) are the means of expressing the Self in the continuous state of Now, while the two others (Becoming and Receiving) are the means of expressing the unlimited and unknown possibilities for that Self.

But here is where my discussion about the metaphors in the book will end. If I tell you more, it would undermine the organic process in which you, as the reader, are about to engage. Metaphors can and do and *must* be allowed to grow naturally and take on a life of their own if they are to have any impact. I believe it is not actually ethical, effective or artistic for an artist to explain their metaphors to an audience. A few months before this book was finished, I read the story 'The Very Good King' at an art gallery here in Bedford, England. After the reading, a woman from the audience very excitedly came up to ask me whether I had intended to put what she identified as Biblical references in the story. I told her that, no, I had not intentionally put any Biblical metaphors or references in the story. But she quoted some Bible verses, and compared them to parts of my story, and was quite insistent that I must have thought of them, even if unconsciously, when I wrote 'The Very Good King.' At first, I wasn't quite sure where this conversation would lead, but inspired by her passionate enthusiasm, I took out a page from my unfinished manuscript and read her this piece, which I call my 'Artist's Manifesto':

An artist is a person who has awakened
to the thrilling realisation
that the real meaning of what he creates
can only manifest via the multicoloured perspectives
of those other than himself.

In this state of being,
he releases his vision,
unattached to its destination.

Until that moment,
he is not yet an artist,
but a dreamer.

The true beauty of his art takes birth
in the things others see in it
that he does not.

I said to her, 'So, you see, it doesn't matter whether I put those symbols in intentionally, unintentionally or not at all. This is art. If you see it there, then it is there. If I told you that what you were seeing was not present in the story, then I would not be an artist.' She seemed very pleased by this answer. The manifesto gave each of us a tremendous amount of freedom to see, to experience and to understand Truth in our own way, and for both of us to be 'right,' even if it appears to the onlooker that our viewpoints are not at all the same.

This is the essential point I wish to make. Creation is not, and never is, a one-way act. Creation can only fully manifest when it is given away and received by another. It can only fulfil its destiny when that which is created becomes something more than it was when it first came to be. And so, art is by its very nature a complete manifestation of Give-Receive-Become-Be— the Four Principles in *The Garden of the Soul*.

And this, dear reader, is the beauty and the power of Give-Receive-Become-Be. I am giving this book to you, and you are receiving it. You are giving back to me what you will inevitably see within its pages that I do not, and I am receiving that. And through this process, while the work I have written does not change, it becomes something far greater every time it is read. And thus, this book itself is the Garden, and we are growing it together, you and I.

So now, I release my vision to you, unattached to its destination. You will decide what this book is really about. You will decide what the metaphors actually mean. And if you think you see something within these words, know with confidence that it is indeed there. And in this way, you are also the author of this book. Together we will write our stories. Together we will meet the heroes of our own lives.

And if you ever doubt your own understanding of the Four Flowers, as I once did, just let go of needing to figure it out, and trust what the Flowers repeatedly tell us throughout the pages of this book—

'Oh, but there is much you already know!
Just look 'round your own Garden to see what is already there.'

It is only within your own Garden that you will find the Four Flowers; only there will you find the hero who is calling them forth to blossom.

With blessings,
Lynn Serafinn
3 July 2008

* * * * *

Guide to the Four Flowers

Flower	Principle	Attributes and characteristics
Rose	**Giving**	Sensuality, love, passion, drive, energy, loyalty, bravery, action, boldness, direction, vitality, achievement, expressiveness, emotiveness, confidence, generosity, life purpose, authenticity
Iris	**Receiving**	Beauty, elegance, taste, refinement, attraction, poise, aesthetics, artistry, uniqueness, excellence, relishing, allowing, appreciation, abundance, cherishing, heartfelt thankfulness
Daffodil	**Becoming**	Joy, curiosity, play, creativity, laughter, fun, growth, spontaneity, silliness, discovery, youth, freshness, exploration, innovation, inspiration, rebirth, regeneration, newness, delight imagination, eccentricity
Lily	**Being**	Serenity, peace, tranquillity, satisfaction, wisdom, patience, smiling, compassion, bliss, understanding, reflection, wholeness, intuition, maturity, self-awareness, spirituality, continuity, acceptance, non-attachment

Prologue:
The Very Good King

THE VERY GOOD KING

Long ago, in a faraway land, there was a Meadow full of beautiful flowers. They lived there peacefully and gracefully, warmed by the passion of the Sun and cooled by the kiss of the Moon. Throughout their blissful lives, they felt the touch of soft gentle Breezes, the nourishment of soothing Rains and the protection of the firmness of the Earth, who kept them safe within her embrace. The rhythms of life within this Meadow pulsed to the tempo of the seasons, to the ancient dance between Earth, Sun and Moon. This enduring tempo gave the little flowers much comfort, as they danced in great delight year in and year out, feeling what it meant to be alive.

But then one day, a change in the tempo of life came upon them quite unexpectedly. A new entity entered their Meadow, someone quite hostile and strange. This entity resembled, a bit, their sweet friend the soft Wind, but he was not at all friendly. He spun around and around like some strange sort of top, and he laughed at the little flowers.

'I am going to grab you! Grab you all!' he laughed aloud. And he spun faster and faster.

The little flowers shuddered. This was not friendly at all. It was very confusing to them. They had never seen such a strange being before.

The Wind Demon came closer and closer. His feverish laughter seemed sinister as he approached them. Suddenly, the little flowers felt fear for the very first time in their idyllic lives.

What to do? they thought. *He is coming so close to us. If we are to escape him, we will have to run away, like the Rains run off our petals in springtime.* But since the beginning of time, the Earth had always held them tightly and lovingly in her embrace, so the little flowers had no knowledge of how to run.

The Demon spun faster and faster. The poor little flowers trembled as they felt his breath upon them. Suddenly, they felt his sinewy arms grab them and rip them from the Earth. Now rootless and groundless, the terrified little flowers spun helplessly in his grasp as he hurled them in all directions. He tore them apart, piece by piece, and flung their softness into the sky.

'Our petals! Our petals!' cried the Roses.

'Our lovely leaves!' cried the Irises.

'We cannot feel our stems!' called the Daffodils.

'Our roots are gone! We are dying!' sighed the Lilies.

Laughing all the while, the horrifying Wind Demon plucked their petals, one by one, ridiculing them as he chanted, 'She loves me, she loves me not, she loves me....'

But then, before he could complete his taunting game, he suddenly lost all of his strength and died. The spinning stopped. The laughter ceased. His short destructive life was over and he returned to the totality of the air around him. The remains of the little flowers flew in all directions, and eventually fell to Earth. The petals of the lovely, silken crimson Roses curled in the heat and disappeared. The leaves of the sensuous and velvety purple Irises drowned amongst the reeds in the rivers. The stems of the cheerful, sunny yellow Daffodils vanished amongst the tall grasses of the fields. The roots of the regal and most elegant white Lilies dissolved back into the Earth. All seemed lost for the little flowers.

But something remained of them. When the Demon had torn the flowers apart, the seeds that had been lodged deep within their flowery chambers had also been cast into the air. As the Demon returned to the windy womb from which he came, the sleepy little seeds, not as heavy as the petals, the leaves, the stems or the roots, kept ascending into the skies. The West Wind carried half of them to the west, and the East Wind carried the other half to the east. Carried by these Winds, the little seeds, lost in dreams the whole time, flew higher and higher and further and further, until they were far from home. They flew so far, in fact, that when they finally fell back to Earth, they woke up to find themselves in strange and foreign places—places where no one had ever heard of Meadows, nor even of flowers at all.

Now, the little seeds were not like the flowers. They had no memory of the Meadow or, indeed, of who they were. They were only just born, you see. They had no knowledge that they were flowers, meant to be warmed by the passion of the Sun and cooled by the kiss of the Moon. They had never felt the touch of soft gentle Breezes, the nourishment of gentle Rains and the protection of the firmness of the Earth, who kept them safe within her embrace. All they could recall was waking from the slumber of forgetfulness and the descent into these foreign lands.

The West Wind had dropped his handful of seeds into the court of a King. He was the absolute ruler of this Kingdom of the West. He looked in bewilderment at the little seeds, who had just landed at his feet.

Who are you?' he asked them.

'We do not know!' cried the little seeds. 'But we ask that you may protect us in your kingdom, as we do not have a home.'

The King was not unkindly, but he was a firm ruler. 'If you wish to live in my kingdom,' said the King of the West, 'you must obey my orders like faithful subjects.'

'Oh, yes, of course,' said the little seeds humbly. 'We are only too happy to obey you. We have no knowledge of what is right or wrong. Kindly direct us, dear King.'

The King thought for a moment. Then he spoke with firm conviction. 'First,' he said, 'we must decide where you are to live.'

'Yes, yes,' said the little seeds. 'We must have a home.'

'Do you know what kind of home you came from?' inquired the King.

'No, we do not,' replied the little seeds, 'but the Earth beneath us feels safe and pleasant.'

The King thought again. Then he spoke again with firm conviction. 'No, no, no,' he pronounced. 'There are too many of my subjects living on the Earth already. If you stay there, it will become too crowded. I think that you should live in the River.'

'We are happy to obey your command,' said the seeds. And they went to the River to make their home.

But the River was not at all safe or pleasant for the little seeds. The current of the waters swept many of them away, as they cried for help. Others shivered as they clung to rocks, while still others were swallowed by fishes. A few of the seeds, seeing the plight of their companions, would not enter the water, but stood on the bank of the River, fearful of the situation.

Some days later, the King of the West came to the River to see how the seeds were faring in their new homes. He became angry when he saw that some of the seeds were standing on the bank of the River.

'I told you that if you are to live in my kingdom, you must obey my every order,' he said firmly.

The little seeds who were on the River bank cried pitifully, 'We are very, very sorry, oh kindly King! Truly we tried to do as you commanded. But when we did, some of us were swept away and drowned by the River. Others are still trying desperately to obey you and are clinging to the rocks. Some of us have been eaten by the fishes. We were afraid to enter the water and now, it seems that those of us who stayed on the shore have somehow become tied to the Earth and cannot move.' The little seeds who had stayed on the shore showed the King that they had sprouted roots, and were now unable to budge from their places.

'Oh, kind King!' lamented the seeds, 'how can we obey you now when we are unable to move? We are most unfortunate, as we are unable to please you!'

The King thought about this situation. He felt some compassion for the seeds, as he was not an unkindly man. Then he spoke again with firm conviction.

'If I am to be a good King, my subjects must obey me. It is simply not acceptable that you are here on the Earth as I had forbidden you. So, I will take you back with me to my palace to live, so I may be sure you are behaving like good subjects.'

'Yes, yes,' said the seeds. 'We are happy to obey you.'

The King could see that the seeds had changed. They were, in fact, no longer seeds at all. In truth, they had become sprouts, but he had never seen such a thing before. He tried to pull them from the Earth, but he soon found that there was no way to separate the seeds from the Earth's embrace. So the King had his servants dig up the young sprouts and put them into pots. They carried the potted sprouts back to the palace of this King of the West.

When they arrived at the palace, the King wondered aloud. 'So, now how shall I keep you at the palace?'

The sprouts replied, 'You may do with us as you wish, dear King, but when we were living near the River, we enjoyed the warmth of the Sun in the day and the coolness of the Moon at night. Perhaps you could put us in a small corner of the palace courtyard so we may feel this all the time?'

'No, no, no,' the King replied. 'It is not fitting that my palace servants remain outdoors at night. It is not proper. It is not a dignified way to live. And during the day, the Sun is too hot. I think it is best for you to remain inside my courtroom.'

'Yes, oh kind King,' the sprouts replied. 'We are most happy to do as you wish.'

So the little sprouts remained indoors. But after some days, they started to whither. Some of them curled up and disintegrated back into the Earth. The remaining sprouts gasped as they tried to save themselves. They stretched out towards the light coming through the window of the King's courtroom. And as they stretched and stretched, something strange happened. New limbs appeared from the sprouts as they now turned into tiny plants with tiny leaves, with palms turned upwards towards the Sun and the Moon. Eventually, they stretched so far that they reached the window and pushed their leafy limbs into the open air of the outdoors. Very few of the original seeds remained, but these few brave, little plants pushed higher and higher towards the endless Sky. They pushed so high that, eventually, they became quite noticeable to the King.

At first the King was distressed to see that most of the sprouts had withered up and died. But then, he felt even more distressed to see that the surviving sprouts had defied his orders about staying indoors.

'Oh, little creatures,' he said disapprovingly, 'how can you remain in my kingdom unless you do as you are told? If I permit all within my kingdom to do as they wish, I would not be a very good King at all. I have taken you in. I have given you a home. Why do you not obey my orders?'

'Alas! We are sorry!' cried the tiny plants. 'We have tried to do as you commanded, but we began to suffocate. We did not mean to disobey, but without our knowing how, these leaves started to grow towards the Sun and the Moon. We did not do it intentionally. Please do not abandon us, kindly King.'

The King was indeed not unkindly, but he now looked at the little plants with a fair amount of trepidation. He had never seen such odd little creatures before and he had no idea what to do for them. Although something about the little plants pleased him, he did not wish them to become untamed and to grow out of his control.

As he was pondering what to do, the little plants cried out in a weak and pitiful voice.

'Oh, King, we are very, very hungry! Please feed us!'

Well! The thought of feeding the plants had never even crossed the King's mind. When they had come to him, they were just little round seeds... nothing that appeared to need feeding. He had no experience in such matters. Still, it was very important that, if he were to be a good King, he could not appear to be confused or weak in front of his subjects.

'Well then,' he said, 'what do you creatures like to eat?'

'We do not know,' said the little plants, 'but when we were at the River's edge, for many days we enjoyed the delicious taste of the Waters that fell from the Rains.'

'No, no, no,' said the King. 'Water is not food. In my kingdom, we drink wine. How would it look if my subjects lived on nothing but Rainwater? It is uncivilised. People would say that I am not a very good King at all. I will give you wine instead.'

'Yes, yes,' cried the plants. 'We are very hungry, so please feed us soon!'

Daily, the servants of the King brought wine and poured it over the plants. Most of the plants became poisoned from the wine and died very quickly. One of the servants, however, was not a very good subject and he disobeyed the King. He wanted the wine for himself. So, when he went to feed the little plants, he drank up all the wine in his pitcher and fed Rainwater to the plants instead.

After many days, the King came back into the courtroom only to find an unconscious, drunken servant and many withered plants. His anger knew no bounds. He had the servant thrown into jail to sober up, and then he approached the withered plants. But as he approached them, in one corner of the room was something very strange indeed. There were now only four surviving plants, and they had become quite incomprehensible to him. No longer were they little round seeds or sprouts or even plants. No longer did they all look alike. Instead, atop each thriving plant—stretched fully towards the Sun and the Moon, rooted in the Earth, and nourished by the Waters of the Rains—was a beautiful flower.

There was one flower atop each of the four plants—

A lovely silken crimson Rose —

A sensuous and velvety purple Iris —

A cheerful sunny yellow Daffodil—

—and a regal and most elegant pure white Lily.

The King blinked in astonishment.

He had never before known such bewitching creatures as these. He felt dangerously attracted to them. Never before had he seen such enchanting colours, nor such soft textures. Never before had he smelled such intoxicating aromas. They captivated him. He wondered what they were and how they got there.

But he also wondered what in Heaven's name he was supposed to do with them.

Then, slowly, without knowing why, a feeling of terror crept over him as he felt the trembling words emerge uncontrollably from his lips—

'Who... *are* you?'

He said this softly, but nonetheless audibly.

Then the King became quite nervous. He realised he had visibly displayed his fear and confusion in front of his subjects. This was not a good thing at all. If his subjects thought he was not in control of the situation, how could he make them obey him? And if they did not obey him, how was he to be a very good King?

What to do? What to do? he thought in a panic. Then, his kingly instinct helped him regain his composure once again. He took a breath, stood very tall and began to speak.

'How is it,' he said with much authority, 'that this came to happen? It appears to me that you did not follow my orders once again! I have taken you in, I have given you a home, I have protected you, I have fed you and all you do is disobey me! In this kingdom, there cannot be anarchy. There must be order or everything will fall apart. Why are you so defiant? Your present state tells me that you have not been drinking the wine I ordered you to drink!'

'Oh, King,' the flowers pleaded, 'please do not be angry! We tried and tried to drink the wine, but those of us who did died. The rest of us tried to obey, we did, honestly we did. But your servant fed us the Waters of the Rains and now we find ourselves in this sorrowful state! Oh what shame we feel! We have no power to conceal our disobedience from you. Please forgive us, oh King! We are so sorry!'

The King, who was not truly unkindly, felt some pity for the flowers. But at the same time he felt that their power to enchant and bewilder him was a very dangerous thing indeed. What would happen to the kingdom should he become susceptible to their mysterious powers? Would he lose his mind, his sanity in thinking about them? In truth, he could not take his eyes off them. This alone was not something that could be allowed to continue. What kind of magic did these beings possess that they could transform into something so captivating without his kingly sanction? Would his other subjects become captivated as well? If they did, they would no longer follow his orders. They would fall under the power of these strange and wonderful creatures, who had no name. If this were to happen, if he were not supreme in his own kingdom, how could he remain a very good King?

His kingly instincts took hold of his entire being now, as he addressed the flowers sternly.

'I cannot allow you to do as you please! This kind of open insurrection must cease immediately! I order you to stop this ostentatious display of lawlessness at once! You must never show these brazen colours, nor give off that shameless scent again. You must stop drinking Rainwater at once! You must stop stretching to the Sun and the Moon! You must stop reaching out to touch the Breezes and stop rooting yourself in the Earth!'

The flowers cried pitifully. 'Oh, dear King! Yes, yes! We will do all you request of us. We are but ignorant creatures. We fell from the sky, asleep and uncultured. We have no knowledge of who we are or how we should behave. We are simply out of control. You took us in when we had no place to go. We owe our lives to you. We will gladly, willingly, do whatever you ask! We have no wish to displease you!'

Then the King, for the sake of the kingdom, uprooted the Rose, the Iris, the Daffodil and the Lily, one by one, taking them from the protection of the Earth. He took them from the window, away from the light of the Sun and the Moon. He did not allow them to have any Water, but brought them wine instead. He put them in his inner chambers, where he could look at them day and night, alone, and where no one in the kingdom could come under the sway of their mysterious powers.

But very shortly afterwards, the flowers began to lose their beauty.

Their colours faded into brownness. Their lovely textures turned into crisp wafers and then crumbled into dust. Their scents simply vanished as inscrutably as they had appeared. It was as if they had never existed.

Then one day, just after the Sun had set, the King entered his chambers only to find a barely recognisable memory of what had once been the Four Flowers. He called out to them, but this time they did not reply.

The King stood before their silent remains, not understanding the emotion he now felt.

Then, after several moments of perplexed silence, the King shouted out in dire frustration, 'I did not give you permission to die! I order you to live! You *must* live! You...must...'

But there were no flowers—no plants, no sprouts, or even seeds—anymore. There was no obedience or disobedience, no beauty or ugliness.

There was only silence.

Within his heart, this King of the West, who was not entirely unkindly, wept bitterly.

But, as he had to appear to be a very good King, he did not display this to his subjects.

The East Wind had dropped her handful of seeds in the court of a different King. This King was also the absolute ruler of his own kingdom, the Kingdom of the East. The King of the East also looked in bewilderment at the little seeds, who had just landed at his feet.

'Who are you?' he asked them.

'We do not know!' cried the little seeds. 'But we ask that you may protect us in your kingdom, as we do not have a home.'

The King was not unkindly, but he was a firm ruler. 'If you wish to live in my kingdom,' said the King of the East, 'you must obey my orders like faithful subjects.'

'Oh, yes, of course,' said the little seeds humbly. 'We are only too happy to obey you. We have no knowledge of what is right or wrong. Kindly direct us, dear King.'

The King thought for a moment. Then he spoke with firm conviction. 'First,' he said, 'we must decide where you are to live.'

'Yes, yes,' said the little seeds. 'We must have a home.'

"Do you know what kind of home you came from?' inquired the King.

'No, we do not,' replied the little seeds, 'but the Earth beneath us feels safe and pleasant.'

The King thought again. Then he spoke again with firm conviction. 'Alright, then. I command you to live in the Earth!'

'We are happy to obey your command,' said the seeds. And immediately they nestled into the warm, safe Earth.

After some days, the little seeds felt some miraculous changes inside of them. Their shells were cracking and new life shook within their very core. Then, something incredible happened. Tiny green shoots started to break out of the shells of their pods and stretch into the soft Earth beneath them. The Earth embraced them and pulled them downwards into her womb.

'Now, I have you!' she whispered to them in a soft, motherly voice. 'Don't worry, my dears, you are quite safe now!' And she nursed them with great affection.

Some days later, the King of the East came to that place on the Earth to see how the seeds were faring in their new homes. He was astonished to see that the seeds had transformed into thousands of tiny shoots, dotting the countryside with green.

'I am most pleased to see that you have obeyed my orders and taken your home in the Earth,' he said kindly. 'If I am to be a very good King, all my subjects should be obedient. You can see that good leadership is beneficial to all. Look—as a result you have become so green and charming! You look soft and fresh and innocent. Do you see that it is a good thing that you have obeyed me? My other subjects will look at all of you and say that I am a very good King. The entire kingdom will feel happy and safe.'

The little sprouts shimmered in their places, feeling proud of their King's praises of them. They felt like blushing, and would have, had they not been little sprouts, and incapable of blushing.

'Oh, most benevolent King!' sighed the sprouts, 'how easy it is to obey you! To obey your orders is our great delight! Please, guide us more and more.'

The King of the East thought about this. How much these little sprouts moved his heart as they trembled in shyness before him. They were wonderful little things, and so vulnerable. So now it occurred to him that these little sprouts should be protected.

'If I am to be a very good King,' he said, 'my subjects must feel safe. You are all sitting here in the Earth with no protection. I have my robes and my armour to protect me. Tell me, my tiny subjects, do you know how such creatures as yourselves should be clothed?'

'We do not know,' the little sprouts chimed together, 'but as we have been making our home in the Earth, we have been protected by the passionate warmth of the Sun during the day. At night we have been kissed by the sensuous coolness of the Moon. And at all times, we have been embraced by the silky arms of the soft, gentle Breezes of the Four Winds.'

The King of the East responded quite naturally and spoke with firm conviction. 'Alright, then! I command that you be protected by the Sun, the Moon and the Four Winds!'

'Yes, yes,' said the seeds. 'We are so happy to obey you. So happy!'

Very soon afterwards, the sprouts once again began to transform. They stretched and stretched upwards and outwards. And as they stretched, something very strange and wonderful happened to them. New limbs appeared from the sprouts, as they had now turned into tiny plants with tiny leaves, with palms turned upwards towards the Sun and the Moon, as if in glorification, in jubilation, in prayer.

After some days, the King returned to the place on Earth where the seeds had taken root and the sprouts had taken shelter of the Sun, the Moon and the Four Winds. He was now astonished to see an ocean of green in front of him, full of leaves in all directions.

'Oh, most obedient and faithful subjects!' he said lovingly. 'Just see how marvellous you are! You are exemplary citizens, the finest of the fine! The entire kingdom should come and admire you, lovely creatures! Just see how you prosper and flourish under the law! Your loyalty has made me a very good King.'

Then the little plants shouted in a gleeful voice, 'Yes, yes! You are a very good King, a very good King indeed! You have given us a home, you have seen to our protection! We are thriving and we are so happy to obey your every command! Please, please, command us and guide us even more!'

The King of the East thought about this. These brave, little plants were now full of life. They were charming little things and he was beginning to feel quite possessive of them. If they were to continue to thrive, to grow, and to develop, they needed nourishment.

'If I am to be a very good King,' he said, 'my subjects must all be well fed. Tell me, my lovely creatures, do you know what kind of thing gives you strength? What has the power to make you grow?'

'We do not know for sure,' said the little plants. 'but sometimes the Skies open up and we savour the delicious taste of the Waters that fall from the Rains. After the Rains enter our roots, our entire being becomes enlivened. Our leaves become firm, our heads reach higher and higher!'

Immediately the wise King pronounced with great conviction, 'Well then! I command that you shall be nourished by the Rains!'

'Yes! Yes!' the little plants cried ecstatically. 'We will obey you! We will follow you to the ends of the Earth, oh King! To obey you is our only happiness, our only joy, our only hope in this unknown and dangerous universe! What would befall us without such a good King to guide us?' They were so happy that they would have danced for joy if they had had legs.

One day, the King of the East rode back to the place on the Earth where the seeds had made their home, had taken root and thrived beneath the Sun, the Moon and the Four Winds, and had been nourished by the Rains. As he rode towards them, he began to grow excited in anticipation of seeing them once again. Every time he had come to visit his tiny subjects, he had become increasingly amazed at their wondrous development. They were strange, mysterious creatures of unknown potential. He found that he had, somehow, become attracted to them in a way he could not easily explain to himself. He could feel his heart pounding with increasing intensity as he came closer to where they dwelt.

But on that day, as he came nearer, a most indescribable intoxication overcame him. Carried by gentle Breezes, a veritable blanket of deliciously perfumed air filled his lungs to the point of nearly bursting with delight. He could not think. He could not imagine what could possibly be this beautiful, this captivating, this dangerously sensual and irresistible, but so sacred and pure at the same time.

The King of the East dismounted his white steed and stood on a grassy knoll, not far from the place where he had last visited the little plants. But indeed, no longer were they little round seeds or sprouts or even plants. No longer did they all look alike. Instead, atop each thriving plant—stretched fully towards the Sun and the Moon, rooted in the warmth of the Earth, kissed by the Four Winds, and nourished by the Waters of the Rains—was a beautiful flower.

But—

There were *thousands* of flowers!

Tens of thousands!

Uncountable flowers!

Uncountable
  lovely silken crimson Roses—

Uncountable
  sensuous and velvety purple Irises—

Uncountable
  cheerful sunny yellow Daffodils—

—and uncountable
  regal and most elegant pure white Lilies.

The King blinked in astonishment.

He had never before known such bewitching creatures as these. He felt wonderfully attracted to them. Never before had he seen such enchanting colours, nor such soft textures. Never before had he smelled such intoxicating aromas. They held his heart captive. He wondered what they were and how they got there.

But he also wondered how, in Heaven's name, had he been blessed by such a vision of beauty and grace.

Then, slowly, without knowing how, unbounded love filled him as he felt the trembling words emerge uncontrollably from his lips—

'Who *are* you?'

He said this softly, but nonetheless audibly.

'We are FLOWERS!' the Flowers cried in ecstasy. 'We are *your* Flowers!'

The Roses and the Irises and the Daffodils and the Lilies swayed gracefully like the sail of a ship on an ocean of colours. They waved in the tide of the gentle Breezes and glowed in the passion of the warm Sun. The Earth tickled their toes, all the while smiling at the excellence of her fruits.

The exhilarating scent of the sea of Flowers surrounded the King and embraced him tightly. 'Oh, most beloved King,' the Flowers said, 'when we first came to you, we were ignorant of who we were or what we were. You, great King, gave us direction and protection. Because of you, we have found meaning and purpose. Because of you, we are beautiful. Because of you, we are able to serve such a very, very good King. Only a very good King would be wise enough to command us as you have—to command us to become what we truly are, and to be the only thing it is within our nature to be—Flowers. And only Flowers!'

For many wonderful months, the King walked through this plot of Earth that was now known as the Meadow of the Kingdom of the East. It was now the most beautiful spot in all the world, kissed by the petals of his lovely and loving Flowers. It appeared to him that there was no greater reward in being a good King than to see this blossoming of beauty and happiness before him. Feeling like this, he knew that the Flowers had invaded his heart and held him captive.

But after some time, the Flowers began to lose their beauty.

Their lovely heads did not stand quite as high and as prettily as they had in the early summer months. Rose petals started to drop, one by one. The Irises and the Daffodils curled up into odd shapes and the Lilies, once full of nobility and dignity, now seemed to be hiding their faces.

'What is happening to you?' the good King of the East asked them, afraid to hear their reply.

'We do not know,' the Flowers sighed weakly. 'But something is calling us, pulling us into the Earth. We are tired. We do not know why. We need you to command us, to guide us, oh King. We are lost without you!'

The King felt heartbroken. What did this mean? He looked at his lovely Flowers with great affection. They had been so loyal to him and had brought him so much joy. Now, for the first time, it appeared they were suffering. He could not bear to see them suffer so.

'Oh my lovely Flowers,' he said softly, 'tell me, do you know what would end this tiredness you are now feeling?'

'We do not know,' the Flowers said in a whisper. 'But we cannot continue to resist the urge to return to the Earth. We have no more strength to continue resisting...' The weak little

Flowers gasped for breath as the last of their petals dropped to the ground with a soft pop.

'Then...' said the King of the East in a faltering voice and a heaviness of heart, 'I order you... to return... to the Earth.'

'Oh, sweet and gentle King,' the Flowers sighed, 'it has always been our greatest delight and our very purpose in life to follow your wonderful orders, which never go against our nature. You are indeed a very, very good King. And with every particle of our essence, we love you.'

And with those words, the sea of Flowers faded into the Earth, who embraced them and pulled them downwards into her womb.

'Now, I have you!' she whispered to them in a soft, motherly voice.

And then—silence.

Quite openly, this very good King of the East, who had loved the Flowers deeply, felt a profound sense of beauty as he wept to see them disappear. His subjects were touched to see such an affectionate nature in their King.

The next year, on the first day of spring, the Very Good King rode back to the Meadow of the Kingdom of the East on his white steed. When he came near that same site where his beloved Flowers had once flourished, he dismounted and knelt upon the moist earth. He knelt for some time, deep in the memory of the beauty and the charm of his sweet, little Flowers, and of the joy he had felt every time he had come to see them. He remembered how softly and lovingly they had whispered to him just as they had faded back into the Earth, according to the rhythm of the eternal seasons. He listened intently, lest he might hear their voices one more time, but he only heard the gentle rush of the Breezes of the Four Winds as they danced through his hair. His eyes became as moist as the Earth upon which he knelt.

After some time, he stood up to leave.

Then suddenly, he stopped.

The Breezes had hushed with a '*Sshhhhhh...*' and he now heard something new, something he had not noticed before— something barely audible.

He turned his head in the direction of that barely audible something. Slowly, his squinting eyes began to focus upon the source of a tiny, little voice that was calling him from the Earth...

Only then did he notice that he was surrounded by hundreds of thousands, perhaps millions, of innocent, endearing little sprouts...

*   *   *   *   *

SECTION ONE: LESSONS FROM THE ROSE

THE PRINCIPLE OF GIVING

CHARACTERISTICS AND ATTRIBUTES:
sensuality, love, passion, drive, energy, loyalty,
bravery, boldness, direction, vitality,
achievement, expressiveness, emotiveness,
confidence, action, life purpose, authenticity,
stepping fully into the world, generosity of self

GUIDES:
music, composers, Johannes Brahms,
teachers, students, a glass of sherry,
confession, stage fright, leaving, returning,
the flight of Icarus, angels with broken wings

SONG OF THE ROSE: MAYSONG

Good morning, lovely month of May!

You enter me and my heart springs open
    You free me and my chest fills up
You rise until my throat is bathed
    with a wash of bright electric blue

The blue ascends—
    ever upwards and outwards

It leaps from my mouth
    and spreads blueness everywhere
like an iridescent celestial inkblot
    that fills heaven and earth alike

It becomes my voice
    and colours all it touches

It bathes the landscape

It evolves
    It envelops
        It manifests
            It transforms—
                into words.

The words wash like waves upon the shore of your imagination
    The waves become your thoughts

You breathe them in like air
    and we delight in one other

You lie back and allow me to taste you fully
    I lie back and you taste my words

You become the shore,
  the sky,
    the delirious sea gulls

as the waves of my bright blue words
  kiss your sands,
    your breezes,
      your echoing calls

You—
  are my lover,
    my confidant,
      my friend

You—
  stretch forever—
    this sand, sky and sound

I—
  stretch forever—
    my words reaching—

reaching
  ever further
    and further

My words—
  embrace you
  like two arms of the genie
  released from his bottle after countless millennia
    in that dusty cave of secret treasure

And I call out to you crying—
'Pray open this door with the magic word—
  Abracadabra!
    Open sesame!
      Bubblicious!

Oh, let me enter that hidden site
  where nothing but Aladdin's touch
    can set my inner lamp alight!'

And let all that is immeasurable
  pour forth from that bottle

and spread
  and spread
    and spread
      like smoke—

an inky but translucent cloud—
  in all directions
  without restraint.

Both air and smoke now open-mouthed,
  their essence in and with each other

Where beginnings
  and endings
  are simply
  nowhere

Together
  becoming something
  only becomeable

through their tender
  and most uncontainable

—kiss.

*   *   *   *   *

THE ROSE – THE PRINCIPLE OF GIVING

I had been wandering rather aimlessly through my Garden that day.

It was summer and the sun was strongest in the south. As it neared midday, I could feel the heat bearing down on my head, and I started to seek shelter from its rays. I walked for some time without respite, finding not even a tiny corner of coolness in which to rest. After some time, salty sweat began to pour from my forehead into my eyes, and my head began to feel like it was splitting open, as I squinted in the bright light. I began to feel weary from my search when, in a small alcove in the corner of the Garden, I noticed a trellis of dense foliage and I went to find some relief within its shade.

But as I neared the entrance, I saw this was actually a doorway to a very large maze. I jutted my head inside to look, and saw there were numerous directions in which one could go within the maze. Not really sure that I wanted to become lost within this unknown labyrinth, I stopped for a moment at the threshold to consider what I should do next.

But then, I heard her say, 'Don't be afraid. Come over here!'

The Rose spoke to me in a fragrant whisper. I could not see her, but could only hear her call, and breathe in her sweet aroma. But within the sound of her resonant voice, and the strength of her alluring scent, she seemed so sure of herself, that her own confidence made me less unsure both of the situation and of myself.

I took a step forward and entered the maze, trusting the voice and the scent of the Rose to guide me along. At that moment, the path I was to take became evident, and all the others simply faded away.

Following the scent of the Rose, I very soon found her, as she basked luxuriously in the midday sun, which now seemed pleasant and relaxing, and quite unlike the blazing force it had been before I had come into the maze.

'Come and sit with me,' the Rose invited. And I took my place amongst the other admirers in her company. Truly, many other creatures felt the magnetic attraction of this Rose. I watched the ants and ladybirds crawling up and down her sturdy stem. I watched the bees and butterflies taking turns to sip the nectar from her heart. But the Rose seemed, quite frankly, unconcerned with all the adoration. She was completely generous with her presence, and appeared to be inconvenienced by no one. I wondered whether this was, perhaps, because she was so fearless. I myself was mindful of her thorns, understanding without being told that I could not touch the Rose without her permission.

I sat very near to her, wishing simply to take in her essence. I knew she had much to teach me, so I asked her—

'What can I learn from you, lovely Rose?'

The Rose appeared to smile as she fluttered her petals with pleasure.

'From me, you can learn the Principle of Giving,' she replied sweetly.

'What is the Principle of Giving?' I asked her. 'Does it mean to give what you have away? Does it mean to give yourself away?'

The Rose gave a very slight giggle, as if to say, 'We really do have some work ahead of us, you and I.' Her luscious scent began to waft in the summer sun even more strongly than before. Then she spoke with a sudden burst of vigour.

'The Principle of Giving is passion, drive and energy.

'It is loyalty, confidence, bravery and direction.

'It is boldness, vitality, action and achievement.

'It is expressiveness, emotiveness and sensuality.

'It is generosity with your love and with your whole Self.

'It is authenticity.

'It is dedication.

'It is life purpose.'

Then the Rose turned to face me directly and she said—

'The Principle of Giving is all that emanates from you into the world. It is the very breath that you exhale into the universe, so that others may take it in and find their own life within it.'

'In short,' she concluded, 'the Principle of Giving is Love.'

The intensity and power of the Rose had nearly reduced me to a swoon. As the saying goes, you could have knocked me over with a feather at that point.

This sounded like an awful lot to learn! I was starting to feel rather insignificant and vulnerable next to this courageous, thorny Rose. I could feel myself shrinking back and getting smaller. I wondered whether I could just slip away unnoticed. I tried to look backwards to see whether there was a way back out of the maze, but the path was no longer there. It seemed that now I had heard the call I could not turn back.

The Rose giggled again, as if amused by my apparent lack of confidence.

I looked plaintively at her.

'But how can I learn all this?' I asked her in a pleading voice. 'Are there books I will need to read? Are there mentors I will need to find? Is there a spiritual path I will need to follow? How else could I possibly master all those wonderful things you describe?

'Oh, but there is much you already know!' she said quite directly.

The Rose startled me. I couldn't imagine what I already knew about the Principle of Giving.

'Me? What could I know already? Where have I learned it?' I asked.

'Just look 'round your own Garden to see what is already there,' replied the Rose sweetly.

'In my own Garden?' I asked in wonder. I looked around, slightly confused. I couldn't see anything.

'But fearless Rose,' I asked, 'where in my Garden shall I look to find the Principle of Giving?'

The Rose straightened up now, standing more curvaceously than ever, her crepe-like petals fairly bursting from her hips, their colour becoming more and more crimson, like the reddest of lips begging to be kissed. I felt as though I had fallen into an ocean of honey when she sang:

In all directions are your Guides
in unstruck music on all sides.
From angels fallen, broken-winged
you'll hear the song, and rise to sing.

I did not at all understand what she meant, but that night, I slept with my window wide open, so as to let the intoxicating scent of the Rose enter my room. And as I drifted into a beautiful slumber, the Rose continued to sing to me within my dreams.

The next day, when I awoke from those vibrant dreams, I found I could recall many things from my life to that point that had been lessons from the Rose, but I hadn't recognised them as such. I could remember all the times when passion and expressiveness flowed freely in my life, as well as all those times they felt far beyond my reach. I could recall the contrast between numbness and feeling alive. I could hear music at many levels, and remember times when I felt deaf to the music.

It was all there—all that the Rose had described.

The Rose's teachings were indeed, as she said, all to be found within the Garden of my Soul, within the simple stories of my own life. And as I reflected upon these stories, I understood more and more how the Principle of Giving is sometimes flowing, and sometimes hidden from view in life, and how there is much to be learned from both the light and the shadow of our own experience.

And so, I felt the desire to write some of these stories down within these pages...

*   *   *   *   *

ANGELS WITH BROKEN WINGS

*G*et out! *Get out! Get out! Get out!*
That is all I could think when I was 20 years old. I wanted
to get out of where I was and run away as fast as I could
from everything, screaming all the way.

This feeling was within me every moment of my waking and
dreaming life that year. It was my second year living at the
music conservatory in Boston, and everything about the world
in which I was living was pushing me into a box of ever-
decreasing dimensions. And the smaller and smaller the box
became, the less and less I could feel my way around it. Life felt
like a downward spiral, where everything I had originally hoped
would give me joy and stability had become a web of dark
confusion and isolation.

And as I felt sucked into this uncontrolled and
uncontrollable vortex of emptiness, I found myself becoming
increasingly numb.

*   *   *   *   *

For my 9th birthday, my parents bought me a violin. I asked
them for this because I wanted to be able to play pretty songs
like the themes from *Summerplace* or *Mondo Cane*, like I heard
on the easy listening stations on my parents' radio. They found
me a wonderful violin teacher, a very cuddly 50-something
Austrian Jewish gentleman who loved to smoke pipes and wear
Tyrolean hats with feathers in them (which charmed me
because I am half-Tyrolean myself). He said he had never
taught such a young child before. Perhaps that is why, instead
of children's melodies and exercise books, he chose the most
brilliant array of 'grown-up-sounding' classical pieces for me
that allowed me to soar to great heights of expressive reverie.
He opened up a creative world to me that had been unavailable
to me up to that point, and I felt like a real musician within
only a few months of lessons with him. Before the age of 10, I
had played all the simplified 'greatest hits' from Schubert to

Strauss, from Sibelius to Tchaikovsky, and from Ravel to Debussy that a young violinist could possibly have wanted. I loved playing the violin, and even played solo in young people's concerts in front of large audiences from the age of 10.

But of all the compositions my violin teacher assigned me during that first year, my very favourite was a short piece entitled 'Caprice.' 'Caprice' was no classic, but merely a half-page piece in a technique book, intended to introduce the student to the key of A-minor. I don't even have a clue as to who wrote 'Caprice,' and I am sure the author of the practice book merely saw this little piece as a means to an end, rather than as a composition in its own right. But to my 9-year-old heart, 'Caprice' was the most beautiful composition ever written. It allowed me to sail along the strings of my own romantic imagination, and to express the inexplicably passionate emotions of a very unworldly, innocent young girl. Through this short and unassuming little piece, I found a voice that came from the depths of myself. Long after I had finished studying it with my teacher, I would frequently finish off my daily practice session with 'Caprice,' and play it just for the sheer joy of feeling it in my fingers. And whenever I picked up my fiddle to play it, my performance was always different. I would bend the 'rules' by altering rhythms and changing tempos, speeding up and slowing down, dipping lower and swelling louder, and basically reinventing all that was actually printed on the page, to let it sing in a way that I heard it within my heart. In this way, the piece took on a creative life of its own and became mine and mine alone.

Years later in my twenties, when I myself was a violin teacher, I was browsing through a used sheet music shop, and happened to come across that very same exercise book. Excitedly, I opened to the familiar page, and found 'Caprice' printed there, just as it had been when I was a child. I immediately bought the book and brought it home with me so I could teach this very special piece to my favourite student at the time. When she came for her next lesson, I told her she was in for a rare treat. I opened to the page in great anticipation of sharing something truly magical with my young student.

But as I went to demonstrate the piece for her, my excitement was soon changed to disappointment. No, 'disappointment' is not even the right word. It was a complete and total dissolution of all that had been dear, true and important to my young heart for so many years. Because, after years of classical study and performing as a professional orchestral violinist, I was shocked to discover that, as a child, I had played the piece in a way that in no way resembled what was actually written in the score! And now, the highly trained musician in me could easily see how many of the rhythms I had altered, how many tempo changes I had made up, how many embellishments I had added—and how completely 'incorrect' they all were.

I was truly in a twist over this as I tried to play 'Caprice' for my violin student. Here was the piece I had played for so many years, the one I had loved above all, and suddenly I had no idea of how to play it.

Watching me, my young student could see I was struggling, and she looked confused. I stopped playing, and looked at the score objectively. I took a few breaths and, like a good teacher, I played the piece 'correctly' so my student could learn it 'properly'. As a result, she learned it easily and accurately by the next lesson.

But, I found no joy in this. Now that I had fixed all my childish 'mistakes' and played the tune correctly, it sounded stiff and lifeless to me. It was not the beautiful, lyrical, magical composition I remembered. In fact, it was downright boring. It sounded like just an ordinary piece from an exercise book.

Confusion, intense sorrow, along with an odd kind of grief came over me as I realised that the magical composition I had loved for so many years did not even actually exist. It was as if all the expressiveness of my childhood had been invalidated—as if my entire musical life to that point had been a lie.

But now I was faced with a conundrum. How was I to teach this piece to my students—the 'right' way, so they could become good musicians, or the 'wrong' way, so they could become the music?

I found this dilemma so disturbing that I decided not to teach 'Caprice' to any of my students ever again. I stuck to teaching pieces that I knew the 'right' way to play, so as to avoid having to come face to face with such upsetting philosophical questions. 'Caprice' would forever remain in the world of a past life, in the world of childhood. I was an adult now. I was a professional musician. I had a responsibility to my students.

Didn't I?

But it remained a mystery to me why my wonderful feather-capped teacher from my childhood, who always exuded a delicious aroma of fine old wood and rosin whenever he came to give me my violin lesson on Tuesday afternoons, never ever told me that I was playing 'Caprice' incorrectly. He was the concertmaster of the symphony orchestra for the whole county. Surely he could hear I was making artistic 'mistakes'?

I will never know. One day just before my 11th birthday, he told me the time had come for me to find a new violin teacher. He said he had throat cancer and was moving to Florida with his wife to live in the sun and try to get better.

About a year later, I heard that he had passed away. I guess it was from all those delicious-smelling pipes he used to smoke.

*　*　*　*　*

If I could choose one event, one evening, that epitomised that sense of being in completely the wrong place, in the wrong LIFE, it would be the night of the new composers' concert at the music conservatory in the spring of 1975.

Our western society has a strange kind of reverence for composers. Perhaps reverence is not even the right word. I think 'worship' is more appropriate. We worship our composers. We worship them over and above the musicians who play the music. And again, perhaps it is not necessarily true that all of western society worships all composers. But surely some classical musicians worship some classical composers like gods. For instance, if you go to the Boston Symphony Hall you will notice something very peculiar. Above the stage, carved into the proscenium arch itself, in big, bold letters is a single word— a name—'BEETHOVEN.' I often wondered why the heck Ludwig was chosen as the one composer, out of all the composers they could have chosen, who got to be immortalised above the stage of Symphony Hall? But I digress. The main question is, why did someone even think to engrave the name of a composer above the stage at Symphony Hall, like a deity above an altar? It is definitely a sign that the composer as a concept has become the reverential icon. And as an icon of much reverence, the western classical composer has ascended into the pantheon of musical gods. He has become immortal.

Perhaps this is why the composition students at the music conservatory were a bit of an elite society. I say 'elite' only because that is more or less how they regarded themselves, and not necessarily because everyone else regarded them as particularly elite. In fact, it seemed to me at the time that most of the performing musicians had little interest in the composers. As a rule, the other musicians felt most student composers were 'composers by default' who had taken up composing because they were less than competent performers. Of course this was snobbery, and not necessarily true. The music conservatory was full of such 'class' distinctions between the musicians. And truthfully, while the composers were indeed a niche unto themselves, who generally regarded themselves as the lifeblood of the future of music, in reality most of the other students seemed to view them to be just a quirky set of musical outcasts.

But Beethoven, as we know, although now a god in the temple of the classical musician, was also regarded by many as a quirky outcast in his day. And, it appeared to me back then, that the lure of attaining such an iconic status was the driving fuel for many of the young composers. They seemed to be more than willing to accept the composer's tragic fate—to be grossly misunderstood by the 'masses' throughout their lives, possibly to be understood only in death, at which time their lifelong suffering would be rewarded by being invited to sit at the right hand of Beethoven in the eternal kingdom of the composer. Ah, to suffer for one's art shows the height of one's dedication to it!

All right—I admit I am being unfair to the poor composers. If I'm honest, my somewhat caustic view of student composers in those days was coloured heavily by my dysfunctional post-adolescent relationship with my 19-year-old composer boyfriend at the time.

My young boyfriend was amongst the composers featured at that evening's concert. He had been writing his compositional manifesto now for many months, in preparation for this special evening. In the true spirit of the times, his piece—an oratorio featuring a female vocalist—was extremely 'contemporary.' In those days, to be respectably 'contemporary' meant your composition had to be devoid of any kind of recognisable tune, rhythm or structure. Or, at least that is how it seemed to me. In order to be a contemporary composer, your music had to defy all pre-conceived notions of what 'music' might have meant.

Because of this, 'contemporary' music in the 1970s was not exactly easy listening. Let's be honest—it was downright challenging listening. It challenged all the bodily senses, and it seemed to bypass the heart. In fact, to me, at the time, 'contemporary' was not meant to appeal to the ears, heart or body—it was from and for the brain.

At that time, I felt like my social relationships and my life in general were just like this music. Everyone in the conservatory was busy trying to outdo one another. Human communication mainly entailed the bantering between intellects. The senses were almost continually subdued by intoxicants of various kinds, rendering them ineffective. Matters of the heart were simply a tangled web of stress and hormones. Bodily well-being was not even on the list of priorities. Thus, the analytical brain was the only really functioning organ, without the benefit of the guidance of the senses, heart or body. And when senses, heart and body are unavailable to us, genuine feeling is impossible, and we become emotionally and spiritually numb.

Although I was not able to see my way out of this numbing void at the time, somehow I knew within me that a brain divorced from sense, heart and body does not connect us; rather, it dissects us.

*   *   *   *   *

Someone calls out my name. I stumble blindly onto the brightly lit stage and I feel my hands turning into ice. Somehow I manage to put my sheet music on the black metal stand that is there in front of the piano. My brain ceases to function and the notes on the printed page look like a mass of inscrutable inkblots. My whole body begins to tremble uncontrollably like the last leaf clinging to the branch before a winter storm. I have absolutely no memory of ever having learnt what I was about to attempt to play.

Blinded by the glaring stage lights, I squint to try to make out the figures sitting in the back of the otherwise empty auditorium. Eventually I hear a disembodied voice from the darkened void, as someone cues me to start playing. I do so, automatically and unthinkingly, as if in a dream. Oh, if only this were one of those awful dreams you have about being on stage and not knowing your lines. But this is not a dream. This is real.

I begin to play, but my fingers do not fall on the right places on the strings. I feel like I am drifting above my body, looking down. I am appalled at the horrible sound I am hearing coming out of my violin. This is not what it sounded like in my practice room. Why can't I hit any of the notes right? As I look at myself, I become certain that my numb, shaking hands will simply drop the bow right there on stage to my utter embarrassment. But this never actually happens.

The panel of judges wait for me to play. They sit in the back of the dark 19th century auditorium, clipboards in hand, ready to score my performance. I deliver a nerve-driven, painful, out-of-tune rendition of the first movement of the Mendelssohn Violin Concerto. My vibrato is so quivery it sounds like a mosquito buzzing in my ear. The whole torturous experience seems to last forever, and feels like involuntary paralysis mixed with blindness, deafness, amnesia and abject terror.

They say that when you are afraid, your body reacts with either 'fight' or 'flight.' But what do you do when your heart and soul flee, and your body is still left behind to deal with the situation without you? And as your body is standing there deaf, blind and numb, your mind is shouting, 'Get out! Get out now!'

This is stage fright.

It is not a dream. It is a nightmare. And for a musician, it is the ultimate nemesis.

*   *   *   *   *

Dissected.

That is how I felt as I sat in the audience at the composer's concert that evening.

I sat there thinking critically, *This music is unlistenable.* But I knew if I voiced such an opinion to my boyfriend or any of the other composers, they would think I was just an ignoramus with no musical taste. And so I kept my criticisms to myself. My mind drifted to memories of the Hans Christian Anderson story 'The Emperor's New Clothes.' Everybody knew the Emperor was stark naked, but no one had the audacity to speak up, lest he look like an idiot. Eventually, a little boy, who wasn't old enough to know how to lie, ran up and pointed at the Emperor shouting, 'Look! He's naked!' Just like that, with every nerve in my body, I wanted to stand up in the middle of the concert and scream at the top of my lungs, 'How can you people take this stuff seriously?! It's bloody AWFUL!'

But of course, I didn't.

The concert was held in a lovely old wooden recital hall. Normally I loved this room. But that night, the discordant music and the dark, nihilistic words of the vocal pieces did

nothing but fill my mind with morose, foreboding messages—
*The world sucks... We're all gonna die... There's no point to
anything... Might as well be hedonists.... Who gives a flying* ****?

Ugh. This is really depressing, I thought. *Small wonder
everyone's on drugs.*

Clearly, I was not enjoying myself.

About 45 minutes into the concert, I glanced at the printed
programme to see when my boyfriend's piece was due to come
on. I took note that there were only three acts remaining
(*Thank, God,* I said to myself) and that his was next to last in
the sequence. Coming up next was a short vocal piece with
acoustic guitar by one of the first-year composers. I still
remember this young lad because he was a bit of a 'rebel'
amongst the others as he refused to compose in the
'contemporary' style. His music had traditional chords,
melodies and rhythms. It was, in fact, kind of folksy, and
sounded a bit like Cat Stevens to me. Of course, all the other
composers used to snub him as not being a 'serious' composer.
When he was preparing to go on stage, I could see and hear the
other composers, including my boyfriend, sniggering amongst
themselves, and verbally patting themselves on the back for
being the 'real' composers in the programme that night. I could
hear them say things like, 'How can he call himself a
composer?' and 'How can he imagine he has a future in
composition?' Hearing this kind of talk around me as I sat in
the audience, I felt both uncomfortable and angry, and
increasingly desirous to escape it altogether.

The young folk composer's piece was performed nicely, but it
attracted little attention from the audience, who applauded
politely when it was finished. Then, the small musical ensemble
that was to play my boyfriend's composition started to enter the
stage area. I am not sure how he did it, but my boyfriend had
managed to assemble a group of five or six musicians
comprised of some of the best players in the conservatory. It
was an unusual combo of violin, trumpet and other
instruments that I cannot remember. But the one thing I do
remember very well is the vocalist—a young female singer who

had the uncanny ability to screech at least an octave (or was it two?) higher than any 'normal' human being could sing. I remember a group of us being at a party one night (all of us quite drunk) when we first heard this girl's unusual vocal technique. To be fair, it was a bit otherworldly to hear such a sound coming out of the mouth of a rather petite 23-year-old girl, but I cannot say I found it to be a very pleasant auditory experience. But my boyfriend was completely enamoured. He thought her screeching was simply amazing, so he wrote his entire composition based upon this girl's rather unconventional talent.

Unlike the folk composer, my boyfriend considered himself to be a 'serious' composer of 'contemporary' music. I had never heard his composition performed by the ensemble, but as I had heard him play the piece on the piano daily as he had been writing it, I knew what to expect—eight or ten minutes of dark, depressing gurgle, devoid of any recognisable structure, theme or development, climaxing with the girl vocalist screeching a double High-C at the top of her lungs for several pain-inducing seconds while trying her best to articulate this single word:

'DEATH!'

Screeching the word 'DEATH!' in such a way that even the audience would feel physical pain was a true testament to the fashionably decadent voidism of 1975.

To appreciate the irony of what actually happened, you need to get a full picture of the all that had transpired before the big night. My young boyfriend had languished over this composition for many months. He held the piece and the lyrics as something sacred. He felt this piece would be his supreme existential message of nothingness, of bleakness, of pointlessness. It was to be his ultimate 'Piss off!' message to the universe (and perhaps to the audience as well).

For weeks he had been waiting in eager anticipation for that singular, most spectacular moment when this bizarre singer would screech the word 'death' to a captive audience. In our private moments together, he would tell me how he imagined the concert to run—how breathtaking that climactic moment would be, how astounded the audience would feel, and how they would shower praises upon him about what an amazing composer he was. It would be his *pièce de résistance*, his masterpiece, his signature composition. It would be the thing that would make people talk about him, remember him, revere him—perhaps just like Beethoven...

But the ultimate irony was that, in the concert, when the singer hit the screech note, it was so high and shrill no one could actually *understand* the word she was screeching, and the profound, existential message my boyfriend had wanted to convey was completely lost on the audience. All they heard was a girl screaming.

And it didn't feel particularly good on the ears.

In fact, when the girl shrieked, far from taking their breath away, the moment compelled many people to cover their ears, or to laugh under their breaths, because it all seemed just so damned ridiculous.

I sat in the audience, squirming in my seat—not only because this ultrasonic death tone was actually quite physically painful, but also because I felt utterly embarrassed and uncomfortable by the whole performance, full stop. I felt my boyfriend's attitude was soulless and that his primary desire was to appear to be clever. And now, after so many months, after all the anticipation, this was his big moment—and no one in the audience 'got it.'

Death indeed, I thought. *This is the death of art.*

* * * * *

I was ecstatic when I found out I had been accepted into the conservatory. I had just turned 18. I knew I had played a brilliant audition. I had prepared for it for over a year with a wonderfully warm and slightly eccentric violin teacher who lived up in the Bronx. He chose two audition pieces for me—Mozart's *Concerto Number 5 in A-Major* and Fritz Kreisler's *Praeludium and Allegro.* At the time I felt the Mozart was more or less something I was 'obligated' to play to display my standard repertoire; it was pleasant and fun, but not particularly compelling to my teenage disposition. The Kreisler, on the other hand, was an entirely different story. When I played that piece, I felt like there were threads of liquid silver running beneath my fingertips, and that my playing was capable of weaving an intricate pattern of glistening filigree. I actually could taste the silver. I could touch it. It was smooth and shiny and slightly cool. Whenever I played the Kreisler, I felt like I was deep within an ancient pine wood at dawn, dressed in nothing but a long, thin, white gossamer dress, dancing barefoot in a gentle autumnal rain like some sort of Druidic priestess. Honestly, that piece gave me shivers every time I played it, as I felt the notes run up and down my body like tiny little tongues. I felt that I myself had turned into an irresistibly sensual feminine creature, which was not something I normally felt in my day-to-day life. It was an empowering piece.

But a strange twist of fate happened just one month before I was to start my studies at the conservatory. I remember the very day it happened. Before I began my studies in Boston, I was accepted onto a very elite programme studying orchestral repertoire with members of the Philadelphia Orchestra while they were in summer residency at Saratoga Springs. I was full of confidence and high spirits that August, and my entry audition for the programme went so well I earned the place of assistant concertmaster—the second highest chair. I had never earned such a high ranking before, except in my own hometown. To add to the honour, I was also accepted for private violin lessons with one of the orchestra's top players. This was to be my very first experience with a truly world-class professional. I was extremely excited when I walked into my first lesson with him.

We exchanged friendly greetings. I could scarcely contain my excitement as my stomach fluttered with nervous anticipation. My teacher smiled and sat down comfortably, and then asked me to play for him. *This is the moment—the turning point—I* thought. *This is when I will finally discover the hidden treasure that only a teacher of this calibre can unlock from within me.* I wanted him to set the music free from within my heart and raise me up until I could play like Fritz Kreisler himself. This was the first day of my new life as a professional musician.

Joyfully, I took out the Fritz Kreisler piece and started to play.

But within less than a minute, the music stopped.

'Stop!' he said, after I had played a few bars. 'Go back to the beginning.'

I was thrown a bit off balance when he did this. I was just getting into the piece and he pulled the plug just as I was getting going. I must have looked at him confusedly, but I did as I was told, and went back to the top of the piece and started again without protest.

Two bars into my playing he stopped me again.

'Oh, stop, stop, stop!' he said, getting out of his chair.

'Why are you stopping me? I've just barely gotten started. I want to show you what I can do with the piece.'

'But what's the point of keeping on going when you're just playing mistake after mistake?' he said.

'Mistake? I know this piece inside out,' I said.

'Just start again. And this time, play it half tempo.'

'Half tempo? But then how can I put any of the feeling into it?' I asked.

'Feeling? Who cares about the feeling when it's unlistenable,' he replied.

Unlistenable? I thought. *Is this what a world-class professional thinks of my playing?*

'Go back to the top.' He turned his back to me and walked to the other side of the room. Without looking, he waved his hand dismissively in my direction.

'Start again,' he said.

I started again from the top and began to play the piece at half tempo. I felt as if I were trying to dance while hovering in mid-air in between steps without falling down. I stumbled and tripped all over myself. The notes began to fall clumsily in all directions. I just couldn't do it. It sounded worse than ever. I felt myself starting to shut down.

'Ach! Please STOP!' he said again, with some impatience.

I could feel my insides shaking with a type of nervousness quite different from the friendly butterflies I had had when I first entered the room.

'Just put the piece away,' he said. 'You're not ready to play music yet.'

I'm not ready to play music yet? I echoed in my head.

My eyes held back the big gulping tears that wanted to come streaming down my face.

'I want you to play me a 3-octave G-Major scale very slowly without any vibrato,' he ordered.

'No vibrato?' I asked. 'But I've always been told that my vibrato is excellent.'

'But what's the point of playing nice vibrato when it is only masking your appalling intonation?' he countered. 'The fact is, you haven't yet played a single note in tune since you started.'

Not a single note? I thought. *Not one? Am I really that incompetent? Were all my teachers lying to me all these years?*

I stood there looking and feeling very stupid and embarrassed. Never in my life had any teacher spoken to me like this before, and I didn't know what to make of it. My insides were shaking quite intensely now, and I felt as though a tunnel was forming around me. My teacher was standing just a couple of feet to my right, but I was no longer able to see him, nor anything else around me. I could only hear his words as if they were coming from another room. I had vacated my body and couldn't come back.

Somehow, I managed to raise my bow again and I started to play a scale at a snail-paced tempo, without a stitch of emotion. I felt like none of my fingers were falling in the right places. I didn't recognise the sound of my own playing. It sounded horrible.

After only three notes, he decided he had had enough.

'Just stop altogether,' he said with finality.

I stopped.

I stared vacantly into space, waiting for him to speak.

'Your intonation is completely unacceptable,' he said. 'In your practice sessions, I don't want you to play any music at all this week. And no vibrato. Just play a G-Major scale. Every time a note is out of tune, stop and go back to the beginning. It's really too bad you are here doing orchestra classes all month. You'll never get over all these bad habits if you keep playing in the orchestra.'

I felt my head stooping downwards. I couldn't look at him. I wanted to run away. To the bathroom. To anywhere. But instead, my feet were stuck to the ground and I could neither run nor speak.

Then he added, 'I actually can't believe you are the assistant concertmistress here at Saratoga. You must have had a really lucky day when you auditioned. And you said you were accepted into the conservatory? You are not on scholarship? Hmm...yes, I heard they were having financial difficulties....'

Do you mean I am not really a musician? I asked without speaking aloud.

My whole body felt like it was weeping. I wanted to sink into the earth.

Dissected.

That is how I felt in that moment.

And that is also how I continued to feel for the next three years, throughout my studies at the conservatory. On the very threshold of my professional career, I found I was suddenly incapable of playing my violin in front of anyone.

Stage fright. That's how it started.

* * * * *

Oblivious to my silent contempt, my boyfriend and the other composers were in a celebratory mood as the concert neared its conclusion. I heard them whispering about going over to the local pub along with the musicians for an after-show party.

Oh no, I thought. *I'm going to be stuck having to play the wide-eyed adoring girlfriend. I'm going to have to stand around and smile and say how absolutely wonderful the music was. I'll hide behind my Singapore Sling with a frozen smile on my face while watching all the composers pat each other on the back and joke around, pretending they actually like and respect each other. Then I'll pretend to laugh when they start to criticise each other behind each other's backs...*

No way! I told myself. This simply could not be allowed to happen. There was no way in hell I was going to go to that party. Absolutely not! I HAD to get out. Get out of the concert. Get out of this society. Get out of this life.

Get out! Get out! Get out! Get out! I told myself. *Get out of this hall now before the last number on the programme ends and you're stuck. Slip away fast before anyone notices you. You simply cannot go to this party. Get out NOW! RUN!*

But running would have been far too noticeable. Instead, while everyone else was pre-occupied with the grand finale for the evening, I slid nonchalantly to behind the back row of seats in the audience. Then, slowly creeping along the back wall of the recital hall, trying to look as inconspicuous as possible, I managed to get to the exit door. The final performance was winding down, and I could tell it was coming up to the last few bars. I could feel my groin tighten with anxiety. I simply had to get out of this door while people's eyes were still focussed upon the musicians.

I cracked open the exit door as narrowly as possible, so as not to let the light from the lobby enter the hall and attract attention. Then, just as the final cadence was played, I managed to get out the door. As soon as I slid myself around the heavy wooden door and shut it behind me, I could hear thunderous applause rising as the composers were called onto the stage for a collective bow. *Yes, keep on clapping,* I thought, *Go on—give them at least three curtain calls. Bravo! Bravo! Give me time to get away!*

Now on the other side of the door, I could feel the adrenaline pulsing in my brain, and in one breath I ran out of the lobby and into the corridor. Suddenly, the light and sound were completely different. It was night time and the incandescent lighting felt a bit depressing against the institutional green walls. The echoes of the audience were distant and somehow absurd against the din of the traffic outside.

Then, getting my bearings, I turned right and bolted away as fast as I could.

I ran down the antique corridors of the conservatory like a gazelle running from a lion, all the while hearing the ever-decreasing applause echoing through the stairwells and walls of marble, plaster and polished wood. I felt a rising sense of panic, knowing I simply had to become unfindable before the applause completely died out, and my absence noticed. I ran past all the portraits and stone sculptures of the conservatory founders, past the main entrance to the building, and then turned impulsively down a corridor that would take me out of the line of vision of the recital hall exit.

I ran blindly with only one thought, *You've got to find a place to hide before they find you, and stay there!*

It was at that moment that I bumped into Mr Hat.

We nearly crashed into each other as I hurtled around the corner of the hidden corridor. He grasped me lightly by the shoulders and laughed saying, 'Whoa! Hold on! What's the matter? You look like you are running away from someone.'

'I am!' I managed to choke out breathlessly. 'Help me! You've got to help me get out of here!'

This began my most amazing evening with Mr Hat.

* * * * *

During my first year-and-a-half at the conservatory, I had felt cut off from all that I had once loved. I found the culture at the school to be toxic. Nearly every conversation I had with the other musicians involved either critiquing a composition or a musical performance. And most of the critiques were negative. This, of course, demonstrated our ability to be discriminating— or at least this is how we rationalised it. That is how our teachers rationalised it too, especially when they criticised our performances as students. How could we become professional musicians unless we maintained a rigorously high standard? And how could we maintain that high standard without rejecting 99.9% of everything produced, just as a matter of policy? And to be able to do this, we had to develop an extremely discriminating sense of hearing. We took countless courses on this. I excelled at ear training, analysis and theory. I became one of the best critical listeners I knew.

But throughout that time, what I sensed, but could not express, was that while I was indeed learning how to hear the *sound* in great detail, bit by bit I was forgetting how to hear the *music*.

Then finally, in the middle of my second year, a new teacher came to the conservatory. His name was Mr Hat. Of course, 'Mr Hat' was not his real name, but for years I have called him this name in my head, not because he wore a hat, but as a kind of secret alias I assigned him, so as to allow him to remain a man of mystery both to myself and to others.

Mr Hat was an art curator, collector and historian. He had only just begun his post at the conservatory as the art history teacher. My friends Janina and Mary Beth had heard about the new course, and convinced my boyfriend and me to sign up. Then, on a bleak, dismal and non-descript Monday evening in late January, we went to the museum after closing hours to attend our first class.

Within moments, my whole life changed.

The evening I went to Mr Hat's first class, it was as if life had been breathed back into my soul. Here was art at last!

Mr Hat had the ability to see the soul and mystery of any work of art. Week after week he would take us through the museum collections and special exhibitions, and teach us how to look at art. I remember standing transfixed before a massive 6th century Celtic arch, as Mr Hat spoke of its esoteric symbolism and hidden meaning, which could only be understood by someone who had allowed himself to be transported back into the time, hearts and minds of its creators. As I listened to him speak, I could truly feel myself standing on the mystical windswept downs of early Christian

Britain. I could see the fog on the horizon and feel the mist against my skin just by listening to the melodious sound of his romantic words. I was there in the monastery from which this enigmatic arch had come. I could hear the sound of the chapel bells. I could smell the aroma of incense mingling with the scent of the damp, moss-covered Anglo-Saxon earth.

Every Monday evening, Mr Hat took a room full of confused, middle-class, post-adolescent classical musicians on a unique and magical journey through time. And on those journeys, I became one with the art, one with the artists, one with myself, one with the world, one with the embrace of the Divine—and one with Mr Hat. For a few hours each week, I got to leave my numb, mundane existence and become the person who had touched the stone, the brush, the paint and the canvas. I learned to see through their eyes, feel what they felt, know what they knew.

I was one with this art. I was one with this time.

I was one with the artist—especially those who had faded into the annals of posterity and anonymity—those whose names were unknown and forgotten, but whose souls, hearts and voices remained within...

—a block of stone
   —a minute chip of detail
      —a single brush stroke
         —an impeccably placed shadow against the light.

In those precious, precious moments, I truly knew passion. It was a seduction of the highest order. I was swept into a totality of being, of sensing, of knowing, of loving, of tasting, of marvelling, of cherishing. It was an ecstasy of spirit my body and soul craved and longed for and found only—only—in those weekly art lectures.

Passion—
   that point in time and space
   where body and soul are indiscernible

That elusive moment
  when the only thing you are aware of
  is the fact you are aware.
  you are alive

And within that aliveness
  is contained
  everything.

In a word, Mr Hat's classes were spiritual.

But all spirituality aside, every girl in our art history class was madly in love with this man—including myself.

*   *   *   *   *

I felt my heart pounding as I tried to catch my breath.

I've got to get out of this building before he notices I've gone. I've got to go somewhere he can't find me. I can't just go back to my dorm room. He'll find me there. What would I say to him? How could I explain? Then I'll really be stuck. Where can I go? I've got to get out of here right now...

Babbling thusly, I tried to explain my predicament to Mr Hat, but I felt frustratingly sure I was making no sense at all to him. How could I possibly explain the real reasons why I was running down the corridor? I felt embarrassed. I felt very childish to be seen this way in front of him.

But Mr Hat was a kind and compassionate man. He could see I was distressed, and that was all that really mattered to him. He didn't question my reasons for needing a hideaway, and he certainly didn't act as if he thought I was being silly.

'Look, I'm on my way home,' he said warmly. 'I live just around the corner. If you want, you can come over and hide there for a little while until the coast is clear.'

Now my heart started beating even louder. *Go home with Mr Hat? Oh my God! Am I dreaming?*

My breath gradually slowed down, and I began to take stock of my current situation. *Let's see—only a minute ago I was in a state of utter panic, desperately trying to find a place to hide before my boyfriend could find me. And now, I not only had found a hiding place, but I was also being invited to hang out with my very favourite teacher at his home. Not just any teacher—Mr Hat! The gorgeous art historian who is the heartthrob of every girl in our dorm. 'Wow! Janina and Mary Beth will never believe this!*

I couldn't believe my luck. Things couldn't have gotten any better for me at that moment.

We left the building, turned down the street and headed for his flat. As I turned the corner and was out of sight of the building, I could finally feel my heartbeat returning to normal, and I could breathe freely again. I finally started to relax.

As we walked casually down the unpretentious, if not slightly rundown-looking, street towards his home, I found myself surprised that Mr Hat lived in this particular neighbourhood. I don't know what I had imagined (if I had imagined anything) about how Mr Hat lived, but his naturally cultured and genteel nature made me assume he lived in a place of great material comfort and refinement—not at all reflective of the environment in which we now walked. But it didn't really matter. The real wealth was in the richness of the conversation. I found out that Mr Hat had also been at the concert, standing in the back row. As we strolled, we chatted about the compositions, the composers, the musicians, the audience and our own feelings about it all. This had a calming effect on me, and in sharing my discomfort with Mr Hat, who was most sympathetic, I felt my discomfort dissipate.

Eventually, we came to his building, one of dozens of other turn-of-the-century blocks of walk-up apartments that populated much of this part of Boston. I walked into the tiny, one-bedroom flat on the fringes of Roxbury in which Mr Hat had made his home. He lived alone here, and as he was a newcomer to the city, it was still somewhat sparsely decorated. The flat had unfinished wooden floors and was rather dimly lit. There wasn't an awful lot of furniture either. Overall, it felt a bit spartan, but it was nonetheless still very tidy, warm, welcoming and, above all, traditional.

As he took my coat, Mr Hat asked, 'Would you like a glass of sherry?' At age 20, I had never had sherry before but I thought it sounded awfully sophisticated.

'Sure,' I said, pretending that drinking sherry was something I did all the time. The last thing I wanted was to appear to be naïve.

Mr Hat went off to the kitchen to prepare the sherry, and I wandered into the lounge area. It had a large bay window facing the street, something quite common in older Boston architecture. I walked over to the window and looked out at the street below. After gazing rather mindlessly out the window for a few moments, I felt my eyes drawn inexplicably towards the floor, until they caught sight of something peculiar, and out of place. What I saw was a fairly substantial stone statue of an angel—the kind you might see in an old historic church— standing on the floor, looking directly at me.

I felt a bit taken aback by the sight of this angel. *What an extraordinary thing to see in one's living room!* I thought. But then I considered the fact that I was in the home of one Mr Hat, who was himself also quite extraordinary.

I was just about to comment on this angel, but as I turned my head towards the kitchen, I was stopped by the sight of more angels on the mantelpiece above the fireplace—a row of angels.

And then, my eyes fell upon the sight of still more angel statues sitting at the base of the fireplace.

I whirled around the room to find, quite to my astonishment, that the entire lounge was a veritable shrine of angels in all directions—angels of all sizes and shapes and materials.

As Mr Hat re-entered the room with two very modest but elegantly contoured crystal glasses of deep golden-coloured sherry in his hands, I could not contain my curiosity.

'Where did you get all these angels from?' I asked. *Silly question!* I thought. *The man is an art collector!*

'Oh, here and there,' he said, handing me my glass. 'Auctions, estate sales, antique shows, gifts—everywhere.'

I nodded as if to say, 'Oh,' and I took a sip of my sherry. *Wow, this stuff is really strong,* I thought, stifling the urge to choke, so as not to give myself away.

But as I was ruminating over my first taste of sherry, Mr Hat asked, 'Have you noticed that these are all very *special* angels?'

'Special? What did he mean? Is this some sort of art history question?'

I looked again at the angels around the room, but I couldn't see what 'special' thing these angels might have in common. They were not all the same kind of angel; they ranged from the large and majestic to the small and childlike. They were all different in appearance—different colours, sizes, shapes, styles, era. Some were obviously antique while others were not so old. Some were porcelain, while others more rough and unfinished. Some were unpainted, some of single glaze, while others were painted in great detail and full colour. Some were statues, while others served some functional purpose. I think one was a candle-holder, and I think I remember seeing one angel standing in a panel of stained glass.

Special?

Gosh, I really wanted to look smart in front of my art history teacher. But I couldn't answer his question. Instead, I very nonchalantly took another sip of sherry and, trying really hard not to look as dumb as I felt, I said, 'I'm afraid the only thing I can see that they have in common is that they are all angels.'

Mr Hat smiled charmingly. Then he leaned slightly towards me, with a devilish grin on his bearded face, and said in a subdued and slightly hushed tone:

'They're not just *any* angels,' he whispered. 'They're all *angels with broken wings.'*

Mr Hat said this with an air of such significance, that I felt myself bolt upright with a short intake of breath—ha! And, fumbling for words, the only thing I could muster up to say, in a very small voice, was '—Oh!'

But then, I surveyed the room once again, looking more carefully at the hosts of angels surrounding me, and the words, much louder this time, came from my lips, '—Oh my!'

Mr Hat sipped his sherry.

'I only buy damaged angels, whose wings are broken in some way. If they are perfect,' he said, 'I leave them for someone else to buy.'

I walked from angel to angel, and found that all of them were indeed angels with broken wings. I really took them in now, but with very different eyes. I examined the uniqueness of each one. Some angels had just lost the very tip of their pointed wings. Others had cracks running through one or both of their wings. Still others were missing large chunks from their wings, or even had a full wing broken off.

No longer were they works of art or fragments of history. What I now saw were angels in their own right.

Well! This is truly remarkable.

I felt both transfixed and transported. No longer was I in a low-rent walk-up on the fringes of Roxbury, but rather in a very special rescue home for fallen angels. It was as if all these angels shared this humble flat with Mr Hat, and in doing so this was not a flat at all, but a very special place on earth, unique in all the world.

And tonight, I am here with Mr Hat and the angels.

We took our sherry and sat on the sofa facing the mantle. Mr Hat continued.

'They are like us, you know,' he said, 'these angels.'

I watched Mr Hat's face light up as it always did whenever he felt inspired.

'How are they like us?' I asked.

'Well, look at them. Each one has some slight imperfection, just like we do. Some tiny tragic flaw—a break with Divinity. You know the story—the fall from heaven and all that kind of "stuff".'

He took a sip of his sherry. Looking into his glass, he gave the very slightest hint of a laugh. Within that hint was just a pinch of sarcasm mixed with a faint shadow of melancholy, all at the same time.

'Our wings get broken, and so we fall. We land on earth. And, here we are.'

* * * * *

When I first came to the conservatory, I saw it as the answer to my prayers. Here was the place where I could eat, breathe and dream music 24 hours a day. But very shortly after beginning my studies, it became the place where all my passion, creativity and joy for music collapsed. Instead of discovering an idyllic land full of love for art, I found a social environment filled with gossip, snobbery, competitiveness, alcohol, drugs, and a level of sexual promiscuity that my tender, idealistic disposition could not handle at the time.

Combined with this, my stage fright had prevented me from passing my final exams at the end of my first year, even though I was a very good violinist. This caused my already shattered nerves to get even worse, and the infirmary nurse periodically gave me Valium, which was the prescription drug of choice back in the 70s, much like Prozac is today. The Valium affected my sleep patterns and gave me nightmares. Within my dreams I saw disturbing, violent images that terrified me.

Then, to make matters even worse, just before I started my second year, my parents' already troubled marriage was going through a particularly turbulent period. They were threatening divorce (they never actually went through with it), but then simply went silent about it when I went back to college, making me feel frustrated, isolated and even more frightened. Only a few months before I met Mr Hat, I lapsed into a depression where I could do nothing much more than eat, sleep and cry. I drank a lot of alcohol. I ate a lot of coconut donuts. I gained a lot of weight. I latched onto my boyfriend who himself had many emotional issues. In a desperate attempt to connect, I entered quite miserably into the adult world of sexual relations with this boy whom I did not love, which left me feeling even more isolated.

And all around me I saw young people who were just as messed up as I was. Wherever I walked, I felt like there was a black fog that cloaked everyone I knew. I could see no sunshine in my life.

Over the months, my nerves went from bad to worse. My violin playing deteriorated proportionately. Believing I could not handle professional-level pieces, my violin teacher kept assigning me easier and easier compositions—things I could have played with ease years earlier. My heart shut down more and more, day after day, and I went into an even deeper depression. I slept more. I cried more. The infirmary nurse no longer knew what to do for me, so she sent me off to various doctors who put me on a steady diet of tranquilisers from Darvon to Librium. Sometimes, these drugs knocked me out for two days at a time. Of course, this didn't help my problems. In fact, they made them far worse. Things became dangerous, and once I even passed out in the middle of a crowded city street, as I was just so heavily doped up.

Then finally, one day, I was in the room of one of my friends in the dormitory, and I suddenly keeled over unconscious without warning. Apparently, several panic-stricken students carried me back to my room. I became mildly aware of being moved and placed on a bed, but I was completely disoriented. Somehow I managed to open my eyes, but I could see nothing, hear nothing. All I was aware of was a single impulse:

Get out! Get out! Get out! Get out!

That is all I could think at that moment. All I wanted was to get out of where I was and run away as fast as I could from everything, screaming all the way.

And I did start to scream.

I screamed and screamed and screamed.

I screamed blindly and uncontrollably, the sound of my voice echoing throughout the dormitory corridors. But it was not me who was screaming; it was my voice. That voice, which had become progressively and systematically subdued over the past year-and-a-half, was now finally rebelling, finally breaking free, and simply wanted to get out of the dark void into which it had fallen.

My screams frightened the student onlookers. Not knowing what else to do, they called the infirmary nurse.

But after a few moments of screaming, my vision started to return. My breathing returned to normal and I started to feel amazingly alert. I gradually became aware of my surroundings. I saw that I was on my own bed in my bedroom, with a half-dozen pairs of eyes looking at me. My head started to clear. I felt an odd sort of shift inside me. The scream had shifted my awareness from a passive, inward-driven depression to an active, outward-reaching rage.

I was angry. No, I was way beyond angry. I was absolutely furious.

When the infirmary nurse received the report from the other students, she freaked out. Students can't just collapse and then wake up screaming. Something radical had to be done. Drawing no connection whatsoever between my worsening depression and the ever-increasing cocktail of drugs she and the doctors were feeding me, within 12 hours she shipped me off to a hospital to get myself 'sorted out'.

At the hospital, they tried to give me still more drugs. But this time, I adamantly refused to take them. The other 14 patients in this upscale ward were all heavily sedated, and very difficult to speak with as a result. All of them were there because they had tried to take their own lives. The counsellors at the hospital tried to convince me I was also suicidal, but I told them I was not suicidal, I was angry. They tried to tell me I was sexually frustrated. I told them they didn't know the half of it, and that if they really wanted to help me, they should stop trying to tell me what was wrong with me and listen instead.

I was there for 10 days. The day I signed out was the first day I had even seen a doctor, as I needed his signature on the release form. As I left the building, and not without a certain amount of self-righteous indignation, I handed this poem to the attending counsellor and walked out the door:

I am strong
I am strong enough to know my limitations
Strength, in part, is tolerance
Patience, the means to that tolerance
To myself do I first owe that patience
For in truth—
the only person
with whom I shall spend all my days
is I.

I never really understood what purpose my going there had. I always felt it was more for the sake of the sanity of the infirmary nurse than for my own. When I returned to the conservatory, I walked around with the feeling that the entire population had branded me with the title, 'That Psycho Girl Who Flipped Out.' Whether they were actually thinking this, I can't say. But this was how I felt.

Yes, I was off the drugs. Yes, my depression had passed its critical mass. But far from being healed, I was now more isolated than ever in my own society. I felt no connection to the people, the place or the ethos of what surrounded me.

I lived within a community of musicians, but felt no connection to the music of my own essence.

* * * * *

Mr Hat and I started our conversation by getting to know more about each other.

He found out I was 20 years old (he had thought I was 19); I found out he was 32.

I found out he was from Ireland (I had thought he was English); he found out I was Irish on my mother's side of the family.

We found out we had both been Catholics earlier in life, but had broken from the Church at some point in the past. Mr Hat referred to himself as a 'Roaming Catholic', believing no one who had been Catholic earlier in life was ever completely able to separate himself from its cultural conditioning.

At that point, we began a rather lengthy discussion about religion. I was surprised to learn that Mr Hat had actually entered an Irish monastery to live as a Catholic monk at the age of 16. He left there when he was 20. *The same age I am,* I thought. I sensed a trace of wistfulness as he described the twelve years since his leaving the monastic life, but perhaps that was just my subjective impression. During those years, he told me, he had married and divorced twice. He had a daughter who was now four years old. Thirty-two years later, as I write these words, I myself have been married and divorced twice, and also had one daughter. Coincidentally, she was also four years old when I was 32.

But, at that moment, I was only 20, and a very young, naïve 20 at that. As I sat there on the sofa, just a few feet from a man I idolised, I became painfully self-conscious about my recent hospitalisation. I started to wonder whether Mr Hat had been told about my 'flipping out', which had happened only a few weeks earlier. *Had he noticed I missed two of his classes? Did the other students tell him why?* I started to feel uncomfortable with these thoughts.

But if Mr Hat did know, he showed no signs of it whatsoever. He did not speak to me the way people do when they think you are 'close to the edge'. He seemed to feel no need to divert his eyes or to talk about 'safe' things like the weather. He seemed completely normal. He was free and expressive with me. He was kind-hearted, uplifting and made lots of jokes. He was warm, sometimes a bit risqué, and continuously fascinating.

This man is the opposite of everything I have in my life right now, I thought. *This man is the embodiment of everything I passionately crave.*

I looked at Mr Hat as he sipped his sherry, and felt as though he were indeed an angel sitting there, trapped in a modest wooden-floored flat in a not-so-very-nice part of Boston, who was sent there on a mission to breathe some life back into the comatose souls of a group of mixed-up post-adolescent musicians—and especially one particular 20-year-old girl.

But of course, he was also just a 32-year-old man. And that man seemed to be full of his own unspoken human longing, to which I had no access.

* * * * *

As a child, I loved going to church. I was the kind of kid who would go to 7 AM Mass every day before school, when the only people in the church besides myself was the priest and a little, old Italian woman who always wore a black mantilla. I never saw any other children at these morning Masses, and I was quite content to be silent in the warm, glowing ambience of the century-old wooden church. There were gothic-shaped stained glass windows lining the walls, and amber-coloured glass lanterns hanging from the high-pitched ceiling. Behind the altar was a tall bas-relief of polished white marble. It always reminded me of stalactites (or is it stalagmites?) that you might see in an underground cavern. I used to love to go to Mass. For me, the ritual was elegant and wonderful to watch. I went to every 'First Friday' Mass, and loved to go to all the special ceremonies, like the 'Stations of the Cross', that happened just before Easter, because that is when the priest would carry those massive lamps filled with frankincense, which would waft through the room in an intoxicating vapour. I loved hearing the long 'Passions of Christ' that were told during that time, as each one revealed a different part of the story in a different way.

Oh, I loved the stories! The drama of them made my young heart pound.

I had a huge cloth-bound 'missal' that contained the liturgy of every Mass or ceremony for the entire year. I remember I spent months saving my allowance money to buy it from the school shop. When I finally got it, I lovingly stroked the multicoloured fabric bookmarks attached to its carefully sewn binding, and placed them in my favourite places throughout the book. I can still remember their vivid colours—all matched to the liturgical vestments—green, white, red, purple, black. Just looking at the missal gave me the same sense of wonderment and thrill I would feel whenever I was at High Mass. For me, going to church was a step into the past, a step into the unknown, and a step into the world of the mysterious and the inexplicable. It was a world full of magical creatures called angels—all kinds of them! But it was also a step into the world of the deliciously sensual, the beautiful, the artistic, the fearful, the intense and the joyful. It was a world where extreme was ok. It was a place where I could 'feel' without restriction or censorship. This was the world of spirit, of art, of soul—everything was possible here.

Between the ages of 7 through 12, church was my place of 'passion'. It was my world away from the 'normal' world where passion was not socially acceptable.

But then things changed.

Sometime in the 1960s, the Catholic Church made the decision to turn the altar around to face the congregation, and the language was changed from Latin into the local vernacular. Then, our parish started to require all young people to attend the 11 AM 'folk' Mass. This meant that, instead of being allowed to go to my 7 AM mass with no one but myself and the old Italian woman, I had to go to a Mass in which hundreds of us kids were crammed into the modern, and somewhat sterile, chapel to sing modern songs of praise to acoustic guitar accompaniment. I know that the Church did this in response to the diminishing numbers in their parishes in an attempt to make coming to church more comfortable and not so foreign to people's day-to-day life. But in my case, it had the opposite effect. I didn't go to church to feel the same as I did every day. I went to church to feel *different*. I started to lose my interest in going to church. It felt bland to me. I could no longer connect to it.

All this coincided with the blossoming of my own emerging adulthood as I entered my teens. Although still a very modest and immature young girl, I was no longer satisfied with 'passion' being merely an escape from reality; it had become something vital to my very existence. It was then that my real love for music and the arts took hold. I began playing in orchestras, especially on the weekends. Music became my new 'religion' in that it filled my heart with ecstasy and a sense of communion with other artists, with the art, with myself, and with the very source of creation at a deeper level.

As my newfound passion for the arts grew, my interest in the Church began to slip away from me. This was compounded by the fact that, being a musician in New York, I began to make lots of non-Catholic friends, especially Jewish friends. My religious conditioning began to fall away as my social circle expanded, because I could no longer make sense of the clash of ideologies.

Then one day when I was 15, an inexpressible sense of loss led me to one of the first major turning points in my young life.

One Saturday afternoon, I went to our neighbourhood church to go to confession, along with my friend Jane. Generally, people go into the confessional, tell the priest their minor faux-pas of the past month, get their requisite 'penance' of three 'Hail Mary's' or so, and leave. But, on that day, I felt a strong need to break from the norm and speak to the priest personally. The confessor that day was a very young visiting priest, who did not know me, which only helped to give me the courage to speak to him. I cannot remember the exact words I said to him, but I do know I expressed the heaviness of heart I felt because I was simply no longer able to relate to the Church.

I made it clear that I didn't have an 'argument' with the Church. Oh, yes, as my young 'rational mind' started to wake up in my early teens, there were many conflicts of belief. But, in truth, these only gave justification to the real underlying problem—that I *felt* nothing anymore for the Church, neither good nor bad.

To be fair, the young priest did his very best to lift my spirits. I wish I could remember exactly what he said. I think my mind at the time blocked him out, so I cannot remember the actual words he spoke to me. I am sure they were kind words, as he seemed like a very nice man. But the sad thing about his words is that they made me feel tired. They made me feel numb. They made me feel empty. They made me feel—well, nothing really.

I felt sorry for this young visiting priest. I felt sorry that he couldn't understand, and that he was trying so hard to make me feel something. I felt sorry that he, a well-intentioned, kind person, was making no impact on me whatsoever.

And I also felt sorry for myself for feeling nothing.

But nothing this priest could possibly say to me could stop me from doing what I was about to do.

I was about to say, 'Goodbye.'

Goodbye to the place that had been my passion when I was too young to know what passion was.

Goodbye because the passion of my youth was gone, and nothing was going to resurrect it.

And, as we all know, goodbyes to someone or something you have once loved, even when inevitable and necessary, are always difficult. But, as they say, to all things there is a season. It was, quite simply, time for me to leave the Church.

I was in the confessional for more than 20 minutes—an absolutely unheard of amount of time. When I came out, my friend Jane was sitting in the church pews waiting for me. She had long finished her confession and completed her prayers. She was waiting for so long that I think she had started to wonder whether I had already left the building, and she should go home. When she finally saw me come out of the confessional doors, her eyes got huge and she whispered (loudly)—

'My God—what the HECK did you confess to in there?!'

Embarrassed, I brushed it off and said, 'It's nothing. I just wanted to talk to the priest about something.' I said my three Hail Mary's, and we left.

I remember stopping in an ice cream parlour on the way home and bumping into some school chums. Life seemed unchanged. But it had changed forever for me. I never returned to the Church.

* * * * *

I told this story to Mr Hat. I had never shared it with anyone before.

Mr Hat listened attentively and nodded as I spoke.

The angels watched us, without judgement.

Passion—it lures us to religion, to art, to people, to places. It is the essence of mysticism and the key connection to all that is around us.

I confessed to Mr Hat that I had left the Church because my passion had ebbed away and seeped out of my spiritual life.

The lack of passion dries up our hearts and souls.

I confessed to him that I was utterly miserable at the conservatory for exactly the same reasons.

The loss we feel when passion is no longer pulsing within us is unbearably painful.

What I did not have the nerve to say, was that being with him, both at our weekly classes and in this moment, was my only connection with passion in years.

* * * * *

When I was 15, my high-school orchestra conductor invited me to come and play with a teacher's training orchestra at Columbia University in New York, believing it would be a good experience for me. When I arrived, I found I was the youngest person in the orchestra, and I was surrounded by professionals from around the New York City metropolitan area. Professionals and students alike came to the Saturday morning rehearsals simply for the fun of playing a wide range of orchestral repertoire.

I remember sitting down at my stand in the second violin section, next to a girl a few years older than I, and feeling very nervous. The conductor took to the podium and asked us to open to the first page of the 2nd Piano Concerto by Brahms. We were to rehearse it that day before the pianist would come the following week. I had never heard the piece before, and didn't really know what to expect. The conductor's baton went up. I raised my violin, bow perched upon its strings, in slightly fearful anticipation.

I held my breath.

Then the conductor's baton went down. I exhaled to my first taste of musical ecstasy as the first glorious note of that powerful, stormy concerto bellowed from the depths of the orchestra and swept me away in one immeasurable, intoxicating moment. The baton came down again and again upon the irresistible downbeats, pounding away in three-four time, to beckon forth each subsequent note, each more and more powerful than the one before it. Again and again, the trills from the strings and woodwind section wrapped their sinewy fingers around my senses and said, *Fly, damn it! Don't look down! Just jump and fly!*

My heart pounded. My breathing was now so deep and rapid that it nearly took me to the point of shouting, *Oh my GOD! What IS this? Don't stop! Don't stop! Aaaah!*

But the conductor did stop after that first life-changing opening phrase, which now languished and licked the edges of the walls of the old concert hall like some sort of blatantly sensual, purple-coloured Muse who had come to impregnate herself with the seed of Man. I could barely hear the conductor's instructions over her cries of ecstasy, as I tried to recover from this unexpected flight into a world I had not known existed. As the conductor spoke, I blinked vacantly at the score, and fumbled nervously as I picked up my pencil to enter the markings he was requesting us to make. Pencil in hand, I glanced shyly around me, trying to determine whether anyone had noticed the tattletale blush that had flushed across my cheeks.

For on that otherwise unmemorable Saturday morning on the upper west side of Manhattan, I felt conspicuously and irreversibly deflowered by Johannes Brahms.

Music had become my lover. I surrendered to it completely. Now, peering through the portal at the threshold that would lead me into young womanhood, I had found a new kind of passion—one that not only fed my spirit, but also my body and my mind.

I could play music—and it could play me.

*　*　*　*　*

I told Mr Hat about my relationship with music—how it had first seduced me completely and how now I felt as though my lover had left me... or perhaps I had left him. I told him how, since coming to the hyper-critical arena of the conservatory environment, the sheer ecstatic pleasure of the freedom I had once enjoyed had been derailed by the ethos of criticism and competition. I told him that, in my experience, it was the habit amongst musicians to start critiquing music (including each other's) whenever they got together. The toxic behaviour I witnessed on the night of the composers' recital was not at all unusual. In fact, it was the norm. But the fact that it had become so endemic and so unconscious was what frightened me most, and by that time I had come to realise that I was starting to behave in the very way I myself detested.

Thirty years later, I now know this is what I was really running away from that evening. I was not only trying to run from all the things I had allowed to steal my rapture, my love, my delight and joy. I was also, and mostly, running away from myself.

I lost my religion once; now I am losing it again.

I could not have known on that evening that this loss would continue for decades. I could not have known at the time that I would spend years of looking for my lost religion, my spirit, my soul, my lover, and that it would continually elude me until I got much older. But of course I couldn't know this, and barely understood what I felt at the time.

Nor could I have known that, in sitting with Mr Hat that evening, I was already in the process of saying goodbye to the conservatory, although I would not leave it for another year.

Goodbye to the place that had been the promise to fill my soul with the passion of music.

Goodbye because the promise had been unfulfilled, and I felt like a jilted lover.

And goodbyes to promises in which you had vested so much of your heart, even when you know there is no chance of the promises coming true, are always difficult.

I told Mr Hat that my only oasis amidst all of this were his classes, which had the power to transport me to magical kingdoms where music was everywhere.

I told him his class was the only place where I could feel anything.

*   *   *   *   *

Mr Hat offered me another glass of sherry, and I accepted. Several hours had already gone by, and it was past midnight.

He began to speak about his relationship with art, with James Joyce and other wonderful things. He told me about the ancient *Book of Kells*, which had just been reproduced and made available to the public. He was so thrilled by it, that I could not help but be captivated as he spoke. He told me all about its history and significance. Through his words, I could feel the breath of life in the ancient manuscript, even though I had never heard of it before. I could feel myself walking along the medieval Celtic seacoast. I could hear the calls to Matins, the scent of a musty room filled with paints made from crushed lapis lazuli and vermillion.

I was captivated. I could see creation, wonder and ecstasy in all directions. Through Mr Hat's eyes, art was everywhere, just as music had once been everywhere for me in my life. And in those moments, we could feel both the ecstasy and the loss of rapture.

Passion is passion—be it art, religion or sex.

Sex.

Inevitably, we had to come to this topic too. So we talked about our love lives.

I confessed to him how I felt nothing—either physically or emotionally—for the boy I was going out with, and how I was clinging to our relationship simply because my life was otherwise in shambles. I told him about my parents' rocky marriage, and how they had been threatening divorce earlier that year. I told him how, when I thought of 'home', I could only envision a dark, isolated place where I spent all my time alone. I told him about the stage fright, about the prescription drugs, the hospital, all of it. I told him all about this dark period, perhaps the darkest period of my life, and how I felt that every pathway to my spirit was blocked by debris.

Mr Hat shared his own stories of lost loves. As he spoke, I was deeply struck by the fact that Mr Hat had gone from being a monk, to married, to divorced, to married and divorced again so quickly. I tried to imagine the impact this must have had upon him. Quite apart from the emotional turmoil of it all, divorce, at the time, was still a very hot issue for the Catholic Church. If he hadn't left the Church when he left the monastery, surely it would have left him when he got divorced. And leaving the Church is a kind of divorce in itself. *What must it feel like,* I wondered, *this feeling of divorce after divorce after divorce?* I looked at him, and mused that, within all of this rocky sea of emotion, art was his only true and steadfast lover.

Mr Hat made some casual joke about us all 'living in sin'. He laughed and took another sip of sherry. Again, I thought I heard that hint of wistful sarcasm.

I was unsure how he really felt about this. I didn't know whether he actually saw himself as 'fallen', broken, sinful, or whether he was just having a random dig at dogma. Or maybe, he was just making a joke (and perhaps feeling a bit uninhibited from the sherry), and there was nothing very significant to it at all. I didn't really think he felt like a 'sinner', but still there was a distant sadness lurking beneath the words. I found myself wishing I wasn't so young, so shy, so nervous— hmmm, and so sexually inexperienced! I found myself wishing I was mature and sensual. I wanted to embrace him—his soul, his heart, his eyes, his words and, yes, his body too.

But of course, I didn't. He was my teacher. There are some lines we do not cross. At least, that is what I told myself.

Besides, there was something else here between us, something that felt much more intimate. I didn't want sex. I just wanted Mr Hat. All of him. But I didn't know what that could possibly mean.

Thinking this way, I became self-conscious of the collection of earthbound angels surrounding us. They gazed at us silently, and perhaps even a bit sympathetically. Feeling slightly tipsy myself, I motioned towards the angels, and said, 'Maybe we should be more discreet about the topic of our conversation.'

He laughed and said, 'Don't worry. This is why I keep them— to remind us of who we are.'

I had quite forgotten who I was, I thought.

'My surname means angel,' I said simply.

'Yes, indeed,' said Mr Hat.

Blissfully, I listened to his poetic explanation of the history of my name. And as I sat there listening, beneath the watchful eyes of the angels with broken wings, I felt as though he saw me as a living, breathing treasure within his precious collection. I felt at one with these tiny, fallen emissaries of heaven.

The golden ambient light of the room glowed with a warmth only surpassed by the soft, loving words that flowed between us. Our conversation, just like the gentle ripples upon the surface of that golden-coloured sherry swirling in a pair of crystal glasses, touched my lips, awoke my senses, and entered me, filling me with its fire as it went down.

I felt seen. I felt heard. I felt understood. I felt so very special.

I loved this man.

I could not have known this moment would be the beginning of my goodbye to childhood and to all the dark places in which I had lived up to that point.

Nor could I have known that it would take yet another 27 years before I would finally say goodbye to the broken wings of my own passionless world.

Goodbye to earthbound loneliness and isolation.

Goodbye to the emptiness to which I had become accustomed for so many years.

And goodbyes to an old familiar self, even when they are hellos to a new and unknown Self, are always difficult.

*   *   *   *   *

It was now close to 2 AM and well past the time I should have gone back to the dormitory. Mr Hat went to get his coat so he could walk me home, and told me my coat was lying on the bed in the bedroom next door. I went into the bedroom and put on my coat. While I was doing up the buttons, my eyes fell upon a large painting that hung on the wall. It was a surrealistic vision, full of symbolic images. Slowly, I realised this was one of Mr Hat's own works of art, a vibrant expression of who he was and what he saw.

Now in his coat, Mr Hat came into the room and saw me staring at the painting. He started to tell me something about it, but my mind had gone somewhere else entirely. As if in a trance, I found my eyes drawn irresistibly to survey the entire room. I looked in all directions and noticed how simple and tidy and artistically pleasing everything was. There was not a corner of it that was uncared for. There was something magical about this wonderful, private world that made me want to leap into it instead of the world into which I was about to step back.

And then, I said the most bizarre thing.

Well, actually, I wanted to speak, but I couldn't muster up the courage to say what I wanted to say. So instead I just stood there for a few moments without speaking at all. As I had gone suddenly silent, Mr Hat looked at me quizzically.

'Are you ok?' he asked.

'Yes, I'm fine...' I stammered. 'But I...I have to tell you something.'

'Yes?' he queried.

'I have to confess something to you,' I offered.

'What is it?' he asked.

Embarrassed, I looked away. Patiently, Mr Hat waited for me to speak.

'When I came here tonight,' I began, 'well, I had the idea...well...'

I hesitated. I looked away from him. I looked back at the painting. I looked at my feet. I looked at the door. But I had started to speak and now there was no way out.

So I took a breath and just blurted, 'When I came here tonight, I felt like I wanted to... well not exactly to "seduce you", but something like it.'

Instantly, my mind started screaming at me very loudly:

And just what the heck did you MEAN by that ridiculous statement? Precisely what IS 'not exactly, but something like it'? Geez! How could you actually come out and SAY such a dumb thing? Boy do you look stupid right now. This is a man here. You're still a kid. And besides...he's your teacher! What are you THINKING?!

Oh, my young heart pleaded with my mind, *but he is gorgeous, isn't he?*

Fortunately, Mr Hat was not as discourteous as my own mind. He shuffled a bit in obvious discomfort and said something that somehow or other got us out of the bedroom and to the front door. My girlish imagination wanted to remember him saying something like, 'We'd better go now before we do something we'll both regret.' But I am reasonably certain he didn't say that at all. To be honest, I don't have a clue what he said. I was too preoccupied with listening to the voices in my head shouting at me, saying, *You idiot! If he didn't think you were nuts before, he definitely does now!*

Within a few minutes, we were out the door. After my weird behaviour, I had assumed I had ruined everything, and that Mr Hat would not speak to me at all as he walked me home. I assumed I was in for an awful ending to an otherwise perfect evening.

But I was completely wrong. When we got to the street, Mr Hat smiled and offered me his arm, the way a true gentleman would escort a lady back home. I hesitated for just a moment, as I was so surprised by this unexpected offer. Then, realising what a gift I had just been given, I looked fondly into his eyes and took his arm. Instantly, I felt a smile spread across my face that lasted the whole walk home.

And so, we two strolled unhurriedly arm-in-arm back to the dormitory, beneath the dim lamplight of the deserted streets of Roxbury.

I had never been treated this way by a man before. I could hardly believe I had been given such wonderful gifts—respect, honour, compassion, sweetness, affection, delight, protection, patience, kindness, gentleness—what possible grace from heaven did I not own at that moment?

As we walked down St Botolph Street, Mr Hat spoke again like the historian that he was, telling me the story of how Boston got its name. He explained that the word 'Boston' means 'Botolph's town', named after the saint, and that the name 'Botolph' means 'Boat helper'. My fading memory recalls Mr Hat describing a legend about St Botolph having escaped from drowning at sea through divine intervention. *How utterly appropriate to be hearing this story at this moment*, I thought. *I myself feel as though I have been rescued tonight.* Fascinated, I felt our footfalls along this desolate street in the wee hours of the morning to be nothing short of magical.

Finally, we arrived at the doors of the dormitory. At last it was time to say goodnight. Again, I was prepared for my girlish infatuation to be deflated, and I fully expected us to part ways and the evening would simply end without ceremony. But once again, I was to be amazed by just how generous the world can be, when your heart cries loudly and sincerely enough for love.

Mr Hat stopped a few paces from the door, and turned towards me. I looked at him, feeling very young and vulnerable.

Very, very delicately, he embraced my face with both of his hands.

Very, very gently, he kissed me on my left cheek.

Then, just as gently, he kissed me on my right cheek.

Then, a pause.

I felt as though I was in a dream, and I could feel my heart racing. I was frozen on the spot, wondering what would happen next. There was a moment, a micro-second perhaps, where I wondered whether he would kiss me just one last time, and I could feel myself holding my breath in anticipation. And finally, Mr Hat did kiss me again.

And I sighed softly with delight as I felt him kiss me lightly just above my eyes.

It was perfect.

We embraced and I felt the warmth of his scratchy Irish tweed against my face in the chill of the early spring New England air. I allowed myself to linger as I held on to him, my head resting upon his chest, for a few precious moments on that cold, clear night. What he had given me was more than I could ever tell him. I had been living a barren life wherein I could feel neither my own humanity nor my spirit. Here was a beautiful man who had opened his home and his heart to me out of kindness, who was at once both wonderfully divine and wonderfully human. And as I felt the light of his divinely human life pressed against my own, I felt like crying for joy.

But instead, we said goodnight and went back to our respective homes.

As I came back down to earth and entered the harsh fluorescent lighting of the dormitory, I knew the time that had just passed was a gift from the angels themselves.

*   *   *   *   *

I cannot remember what excuse I made to my boyfriend the next day. It mattered very little, as I decided to break up with him a month later.

Not long after, when I turned 21, I decided I was finally an adult and was entitled to my own opinion as to whether I was a good musician or not. I decided that, while I might not be able to play the Tchaikovsky Violin Concerto, there were still plenty of other beautiful compositions I could play really well. And with that fresh perspective on life, my stage fright magically vanished as suddenly as it had appeared.

But in spite of these victories, I had had enough of conservatory life and I left Boston in the summer of 1976. I had reached the somewhat ironic conclusion that if I ever wanted to be a musician, I would need to get away from musicians.

I moved to Texas. I never expected to see Mr Hat again.

* * * * *

Get out! Get out! Get out! Get out!'

That is all I could think when I was 47 years old. I wanted to get out of where I was and run away as fast as I could from everything, screaming all the way. I wanted to run from being in the wrong LIFE.

A lot happens in 26 years. A lot and nothing at the same time. I moved from state to state, from country to country, from religion to religion, from relationship to relationship. But within all that time, I remained a musician, although I moved continuously from musical style to musical style. Over the decades, I went from classical, to medieval music, to Indian music, to middle-eastern music, to east-west-rock fusion, to acid house, to trance and ambient music. By age 47, I was living in England and had been running an electronic recording studio for several years with my husband, who was also a musician. And in spite of my having run from Boston half a lifetime earlier, being married to another musician for 22 years only served to echo the experiences of my past over and over. My husband and I fought incessantly over music. We fought violently. Very violently. Music became a competitive battleground, devoid of joy or delight. Admittedly, it is also true that, over the years, we made some incredibly wonderful music together. But every note of it came at the high price of extreme emotional turmoil. I finally reached a point where I couldn't even listen to what we had composed together, because all I heard within the strained frequencies were the interference patterns of discord from which they were created. All I could hear within our compositions were the arguments, the shouting, the hurt, the anger and the sadness. I could no longer hear the music.

Once again, my experiences with music had left me feeling dissected.

This time, however, I had had enough of all of it. I just couldn't be bothered anymore to fight this hard simply to be miserable. So I decided it was time to announce that I was quitting.

'I am quitting music.'

I stood in the doorway of our studio when I said it. As soon as the words left my lips, I felt my stomach churn as if I was going to be sick. But I stayed with the discomfort and allowed myself to take in the significance of this moment in my life.

'I really mean it, you know. I'm quitting music. I'm finished with it.'

I doubt my husband took me seriously at first. But over the coming months, it became evident that I had indeed quit. I stopped playing and composing music altogether. I even stopped listening to music. The joy of music had completely drained out of me, and I was simply not going to try to resurrect it this time. And as my connection to the music faded, my connection to my musician husband faded as well, and at last I told him I wanted a divorce.

I had finally gotten out—out and away from all I had been trying to escape for decades.

When you are a prisoner, all you can think of is that you want to get out.

But once you are out—then what?

*   *   *   *   *

Healing.

My process of healing began when I started teaching again, after a 20-year hiatus. Although I had quit music, I really didn't know much of anything else, so I started teaching music technology in the London college system. Very soon, I found that my work provided me the means to step away from my own unhappiness and find purpose in my life by nurturing the wounded hearts of others, and building them up to attain their deepest desires. I saw the dreams of others take form within sound. I saw shattered lives mend themselves through harmony. I had lost my passion for playing audible music, but I now found a new musical passion was stirring within me—a passion for the music I heard singing within the hearts of my students. It was as if something that had been planted within me many, many years before had begun to germinate and pierce through the earth to feel the warmth of the daylight.

And within that warmth I found through my teaching, I had at last begun to find the intimacy with the universe I had been seeking. No longer dissected, I felt connected. I felt connected to people, to life, to the world and to myself. I felt connected to my own angel wings, no longer broken, and allowed myself to fly. But this time, I was not flying away, trying to get out. This time I was flying upwards as high as I could go, simply for the sheer joy of flight. This time, instead of leaving people, I was taking them along with me.

One of those people was Chloe.

*   *   *   *   *

When I first met Chloe, she was just a shy 16-year-old in my music technology class, who would blush whenever I called on her to answer a question. She always sat in the front row, right near me, and I felt like she needed to be near her teacher to feel safe. She could play a bit of acoustic guitar, but was just learning how to tune it with an electronic tuner. She sang a bit, but she didn't let anyone hear her very often.

But over the course of the following year, Chloe experienced tragedy that not many young people her age have to bear. Within the space of six months, three people in her life died from unrelated circumstances. One of these people was a very close friend, a young girl, who died very suddenly from meningitis. This impacted Chloe deeply and drove her inwards, as one might expect.

Although Chloe was in a state of shock, she never missed a day of class, and continued to keep up with her coursework. Still, she seemed to be walking around in a fog on automatic pilot, which was understandable. Even for an adult, such things would have been difficult. Many times during class, I could tell that, while her body was sitting in the chair, her heart, mind and soul were somewhere else. Even though she repeatedly said she was fine, it was quite clear she was not.

Many times during those months, I found time to bring Chloe out of class just to talk. At first she didn't open up much. I observed her isolation, and recognised myself when I was her age. I simply could not stand by and watch her go through this pain alone. But I knew it would be wrong to try to force her to speak. Her voice had to be invited, not coerced. So I told her about my own experiences with losing people. I told her about the shock I felt over my father's death, which was only a few years before. I told her about my mother's death and how I watched her die. Gradually, Chloe started to share her pain. Soon, we spoke regularly and openly with each other. Together, over the months, we talked about life, death, dreams, nightmares, beliefs, fears and emotions of all kinds. Sometimes we cried—I more often than she. With time, Chloe's dark shadow of grief seemed to lighten.

Then one day, Chloe came into class all excited. She showed me a demo CD of a new song she had recorded in a studio. Chloe had written the song herself, and played acoustic guitar and sang on the track. A professional bass player and drummer accompanied her on the recording. The song had been born from the emotions she had felt over the death of her friend, and was written as a gift for the girl's brother. I listened attentively to the mesmerising track and felt it was very powerful—and surprisingly commercial.

'Chloe, you've got to perform this song at the end-of-year showcase,' I told her.

'What? Me get up in front of an audience?' Chloe looked petrified and her face turned a bright shade of red. She had never performed on a stage before. 'No. No way. I could never.'

'Of course you could, Chloe. You've got to share this track with people.'

Chloe continued to resist the idea, but at the same time she seemed tantalisingly tempted by the thought of it. I told her the saga of my earlier years when I had stage fright at the conservatory. I told her how I had overcome it by realising I had something valuable to express to the world.

'And now you have something you must express, Chloe. Allowing your voice to speak is the most important thing in life. Especially now.'

'Why now?' she asked.

'Because it is the thing—the most vital thing—that will heal you now. Believe me, I know what I am talking about. When we do not speak, we cannot heal. I went for years not speaking out, and it actually made me physically ill. If you learn nothing else from me this year, learn this single lesson—never, ever, lose your voice. Never!'

Chloe considered this for a few moments, strumming somewhat mindlessly on her guitar as she thought.

'Hmm...I'm still not sure,' she said, looking down at her hands as they played lightly upon the strings.

'I don't like people looking at me,' she said, with her blonde hair covering her face.'

She continued to strum.

'Besides, I'll get up there and they'll all be thinking, *Who does she think she is? She's nothing special.* They'll all be thinking, *She must be really big-headed.* I'll just make a fool of myself.'

She gave a nervous, ironic laugh. 'Why would anyone want to listen to *me*, anyway?' she asked.

I became very animated hearing Chloe speak like this.

'Chloe, listen carefully to me. You have no idea of the power of this song. Everyone in the world goes through grief. Everyone. This song—your song—has the power to speak directly to people's hearts. It will weep with them. By expressing your pain, you will release their pain. If you send your pain outwards and let it be heard, you will heal the pain of others. Your song will heal their hearts. It has nothing to do with being big-headed. It is actually the most generous thing you could possibly do for them. It will be a great gift to the audience.

'Chloe,' I said, 'you simply *must* sing this song.'

She stopped playing and looked at me, her bright blue eyes blazing with both terror and excitement.

Taking a deep breath, Chloe at last agreed to sing her song on the night of the showcase. For many days we worked together rehearsing her 'stage persona', so she would feel comfortable on stage. Throughout the process, I trusted that Chloe's recent experiences gave her the ability to rise above whatever fears she may have had about performing. And truly, the more we worked together, the more fluid her playing sounded, and the more confident she became.

Finally the evening of the showcase arrived. When it was her turn on the programme, Chloe walked out onto the stage. She sat down coyly and looked slightly away from the audience, hiding her porcelain complexion behind her long blonde fringe as she strummed the first few notes of the song on her guitar. As I stood in the back of the auditorium, I felt the sombre ambience that had taken over the room. Chloe's face may have been hidden, but nothing could hide the haunting tune and melancholy lyrics of the song from the audience. Just as I had predicted, I could see the song touch their hearts. I could see this song cry for them, reach out to them, embrace them.

When the song was over, Chloe's performance was met with thunderous applause. The somewhat shocked expression on her face showed she could hardly believe all that applause was for her. Nervously, Chloe rose to her feet and took an awkward bow, blushing profusely. After the performance, dozens of people came up to her and told her how much her song had touched them. The parents of the girl who had died came and thanked her, and told her what a wonderful gift this was for them. This was a significant turning point for young Chloe, because in a single evening she learned how seeming tragedy could be transformed into something full of love and joy.

She went on for several years after that, playing this same song to raise money for meningitis research.

But the one thing Chloe could not have understood at the time was how, in allowing me to help her through this time of her life, she was helping me to heal as well. By helping Chloe to perform on stage, I had been able to heal the wounds of my 'stage fright days'. By drawing out Chloe's authentic voice, I had been able to undo the feelings of voicelessness I had felt when I had not allowed myself to speak through my music in the past.

And in the process, I had discovered a great and wonderful paradox—the more I gave of my true Self, the greater and truer my Self became. After decades of feeling disconnected and dissected, I now found that by giving away what I could barely find before, I had tapped into an endless supply of Self.

Where that Self was coming from, I had no idea. But for the first time in my life, I simply loved being alive.

* * * * *

Not long after the showcase, I left Chloe's college in Surrey to take a position up in Bedfordshire. Chloe and I lost touch for a couple of years. Then, one day, I received an invitation to attend Chloe's 21st birthday party. I sent her my R.S.V.P immediately.

During the two years we had been apart, Chloe had been to work in the US, and had also worked as a sound technician at the small local concert venue where her party was being held. When I arrived at the party, I found to my delight that the party was actually a gig, and Chloe was the headline act.

When Chloe walked onto the stage, I felt my heart swell so full it nearly burst. She was so transformed, she was almost unrecognisable. No longer hiding behind a bushel of wheat-coloured hair, she had short-cropped black (almost blue) hair that showed off her stunning blue eyes. No longer a shy, nervous 17-year-old girl, she was now a confident, dynamic adult, who had command of the stage, the guitar, the band, her voice, the sound technician and the audience. No longer dependent upon an electronic tuner to get her strings to play in tune, she was now freely using a variety of tunings on her guitar throughout the concert, and could go casually from one to the next while she spoke to the audience. But even though all of that would have been impressive enough, what I found most remarkable about Chloe that evening was the tone of her stunning and powerful voice, and her ability to communicate everything that was inside her.

At the interval, Chloe made a point of coming up to talk to me privately. With an expression full of sincerity, she told me how grateful she was to me and how important a figure I had been in her life. She told me how much it meant to her that I had listened to all of her grief, her pain, her confusion, her scary dreams and her fears. She told me how much it meant to her that I had convinced her to get out onto a stage, and how I had coached her on how to present herself when performing. She told me how much it meant to her that I had believed in her.

Looking at Chloe, I now saw her as an adult, and no longer felt the need to protect her from parts of me I feared might have frightened her in the past. I told her how important she and the other students had been to me as well. I told her that I believed they had been sent to me at a time in my life when I myself was going through tremendous change. Together, they had allowed me to heal, to find myself. They had allowed me to give something to the world, and to feel valuable. I told her that all of them had given just as much—if not more—to me than they had received from me. I felt this was important for her to know.

But Chloe was very insistent that it was *I* who was to be credited that night, not her. I was extremely moved to hear her speak so affectionately to me.

As teachers, we see our students come and go. After they leave, rarely do they come back to tell us how we have impacted their lives. As such, we teachers learn to become unattached, even though it is not always easy. Chloe and others from her class gave me a priceless gift that evening. What price tag could

I possibly place upon the value of hearing a former student tell me I changed her life?

And then Chloe said something most remarkable.

'When I was in the States, I visited Boston. I loved it there. I've decided I want to go study music there.' She mentioned a college, a different one from the one I went to.

In a single flash of memory, I saw Mr Hat.

I remembered the evening when he had taken me into his care. I remembered the numbness and the isolation I had been feeling, and how he was the only person in the entire universe who made me feel alive.

And now, I saw that, simply by being there for her when she had become numb and isolated, I had given to Chloe the very same gift Mr Hat had given me. Mr Hat had shown me that it was ok to feel. It was not only ok, it was all we had. It was not only all we had, it was marvellous. It was fantastic. It was thrilling. It was stunningly beautiful. It was the touch of two souls upon each other. It was mystical, essential and primordial. It was worth crying for. It was worth screaming out loud for. It was worth running, running, running a million, million miles for.

'It' was life. 'It' was Self. 'It' was everything.

I could feel all my past teachers flowing through me and into my own students, who will invariably pass this 'it' on, and ever onwards.

I leaned towards Chloe as we sat on the stage together during the interval, much as Mr Hat had done when he had asked me to take a closer look at the angels with broken wings, and I whispered to her—

'You *hear* it, don't you?'

Chloe's icy blue eyes looked deeply into my own green eyes. She nodded.

'Yeah,' she said. 'Yeah, I do hear it.'

She looked straight ahead of her, as if she had been transcended to a mystical place.

'Chloe,' I asked, 'do you realise how many people out there don't hear 'it'?

'Yeah...' Chloe said again. 'Yeah, I do.'

'If you hear it,' I said, 'it is your responsibility to sing it.'

She nodded again. She understood. This was her life. This was her vocation. It called her. It said, 'Run to me!' Chloe was running towards it, leaping, jumping and singing towards it.

'It'—was Chloe.

* * * * *

Shortly after Chloe's party, I started to write this story, but somehow I never seemed able to finish it. It felt like something was missing, but I couldn't figure out what it could be.

Then, a few months later, my good friend Marco told me about a coaching course he was attending in Boston. Rather impulsively, I signed up for the course as well, not really knowing why I couldn't just wait for the course to be offered in London. But I always believe that when we act upon strong impulse, there is something important driving us to act. Later that same day, I sat down to attempt to finish this story once again, and in a flash I realised what had been missing—the ending. It was then I understood why I was really going to Boston. I knew in my heart that, to make this story complete, I had to find Mr Hat. I had to tell him how he had impacted my life, just as Chloe had told me how I had impacted hers.

I searched on the Internet to find him. Even though he was now 65 years old, Mr Hat was still teaching. I was amazed to find pages of praise for him written by several of his recent students. My heart started to flutter with joy as I read them. And then, it started to pound when I discovered Mr Hat was now teaching at the very school Chloe had wanted to attend. I located his home telephone number, and one evening, I called him.

He didn't remember me when I told him my name. I wasn't surprised. It had been 33 years, and he had had hundreds, perhaps thousands, of students since we last spoke. But he agreed to meet and before hanging up, he kindly assured me, 'Two things never change about a person: the soul and the eyes.

When I see you and look into your eyes, I am sure I will remember you.'

I had convinced Marco to accompany me to visit Mr Hat at his flat. From the address, I noted Mr Hat no longer lived on the edges of Roxbury, but rather in a very nice part of Back Bay. As we approached his apartment building, we found Mr Hat no longer lived in some rustic flat in a generic walk-up terrace, but rather in a very stately historic building with marble floors, stained glass windows and many elegant period features.

Standing in the entranceway of his building, I saw Mr Hat's name next to the buzzer to his flat. With a belly full of butterflies, I rang the buzzer and held my breath. Over the intercom, I heard his voice, saying he would be right down. As we waited for him to come down the lift to greet us, I could feel my nerves compelling me to pace around the lobby. Would he indeed remember me when he looked into my eyes?

Then I wondered, *Would I remember him?*

But the scarier question was, 'Would this man be as wonderful, as amazing, and as beautiful as I remembered him, or would I find I had been just a mixed-up, deluded young 20-year-old with a distorted sense of reality? Was I going to find the end to my story here, or would I find there never was a story and it was all just a fabrication of my own loneliness?'

The lift arrived at the ground floor. The doors opened and Mr Hat stepped out.

Apart from looking 33 years older, and completely grey-haired, the man who now walked towards me looked exactly the same as I remembered him. In fact, he was just as beautiful, perhaps more so, as he was when he was 32 years old, as the experience of living yet another lifetime's worth of years had given his eyes a wisdom, warmth and depth that could only be the result of all he had learned, felt and experienced throughout the decades.

Feeling something like a post-adolescent schoolgirl, I looked at him shyly as he came towards us, and I asked him in a slightly pleading voice, 'Do you remember me?'

'Let me see your eyes,' he said, putting his hands on my shoulders. He looked deeply into my face. And then he said warmly, 'Of course I remember you!' He embraced me.

'So,' he said, 'what the heck have you been up to for the past 33 years?'

Marco and I went into Mr Hat's flat and we were both immediately astounded by the amazing sights we saw. The entire flat was filled with the finest of art—paintings, statues, antique furniture, fabrics, artefacts, and hundreds upon hundreds of rare books on art, literature, history and culture of all kinds. We felt as if we had just entered a tiny, secret gallery of hidden treasures. We could have spent weeks taking it all in.

Just as I had been more than 30 years earlier, I was once again transfixed and transported to another dimension. This was not a flat at all, but a very special place on earth, unique in all the world.

And once again I was with the extraordinary Mr Hat.

Several wonderful hours passed as we three sat together—sipping Irish whiskey, drinking tea, talking about art, about poetry, about James Joyce, about religion, about life, about the past. There was just so little time, and as I wanted to hear all Mr Hat had to tell us, I never really got around to telling him much about what was going on in my life, or to answer his question about what I had been doing for the past 33 years. But it didn't really matter. The present moment was nothing short of magical. Mr Hat was still just as passionate, just as fascinating, just as mystical, and just as able to transport me to distant lands and ancient times as he had been when I was 20.

I told Mr Hat about my book, and about my story called 'Angels with Broken Wings'.

'Ah, yes,' he said. 'So you saw my collection back then?'

'Yes,' I said. 'Back then, you said you felt they symbolised the human condition. For me, I always felt they represented exactly how I felt about my life back then.'

'Well,' he said, 'these days, those angels like to stay stored away in boxes. I have replaced them with that up there.' He casually pointed to a very elaborate wire sculpture mobile hanging at one end of the room, depicting the ancient Greek myth of the flight of Daedalus and Icarus.

'You see,' Mr Hat continued, sipping his Irish whiskey, 'the father is saying, "You're flying too high, son!" and the son is saying, "No! I want to go higher! Higher!"'

'Ha. That sort of reminds me of what Marco and I do as life coaches,' I said. 'Except it's kind of the opposite, I guess. Sometimes our clients say, "I don't believe I can go as high as that" and we tell them, "No, you can do it. Fly higher, higher!"'

'But of course, in the Greek story, Icarus falls down to earth,' I said with a laugh.

I continued to tell Mr Hat about my book. I told him about the Four Flowers, and that he was in the section of the Rose. He seemed very pleased. As it turned out, Roses were very special to him. He told us about the significance of the different colours of Roses—red, yellow, pink, white. Red was sexual or passionate love; white was pure, platonic love; pink was blushing love and yellow was what he called 'impossible' love. He gave many illustrations of these from literature and his own life. It was lovely to hear him speak about the Rose. It made it even more appropriate that his story appeared in this part of the book.

Then, Mr Hat said, 'After we spoke on the phone, I started to remember things about that evening many years ago. The one thing I remember most is that you were very troubled about something. But I also remember telling you, "If it won't matter in seven years' time, it simply doesn't matter."'

When Mr Hat said this, I sat upright.

'Wow. That's really strange,' I said. 'Back when I was teaching at the college, I used to say the same thing to my students all the time, especially if I saw them getting all stressed out over their grades. The funny thing is, I honestly don't remember you saying this to me, but you must have. Your words became a part of my own teaching, without my even realising it!'

Mr Hat said he was not completely clear as to when we had first met. I clarified it had been 1975, when I was 20 years old, and he was 32. I reminded him I was amongst his very first group of students at the conservatory.

'Well, I find that really amazing,' he said. And he seemed to be pondering something.

'What is amazing?' I asked.

Mr Hat seemed absorbed within his own reflections, as he continued to speak.

'You know,' he said, 'the root of the word "education" is the Latin *edu care*. It means "to draw out" knowledge. When I teach my students, I know I am not really teaching them anything. I am only drawing out the wisdom that is already there. I cannot tell anyone anything about anything.

'So what really amazes me,' he continued, 'is that I am only 12 years older than you. I mean, there's only half a generation between us. And there I was, barely any older than the rest of you, and I was standing up in front of the room pretending I could teach you anything about life. How arrogant of me! I mean, really—what did I think I was doing?' And he laughed at himself with a hint of scorn.

At this point, it was as if all I had held within my heart for the past 33 years had just exploded inside of me. Without even thinking, I leapt out of my seat, stood directly in front of Mr Hat, and said,

'What did you think you were *doing?* I'll *tell* you what you were doing...

You were showing us how to see...

You were showing us how to feel, how to think, how to taste, how to appreciate...

You were showing us raw passion...

You were showing us both the sacred and the profane and how they fit within each other...

You were opening our eyes to the play between light and shadow, to mystery and wonder...

You were transporting us through time...

You were showing us art...

You were showing us LIFE!'

'And that is why I came here to see you today,' I continued, 'I wanted to tell you what you've done. I honestly don't know where my life would be now if you had not appeared when you did. And it is not just my life you have impacted, but the lives of hundreds of others over the decades as well. You have no idea how many people credit you as their beloved mentor. You have changed our lives forever.

'And now, your students are out there in the world changing other people's lives,' I said.

'And that,' I said, looking directly at Mr Hat, 'is what you were doing!'

*   *   *   *   *

It was time to leave for the airport to catch our flights back to Europe. Marco hailed a cab, which stopped immediately, and all too suddenly it was time to say goodbye.

Mr Hat kissed and embraced me, much as he had done 33 years earlier. Once again, I allowed myself to linger as I held on to him, my head resting upon his chest, for a few precious moments. But this time, I sank into him and could feel my heart sighing the word, 'Teacher', with great love and affection, much like the final scene of the play *The Miracle Worker*, where Helen Keller expresses her soul, overflowing with gratitude, to Annie Sullivan for releasing her from the prison of darkness and silence in which she had lived for so long.

In much the same way, Mr Hat had unknowingly come into my life to release me from the prison of isolation within my own heart, to help me return to a place where music, art, love and life itself were still full of the passionate freedom and capriciousness that had always been there—within my true Self. It was only a matter of listening for it.

At last I heard the music.

At last I heard 'it'.

'It' was me, and had been so all along.

As I stepped from the curb to get into my cab, I looked back one last time at Mr Hat. His eyes appeared to be slightly moist. Perhaps it was just the cold winter air?

He said, quite stoically, 'This is not goodbye. It is just the beginning.'

And so, the ending of my story is now the beginning of the next.

As students, we see our teachers come and go. After we leave, rarely do we get the chance to come back to tell them how they have impacted our lives. It is difficult to explain how the act of telling a teacher he changed your life can make you feel complete. What greater privilege can there be than to be able to tell someone, 'You are the person who awakened my soul from its slumber; you were the vessel whence I found my voice.'

I knew it was time to pass that precious gift forward to the next generation. So when I returned to England, I immediately phoned Chloe.

'You must go to Boston,' I said. 'There is someone there I want you to meet.'

*   *   *   *   *

An awkward, blushing 20-year-old girl says to her handsome 32-year-old teacher, *'I came here not exactly to seduce you, but something like it.'*

What she really wanted, but could not express, was to feel his soul, his heart, his body and his mind, and to touch them with her own.

Within his soft embrace, he smoothed her broken wings and held her as sacred—an act of pure love that was to linger, along with the gentle brush of his kiss just above her eyes, for the rest of her life.

And within that most subtle of seductions contained within that sweet and innocent embrace, she felt her wings mend and begin to unfold.

*   *   *   *   *

We fall
   like summer rain
   upon the shattered panes
of the glass roof
   through which
   you see the sky

but from this place
   you cannot fly
   to heaven

Instead oh summer rains
   I open up the shutters
   to let the sky fill my room
   until there is no difference
   between low and high

I let the rain
   nourish all
   that lay dormant within me
and reach out to that sky
that has for so long—
   longed to come in—
   into my heart

And then I join the raindrops
   and dance amongst their cloudy canyons

We knock upon the shutters of the hearts of others
   locked within their own glass boxes

We call
   'Open! Open!'
   And one of them is broken.

She sighs

Surrendering, she opens up her gates

The droplets enter
    just one
        or two
and soon the rain is pouring in
    and melts the ceiling clean away
like sugar candy
    in a bath of warm liquid
that dissolves it
    into a sweetness
    that spreads out like a sea
of joyful sorrows
    or sorrowful joy
or simply sorrow
    or simply joy

All of it!
    I feel all of it!
And life
    is
        everywhere.

Amidst the summer rains
    we fall
        like angels with broken wings
—but angels
    nonetheless.

*   *   *   *   *

REVISITING THE ROSE

The heat was sweltering that evening, and I found it hard to sleep. As I tossed and turned in the darkness, I became vaguely aware of a wonderful scent lingering deliciously in the air of this hot August night. The aroma, I am slightly embarrassed to say, made me somewhat giddy with desire and I could not resist rolling around in my white cotton sheets. It was then I realised it was the scent of the Rose that had captured my awareness.

Such a bold flower, this Rose, I thought. *She makes her way into my room at night, even with the curtains drawn. She infiltrates wherever she pleases, whenever she fancies.*

Soon I found I could resist no longer. The scent of the Rose beckoned me. I put on my slippers, and followed the trail lit by the full moon through the winding maze in my Garden, until at last I found her, holding her midnight court, attended by her ladybirds-in-waiting, at the centre of the winding labyrinth. She stood there proudly singing epic songs of love and valour, as every creature around her stood captive by the rhythmic pulses of her voice. Without thinking, I soon found myself singing rather awkwardly along with this inspirational little Rose, whose ability to express herself seemed at once all-embracing yet unreachable.

Hearing the soft sound of my singing, the Rose turned to look at me as I sat amongst the lilies of the valley that had woken up to hear her midnight concert. Seeing me sitting there, her rosy blush seemed to get redder still, and she called out to me in her luscious voice saying, 'Ah, my friend. Come sit beside me.'

I came closer, and the ladybirds dusted off a spot upon the earth with their spotted wings so I could sit near their queen.

'You look very warm,' she said. 'Your face is all flushed and there are pearls of sweat on your forehead.'

She rustled her petals, as an order to her ladybirds, and quickly they brought me a cooling drink of crystal dewdrops cupped within the folds of a lady's mantle leaf. Very soon, I felt myself settling into the familiar presence of the lovely Rose, as her self-assuredness and inner strength made me feel safe.

'So tell me, my gentle friend,' she began, 'what brings you here this evening?'

I told her the story 'Angels with Broken Wings'. I told her all about the music, the sherry, and of course about the angels. I told her about all the people, places and things in the story. I told her about *Caprice* and the passion I had felt within it. I then told her about my loss of passion, my stage fright, the composers' concert, and about all the times I had felt dissected and disconnected from myself. I told her how I had quit music, and how I had later found a much more subtle music inaudible to physical ears. I told her about my mentor and my student, and how the world had blessed me with the privilege of being a vital link in the transmission of timeless wisdom from one generation to the next.

Hearing all this, the Rose smiled and asked, 'Most fearless and courageous friend! I find your tale extremely inspiring, and I want to know even more. So, now please do tell us, what have you learned about the Principle of Giving?'

I sat and shut my eyes for a moment, so as to feel the Principle enter me.

Finally the learning became clear. I opened my eyes and spoke.

'I have learned the difference between playing the music, and allowing the music to play me,' I said.

'Oh? Please share with us what that difference is,' she bid me. Her ladybirds perked up attentively.

'Well...' I began, trying to find the right words, 'when I play the music, my brain is making all the decisions. My brain is deciding what to play and how to play it. It is busy analysing, evaluating and measuring.'

I stopped for a moment to gather my thoughts.

'Do go on,' the Rose said encouragingly. 'Tell us more. What do you mean by "measuring"?'

The Rose's scent stirred my inspiration.

'Actually, it's really quite simple. Measurement is comparison. It means there is always something bigger and something smaller. There is always something more and something less. And when I look at something and decide it is smaller or less than something else, I am making a judgement of its worth. And when I am judging the worth of something, I am devaluing it. I am criticising it. And when I criticise something, I cannot love it. And if I cannot love it, I also cannot feel it, know it or express it.

'Ok, I am following you so far,' the Rose laughed. 'So what's your conclusion about "playing the music"?' she asked

'My conclusion is—that it is not actually *possible* to play the music!' I pronounced with conviction. 'I mean, how *can* I play the music if my mind is busy criticising it?'

The ladybirds started to flutter their wings more quickly, buzzing noisily, debating this rhetorical question amongst themselves.

The Rose held out her thorny arm and gently hushed her courtiers. Soon, everyone was once again quiet and attentive, as they waited to hear what would come next.

'So,' said the Rose, 'playing the music is impossible. Ha! Yes, I like that. Very good. And what about the other thing you said—about 'the music playing you'?'

Again, I shut my eyes for a moment and simply listened.

I heard the music of my heart as it pulsed through my veins. I listened to the sound of my breathing and felt the rhythm of my own life. Then I opened my eyes and gazed softly at the scene before me—this moonlit night amidst the labyrinth. I listened to the music of the evening—the song of the crickets, the sigh of the summer breezes, the rustle of the leaves within the privet hedge.

Then effortlessly, the words flowed freely from my lips.

'When I let the music play me, it becomes my lover who rapturously seduces my heart, my body and my soul. My whole being swoons to his touch, as I allow him to embrace me, caress me, bend me, unfold me and enter me. I feel him taste me—and I also taste him fully. There are no barriers between us, no limitations or rules saying where we may or may not mingle.

'The music is my beloved, my tormentor, my angel, my demon, my light and my shadow.

'We are both saint and sinner, both sacred and profane, both prince and pauper.

'We are both harmony and dissonance, both point and counterpoint, both suspension and resolution.

'When I let the music play me, we are both the music.

'When I let the music play me, we are both the musician.'

One of the ladybirds fainted. Hastily, her sisters started fanning her with their wings.

The air felt sweet and thick like golden treacle. The Rose stood very still, and smiled at me with her eyes half closed. She nodded her lovely blossom approvingly and spoke to me softly.

'Lovely friend, what is this rapturous music of which you speak?' she asked.

I answered immediately.

'It is my Voice,' I said. 'It is the Voice of my own essence.'

She remained silent for several moments, her shining eyes gazing at me all the while.

'Indeed,' she finally said. 'I can hear *that* Music playing you right in this very moment. And the song is very sweet.'

Then she continued, 'So now, my melodious friend, what can you tell us about the Music itself?'

I let the Music play me for a moment.

'When I was very young, I could feel the cry of my own authentic Voice. That Voice was absolute and without comparison. It was pure and immutable. But somewhere along the way, I learned to measure, to compare, to limit and to reject my own Voice. Eventually, I rejected it so completely that I could no longer feel it or even recognise it. I told myself that by developing a very acute sense of measurement, I was becoming more aware. Limitation became my reality. And in feeling limited, I always felt empty. And when we feel empty, we cannot give.

'I had come to accept that limitation as the truth. I had come to surrender my own will to it, believing the limitation to be greater than myself, and that I could never possibly measure up to it. Feeling I could not even measure up to a mere limitation, I started to believe I had nothing of value to give to the world.

'When I believe I have nothing, I give nothing. When I give nothing, the world becomes poor.

'So the truth of the matter is this—when I choose to remain voiceless, I bring poverty to the world.'

'But it goes even beyond this,' I continued. 'When a child comes from the womb of his mother, the world waits until that first cry emerges from his tiny lungs before it declares he has been born. In the same way, until we break open from the womb of our own isolation, and use our Voice to cry out loudly to the universe that we have arrived, we are not yet fully born.

'And if, by remaining voiceless, I am not born, then I am denying the flow of Life itself. When I am voiceless, there is no pulse, no sound, no vibration. The universe becomes inert. There can be no transmission of wisdom in an inert universe. There can be no Life in a motionless place. There is only darkness and ignorance in that silent place.

'But when I choose to shout my Voice loudly, I break wide open from that silent womb of inertia.

'Voice becomes the hum that sets the universe in motion.

'Voice is the Music that seduces Life to procreate.

'Voice and Life are lovers, and Giving is the Principle that marries them together.

'Like the contents of Pandora's Box, Voice expands and spreads in all directions. It becomes a gift that unwraps itself and is distributed to everyone I meet.

'When I choose to use my Voice, I bring a great treasure to the world.

'When I choose to use my Voice, the world hears that I have taken birth.'

The ladybirds applauded enthusiastically with their spotted wings. Then, they shushed themselves back to a quiet attention, mindful that their Ladyship was getting ready to speak again.

'I am extremely pleased to hear this explanation,' the Rose said kindly. 'And now, I would like to ask you one last question. Could you please tell me, what is the special *power* of this Principle of Giving?'

'The power?' I asked, pausing to reflect upon her question.

'Why, the power of Giving—is that the more I give, the more I have left to give!' I cried out. And my words surprised even me.

I became excited and felt a rush of words come over me.

'Yes, I understand this now. I used to live within a poverty of spirit. Life was always a waiting game for love, pleasure and joy to arrive. But none of these things ever came to me, because I was looking in all the wrong places for them. Because I felt this poverty of spirit, I never thought to give. I withheld all the gifts I had because I believed I had no value, that I had no power to bring love, pleasure and joy to others—or to myself. And because I never thought to give, what I had to give never really grew, because the secret power of Giving is that it grows and grows the more you give it away. Once you open the box, it expands outwards in all directions, and it becomes unstoppable. Once I finally found my Voice, and gave completely and unreservedly of my whole heart and my whole Self, what I had left to give grew more and more and more.

'I used to think I was being humble and selfless by not being bold in the world. But really, now I see that when I remain silent, small and invisible, I am actually a miser, because I am depriving the world of gifts that grow bigger and bigger the more I give them away. In fact, the most selfless and generous thing I can do is to be as bold and as powerful and as visible as I can possibly be—

'The more I show myself in the daylight, the more easily I can see you.

'The more I learn to speak, the more easily I can understand what you have to say.

'The bigger I become, the bigger I need you to be. How else can we hold each other?

'The more we give, the more we have left to give—because what we are giving is immeasurable, and it grows infinitely even as you take from it.

'And this, my lovely Rose, is what I have learned to be the true power, the passion, and the ever-expanding energy of the Principle of Giving.'

At last all my words had been spoken. The air became fragrant with the scent of lilies of the valley, who rang their little, white bonnets like tiny Himalayan prayer bells tinkling in the distance.

A profound silence blanketed us now within the labyrinth. The Rose and I sat together silently for many hours, locked within each other's soft gaze, listening only to the cooling song of the Moon.

Within the heat of the sultry summer eve, I felt the Rose sigh with anguish at the pain of others, shout fiercely against all injustice, and weep for joy at the triumph of true love. And as she sighed and shouted and wept for joy, I felt the tiniest pinch of her thorns upon my own heart, in a bittersweet ecstasy that could only be expressed by this powerful Rose.

Her passionate love filled the world fully and freely in all directions without discrimination, as did the all-pervading cloud of her most intoxicating scent.

Love filled me, and filled me more.

Love was so simple as to be nearly incomprehensible.

And in that Love, I became so full that I had no choice but to love more and more.

'Now I understand it,' I said slowly. 'Years ago, I always felt my life to be devoid of love and passion. But actually, love and passion were always there. I sensed them; I somehow knew they were there in the background, but I couldn't hear them. I really did feel like an angel with broken wings...'

'But you were an angel nonetheless,' she pronounced.

The Rose's eyelids became heavy with dew. Dawn was approaching and the ladybirds started to yawn with sleepiness.

'I told you there was much you already knew!' the Rose said, as her head bobbed up and down, trying to fend off sleep for just one more moment.

'So tell me,' she asked, yawning now as well, 'what will you do next?'

I sat before this regal queen amongst her sleepy night court as the rays of the morning sun now pierced the eastern horizon. I felt my heart swell up with affection for her.

Then, I gave her my sincere promise.

'I will walk daily through the Garden of my own Soul.

'I will nurture it and tend to the weeds that spring up within its flowerbeds.

'I will learn more and more about the Principle of Giving from the simple stories of my own life.

'And,' I concluded, 'I will speak loudly to tell all I meet about the Love they will find when they do the same.'

*   *   *   *   *

SECTION TWO:
LESSONS FROM THE IRIS

THE PRINCIPLE OF RECEIVING

CHARACTERISTICS AND ATTRIBUTES:

beauty, elegance, taste, refinement, attraction, poise,
aesthetics, artistry, uniqueness, excellence, relishing,
appreciation, allowing, abundance, cherishing,
heartfelt thankfulness, acute awareness of being alive,
a sense of awe at the wonder of all things

GUIDES:

air, breath, moon, stars,
canyon, mother, daughter, guru,
dawn, midnight, mockingbird, crow,
birth, coma, sickness, death

SONG of thE Iris: Rainbow

black was the sky
  like night in the day

torrential
  cold
  dramatic lay
  the broad field before me

the path—
  lost
  long ago in the expanse
  of possibilities

direction—
  obscured
  by unlimited directions

purpose—
  cherished
  somewhere within the recesses
  of an optimism
  not quite blinded
  by the darkness of
  this night in day

standing
  on the precipice
  of this plane of unpredictable somethings

staring
  into the beauty of this devastatingly
  pregnant
  emptiness

my eyes were drawn up to the heavens

by some irresistibly
captivating entity—
a little drop
of unpredictability

had I been here
or there
or anywhere else
I'd not have seen him

a slight shift to the right or left
or a moment sooner or later
and his glimmer would not have caught my eye

ephemeral our existence be
a moment in eternity
that comes and passes
just as quickly
as we witness it

but beauty lies within the heart that has seen
and felt
and marvelled
at its sheer simplicity

and its need to exist
for the mere purpose
of being beautiful

for no other reason
did my rainbow
appear
on that black day

no single colour
was his colour

no single frequency
  he sang

his spectrum flashing against the aggressions
  of the lightning and the driving rains

a palette of unrestricted
  and unrestrained
  hues

stretching placidly across
  the torrential skies

amidst the storm—
  the epitome of grace
  the unification of polarities
  amidst the chaos

he is red—
  he is passion
  like blazing fires
  and the burning lips of young maids

he is orange—
  he is warmth and affection
  like smouldering embers
  and the autumnal moon of an October frost

but he is yellow too—
  full of humour and good cheer
  like sunny, yellow daffodils
  along the shore of the spring pond

and green—
  like the moss on a tree of an ancient forest
  like the grass in a painting by Renoir
  a green of quiet dignity and refinement

that is cooling to the spirit

blue he is also—
 full of empathy and depth of heart
 I simply cannot describe
 the unrivalled beauty of this colour—
  oh, I could drown in that ocean of blue

with indigo—
 he is quiet introspection
 like a peaceful, wakeful dream
 in the moments just before the dawn

and with violet—
 that subtlest of celestial colours
 he becomes transcendent beyond earthly thought
 almost invisible—
 like harmonics emanating from a heavenly lyre

and I know—
 as I gaze upon this fleeting image
 that there is more
  and still more that my limited eyes cannot see

I know—
 his spectra of possibilities
 lay far beyond my earthly senses

so what is there?
 what is there?
  what is there?

I had been lost
 in that blackness
 that formless
 directionlessness
 both in the dark

and flashing light
simultaneously

then I realised—
    that had it not been for the rainbow
    I would never have noticed
    the light amidst the storm at all

but for being
    at that point in time and space
    I'd never have seen this marvel
    of light
    and shadow

had I stood
    at but a different angle
    he would not have been visible
    to my limited sight

indeed—
    as I looked around me
    I saw that there were others
    standing on this very same field of possibilities
    but they did not see the rainbow
    at all

how could I possibly describe him to them—
    they who never saw him?

infatuated—
    I ran
    towards him
    only to find that
    the closer I came
    the dimmer he grew

I tried to grasp him—

but could not

better I should stay away
   so that he may exist forever!

he is a phantom—
   a whisper

and exists only
   in our relationship
   within that place in time
   that point in space

then too I realised—
   that had there been no storm
   there would have been no rainbow

they say there is a pot of gold
   at the end of this arch of heaven
   but if you chase it
   the end vanishes
   and you will never find it

but I know otherwise—

today I felt the sun pour through my window
   it shone upon the prism of my heart
   and the rainbow took birth
   within my very soul.

*   *   *   *   *

THE IRIS — THE PRINCIPLE OF RECEIVING

I t looked like rain when I woke that morning, but I didn't take much note of it.

Such was the weather on most of these early autumnal days. We could nearly always expect a shower or two late in the afternoon. It was nothing really unusual. So I made my way out, without any special preparations, intending to make a day of my trek, so I could explore as far as I could within the Garden before sunset. The crisp air, which was only beginning to show signs of the coming coolness of the season, was so inviting that I walked along without much care, delighting in feeling its freshness against my skin.

Small, unthreatening purple clouds came and went overhead, occasionally sprinkling the earth and vegetation with intermittent, but short-lived, showers. As they did, I wrapped my woolly orange-coloured cardigan around me against the occasional gust of chilling wind. The stately maple and horse chestnut trees that lined the back of the Garden and led to the wooded area that lay beyond were only just beginning to turn from green to shades of russet and gold, and provided an ample canopy under which I could shelter myself against these gentle rains until they stopped. As I stood beneath the umbrella formed by the strong, arching arms of these noble trees, the sound of the raindrops upon the leaves overhead made a delicious kind of music that sent shivers up my spine, and made the hair upon my neck stand upright.

The day progressed. Before long it was late in the afternoon. And as I wandered further and further through this forest of stunningly beautiful colour and transformation, I became blissfully unaware of the changing weather around me. So captivated was I by the scent of the earth and the gentle softness of the red-gold carpet of leaves beneath my feet, that I did not notice the gathering blanket of dense, black clouds that were now above my head.

Then, in one sharp burst, I heard a thunderclap—most unusual for this time of year—and the storm began.

I had not been prepared for this. No umbrella. No raincoat. Indeed, my clothes were not warm enough against the sudden coldness. I quickly sought shelter beneath the trees as I had done earlier, but this downfall was much too heavy. After a few moments, a chilling wind came from the north, and I watched hundreds and hundreds of deep red, golden and umber-coloured leaves fly from the branches of the trees and in all directions into the air, leaving nearly bare branches behind them. The rain poured easily through these bony branches, and I started to get drenched.

I was too far from home now to turn back to get shelter from the storm, so I looked in all directions around me for some place, any place, I could run. I was getting soaked to the skin by now, and was starting to shiver. Then suddenly, much to my surprise and delight, I saw a tiny cave, more like a grotto, etched into the western side of a very small hillock. Grateful for this quite random and unexpected good fortune, I ran to it as quickly as my feet would take me.

I reached the shallow grotto, which was so small I had to duck down slightly to enter. I ran my hands along its entranceway, to feel the touch of the craggy earth that formed its walls and ceiling. It was only about eight feet across, and as my eyes strained to see in the blackness all around me, I noted it appeared to be just about the same size in depth, as I could just about make out a faint image of its back wall.

'What an odd little cave!' I said aloud, without thinking.

Then I heard her say, 'Oh, you are just in time! Come quickly or you will miss it!'

I could not see her at first. My eyes were still quite blind amidst all this darkness and I quite nearly jumped when I heard these words resonate from within this featureless void.

And then, as my eyes began to adjust to the minute amount of light within the grotto, I finally saw the Iris. She stood there elegantly poised, bathed in a single beam of sunlight that entered the cave from the west.

The Iris called to me in a velvet voice.

'That's right. Over here! Come quickly!' she urged.

She was a most extraordinary vision, this Iris. Her petals were of the softest, softest purple, each fleeced with a single streak of egg-yolk yellow. She held these petals like gracefully outstretched arms that were accepting all that surrounded her, and all that she could take in. She stood alone and hidden away from the rest of the Garden. She exuded an air of divine grace that attracted me to come closer.

Now in her presence, I immediately forgot all about the storm, the cold and how soggy my feet were.

So, too, I also allowed myself to forget about the fact that Irises are springtime flowers! No Iris blooms in the autumn. This was a singular flower, this Iris. A truly unique flower.

'Come sit! Sit here next to me,' she said with some urgency. I sat down a few inches from her, not knowing what to expect.

'Look!' the Iris said, and she waved one of her velvety petals in the direction of the cave opening.

I turned towards where she was pointing, and saw something that instantly took my breath away.

It was a double rainbow—no, a triple rainbow—a splendid band of arches suspended against a blue-black sky. And just beyond it was an explosive burst of white sunlight shooting like laser beams from behind the towering storm clouds, reaching like outstretched fingers towards the earth. I had never before seen such a hypnotic display of the interplay between light and shadow, between source and reflection, between observer and the observed.

'Isn't it stunning?' the Iris sighed with blissful wonder. 'And how excellent it is you showed up just in time! Here I was, wishing I had someone to share this with me, and then you turn up—right out of the blue! Isn't it all completely and utterly amazing?' she asked.

I found myself somewhat transfixed in this moment, and didn't reply immediately to the Iris. But I knew this was as it should have been. This was a moment when all I was supposed to do is take it all in—all that surrounded me—the air, the rain, the light, the darkness, the chill, the colours, the awe of the fact that this was a moment that would never be repeated, and that the Iris and I were here, now, to witness it together.

And so, we simply sat next to each other for several moments in silence, listening to the rainfall, the distant thunder, the sound of our own breathing and the occasional sighs of amazement we could not help but emit.

After some time, the thunder became more and more distant. The sky began to clear and the sound of the rain was now just a barely audible patter. The birds, who had taken shelter within the canopies of the trees, now began their late-afternoon calls to each other across the Garden. The rainbows grew fainter and fainter until they disappeared altogether, and the sun began its descent on the western horizon.

At that moment I turned to look at my flowery hostess. Now, as the autumnal sun continued to crawl lower and lower in the sky, the tiny cave became illuminated with a warm, golden glow. It was then that I could take in her essence fully, and I was immediately captivated by her simple and graceful elegance. This Iris was indeed very different from the Rose. She had no thorns at all, and her stem and petals were much more delicate and vulnerable looking. There was no court-like array of bees, butterflies, ants and ladybirds to serve and adore her here in this remote grotto. She sat like a humble and hidden gem in this otherwise dark and inscrutable location. Like a fully satisfied hermit-sage whose awareness embraced everything in all directions, she emanated an air of contentment and quiet delight.

I knew she had much to teach me, so I asked her—

'What can I learn from you, gentle Iris?'

'Ah!' the Iris sighed ecstatically, 'how wonderful that you ask me this!'

She spent a moment simply to taste the pleasure of my request. I could hear her say, 'Mmmm,' as if she were relishing something very delicious.

Then, laughingly, she shook her petals as if to shake off her own ecstasy, and returned her attention to me.

'From me,' she replied smilingly, 'you can learn the Principle of Receiving,'

'What is the Principle of Receiving?' I asked her. 'Does it mean to wish for things? Does it mean to have a lot? Does it mean to work hard to get a lot? Does it mean to tell other people what you want?'

The Iris grew even more encouraged by my obvious confusion, as if to say, 'Oh, you and I are going to have such a wonderful time together.' The sun, which was now directly in front of us, wrapped her in a halo of light, and made the last few raindrops in the air glisten like crystal prisms as they nourished the thirsty earth.

The Iris spoke lyrically.

'The Principle of Receiving is beauty, elegance, excellence and taste.

'It is aesthetics, artistry and awareness.

'It is refinement, poise, and inner poetry.

'It is seeing the uniqueness of every moment.

'It is relishing and appreciation.

'It is cherishing.

'It is gratitude and heartfelt thankfulness.

'It is the wonder in both the smallest of the small, and the greatest of the great.

'It is stepping effortlessly into the world, your heart full and open.

'It is rapturously taking in the world, your arms outstretched and ready for everything.

'It is the trust of knowing that everything you need is already there.

'It is sensing the gifts that are at your fingertips.

'It is unlimited abundance.'

Then the Iris turned to face me directly and said—

'The Principle of Receiving is all that emanates from the world and flows into you. It is the magic that dances into you through the senses. It is the life breath that communes with your body, mind and heart.

'In short,' she concluded, 'the Principle of Receiving is Awareness.'

The beauty and gracefulness of the Iris drew me in so gently, I scarcely noticed that the sun had now set completely, and we were in the dark, illuminated only by starlight, by the full moon, and by the brilliance of the unspoken wonder of what was between us.

But then my practical mind began to take me away from this magical moment. This sounded like an awful lot to learn! I was starting to feel rather silly and immature next to this gentle and sweetly satisfied Iris. I had been out all day. It was well past dinnertime and all I could think about was my growing hunger, my soggy shoes, and how I was supposed to get back home in the dark.

The Iris could sense my restlessness, and she cast her glance towards the Garden with a smile. I could not help but look in that direction. To my amazement, the full Moon had risen and was now illuminating the entire Garden like a silver beacon. I could make out every feature of the path back home. It was as if she was trying to tell me that, through this Principle, losing my way was no longer possible. But in spite of this, I found I was still feeling somewhat leery, even though I could see everything quite clearly now.

My stomach started to growl. I think I must have looked embarrassed.

The Iris sighed smilingly once again, as if delighted by my embarrassment.

I looked sympathetically at her.

'Gentle, Iris, how can I learn all that you know?' I asked her in a humble voice. 'How can I possibly be aware? I am always thinking of what is coming next. How can I stop that? Do I need to stop the life I am living now? Do I need to become a hermit and live in a cave? Or do I need to work harder still so I can eventually become free of it all? How else could I possibly master all those wonderful things you describe?'

'Oh, but there is much you already know!' she said with a smile.

The words of the Iris encouraged me, but I had no inkling of what I already knew about the Principle of Receiving.

'Me? What could I possibly know already? Where have I learned it?' I asked.

'Oh, but you already know the answer to that!' said the Iris sweetly. 'Just take a walk through your own Garden to see what is already there.'

Yes, the Rose had told me to look in my own Garden, and I had indeed found many things I hadn't known about the Principle of Giving. Now the Iris was telling me I could find all I needed to know about the Principle of Receiving within the pathways of my own Garden. Still, I felt like I needed a bit more guidance.

'Oh elegant Iris,' I asked, 'where in my Garden shall I look to find the Principle of Receiving?'

The Iris looked upwards, her velvety purple petals stretching out like open arms that wished to catch the moonbeams within their delicate embrace. She shut her eyes and allowed her senses to fill. Then, after a few moments of silent meditation, she shook the moisture from her dewy mantle and spoke in musical tones, with a pleasure that flowed from her as easily and as a freely as a rill in a mountain stream.

In all directions are your Guides
in light and shadow, time and tides.
The dawn, the mockingbird and Crow
can teach you all you wish to know.

I did not at all understand what the Iris meant, but that night, I followed the light of the Moon back to my bed, and slept with my window open, so as to let its platinum beams fill my room. I filled my lungs with the moist autumn air, and allowed the night to fill my senses. And as I snuggled into my bedcovers against the deliciously silvery chill, I drifted into a blissful slumber where the Iris continued to sing to me within my dreams.

The next day, when I awoke from those mystical dreams, I found that, in much the same way I had learned from the Rose, I could indeed recall many simple stories from my life that had been lessons from the Iris, but I hadn't recognised them as such. I could remember times when amazement filled me in the smallest of the small and the greatest of the great. I could remember feelings of abundance in a single moment, and a sense of being alive as if the world had filled my entire being. I could remember how questions had arisen, and how answers had come through the subtle magic of the senses. I could remember moments that would otherwise have been forgotten, had not the Iris inspired me to remember and appreciate them. I could remember my arms being outstretched to the world, accepting without judgement all that was given to me, even things that sometimes felt difficult to bear. I could remember feelings of unbreakable connection, of unimaginable embracing from the universe.

It was all there—all that the Iris had described.

The Iris's teachings were indeed, as she said, all to be found within the Garden of my Soul, within the simple stories of my own life. And as I reflected upon these stories, I understood more and more how the Principle of Receiving may appear to be sometimes joyful and sometimes sorrowful, but how everything within both the light and the shadow of our own experience is equally precious.

And so, I felt the desire to write some of these stories down within these pages...

* * * * *

LEARNING TO BREATHE

This morning I was awakened by a crow. I had my bedroom window open to the cool spring English air. The alarm was set to ring at 7 AM, but before it did, a very large black crow came to perch on the frame of the window, which opens outwards. He cawed six times, in a moderate, even-paced rhythm. I woke up groggy and feeling confused because it almost sounded as if the crow was in my room. As I gained clarity and became more conscious, he crowed again. The same six caws. The same steady rhythm. I have to admit it made me wonder whether crows can count! I wondered whom he was calling and what he was saying. I listened to his raspy voice. Usually we think of crows as having rather nasty sounding voices, compared to other birds. But this is the voice the crow was given. Raspy, nasty or not, his voice stands out amongst all the other songbirds and mourning doves in the dawn chorus. This is the voice Creation had thought to give him to make him different from the other birds. But what was most remarkable this morning was that the crowing of this particular crow was very gentle, and not at all abrasive. It was pleasant sounding and soothing. I couldn't help but think he had actually come with the intention to wake me, because as soon as I was fully awake, he flew off.

The call of Crow had a remarkable effect upon me as the morning air ever so lightly brushed against the net curtains of my bedroom window. I had a sense of having slept outdoors; or perhaps what is more accurate to say is that I felt no barrier or distinction between indoors and outdoors.

The gentle breeze opened the curtains just a fraction further and let the day in just a bit more, tickling my nose and earlobes. And as it let the world into my world, I let my world become that world. I woke to feel that I lived fully in the world. I woke to walk through it, to breathe it in. I woke to feel that there is me and there is everything around me, and that there is no distance, no separation between us. I am in and of this world.

As this wonderful sensation filled my being, I let myself lean back into the softness of my bed and felt the cool summer dawn caress my shoulders. I shut my eyes and very soon, I was no longer in my room. The room dissolved into a place in which there were no insides or outsides. And as the room dissolved, I felt myself rise from my bed to step from the room and onto the threshold of the dawn of possibilities, of being, of Life itself.

And as I stepped onto it, I saw Crow.

* * * * *

He stood there with his head slightly to the side and with a wink in his eye. He leaned upon a silver-headed walking stick and wore a jaunty grey top hat and a red waistcoat. He took out a very oversized pocket watch from his left-hand pocket (which was embroidered with a row of lilies of the valley). Looking at the time, his monocle dropped from his eye, as he chided me.

'You're late!' he said. 'What took you so long?'

'I'm sorry,' I apologised, 'I was asleep.'

'Precisely!' he chastised. 'Now come along. We have places to go.'

I suddenly became aware that I was perched upon the windowsill overlooking my Garden. There was about a 15-foot drop.

'Wait a minute, here,' I protested. 'One more step, and I'll fall.'

'So is *that* what's been stopping you all these years?' he asked reproachfully. And he clucked at me with disapproval. 'Tsk, tsk, tsk!'

Somewhat embarrassed, I looked down at my feet.

'Hmm... so, how *do* I do this?' I asked timidly.

Then I looked up at Crow in front of me. He wasn't flying. He was just standing there outside my window in mid-air. I hadn't noticed that before.

By now Crow was twirling his cane around and whistling Gene Kelly tunes, while tapping his toe impatiently as he waited for me to move.

'Come on, come on,' he said. 'Figure it out, girl!'

I looked back down at my feet on the windowsill. Slowly, a sensation came over me. I felt the air around my feet, my legs, my torso and arms. I felt it on my face. I felt it before me, behind me, and on all sides of me. I felt it fill my lungs and then go out from them. It was the air that was always the same, the air that linked it all.

The air—that was the key.

Crow stood in the air.

I saw the window ledge dissolve away beneath my feet like a mist. Somehow not at all surprised that I hadn't crashed down to the earth below, I looked up and faced Crow directly eye-to-eye. Now, I truly was neither inside nor outside. I too was simply in the air.

Crow and I were both in that same air. We both were breathing it, walking through it, living in it.

I took a breath and felt the air enter me. I tasted it. I let it fill me and nourish me. I felt it give me life.

I lifted my right foot. I released my breath into what lay before me, and simply stepped forward.

I stepped into the dawn.

All at once, Crow tossed his hat into the air. A flock of bluebirds came to play with it. They danced dizzily, chirping their little bluebird melodies. Crow's coat and monocle and cane had all disappeared, and he was now soaring into the sky, like a proper crow would do. I felt myself draw to follow him, and I flew effortlessly into the skies of possibilities behind Crow.

'Where are we going?' I called out to him.

'You see?' he complained. 'That's always the problem, isn't it? You people always think you have to be going somewhere.'

'Ok,' I said, 'then what *should* I be thinking?'

Crow suddenly stopped flying, and turned around to look at me squarely in the eye.

'I don't want you to *think* anything!' Crow said emphatically. Then, somewhat exasperated, he added 'In fact—just *stop* it!'

'Stop?' I asked.

'Yes, stop. Stop thinking altogether!'

I was a bit confused. Stop thinking? Hmm... Just the thought of not thinking made me want to think.

I became aware that I had a very perplexed look on my face as Crow leaned towards me and said—

'Breathe...'

'I *am* breathing,' I protested.

'No, you're not!' said Crow. Then, he put his wings on my shoulders and said, 'Stop thinking and just breeeeeeaaathe.'

Crow pushed me gently away. He shut his eyes, leaned backwards and spread out his black-feathered wings and started floating. He looked like someone bobbing atop the water in a swimming pool. But Crow was floating upon the breezes of timelessness, where there are no markers between here and there. And as he did this, I stood bewildered and amazed as I watched him—well—just *breathe*. He didn't look like a crow anymore. He looked like nothing I had ever seen. I do not think I have the words to describe him.

I tried to imitate what Crow was doing. I spread my arms and lay my head back against the backdrop of the expanse of the world behind me. There was no ground below me, no walls around me, no ceiling above. The horizon was unlimited. My awareness of time itself changed. Time did not stand still— rather I was aware of *all* time—all time simultaneously within this single moment.

Now was always. It has always been Now.

Here is everywhere. I have always been Here.

I took a breath and felt Here-and-Now enter my being.

I released it and felt my being tickle and kiss Here-and-Now.

Here-and-Now laughed and blushed like a shy, young lover, as it entered the lungs of my awareness again and again, and I again filled the world with all that I was.

Now I started to understand what Crow meant about breathing. I felt as though I had taken my very first breath of the world. Yes, to breathe was to take in, to taste, to live—and to release oneself back into that totality as well.

But to breathe was not only that—it was also to allow your soul to be tasted, to allow yourself to *be* loved.

Full of breath, I opened my eyes to see Crow hovering in front of me. Now, he had a sly, little grin on his face, with one eyebrow cocked as if inspecting me.

'Uh-huh,' he said, 'I can see you are just about ready to fly now.'

'Fly?' I asked. 'I thought we *were* flying.'

But before I could get an answer, or even ask the question, Crow was off like a rocket and I found myself pulled into the back draft of his flight.

'Whoa!' I cried. 'Hold on, Crow! Help!'

Crow just laughed. He flew higher and faster and further and more vigorously. The world of possibilities became a dizzying kaleidoscope around me on all sides. There was so much to look at, I couldn't catch my breath.

'Stop!' I called to Crow.

This time he complied. Crow stopped suddenly.

And what I now saw took my breath away.

I do not know how I can possibly do justice in trying to describe the vision I saw in that moment. For what I saw before me was a panorama of every dawn I had ever lived. Here they were all at once, co-existing in a seamless tapestry of colour, sound and sense. There were some I couldn't quite make out and I could only assume these were dawns yet to come, or perhaps dawns that might have been, or that could be. There, in that moment, I saw the endless dawn of possibilities.

With a smile on his face, Crow stood silently before me, watching knowingly, as I took this all in.

'What do you see?' asked Crow.

'I see my life,' I replied, without thinking.

'Only that?' he asked.

'Only that?' I queried. *What more could there be? I wondered.*

Crow now cocked his head to the left and gave me another one of his crooked smiles. I was coming to understand that this expression of his meant he approved on some strange level. In fact, he seemed quite satisfied that I was confused.

'Come here,' said Crow, with a sudden softening of his tone of voice. He reached out his black feathery wing and took me by the crook of my right arm. He walked me a few steps towards a pale yellow dawn that I remembered from my youth.

'What is here?' Crow asked, nodding towards that distant dawn.

I strained to see that dawn. It was a long time ago—almost 40 years now. I was in my bedroom in my parents' home. I was about 14 or 15 years old, I guess. I could see myself tossing and turning in the bed at the end of a long, sleepless summer night, just before the sun was to rise.

'Yes...' I said dreamily as the image became clearer, 'Yes, I remember that night. I remember that something kept me awake all night long. It was a really hot night in August. We didn't have air conditioning in those days, so I had my window wide open. My bedroom faced our garden, and just outside the window was a young mimosa tree. That night, a bird came and perched himself in the mimosa and sang all night long.'

Crow chuckled knowingly.

'And then what happened?' he prompted.

I looked at Crow with suspicion. I got the impression he already knew, but just wanted to make me remember.

'Hmm...' I said, recalling that night, 'Well, I felt angry at the bird actually, because he kept me awake all night and I was really tired by morning. I mean, all the other birds had the decency to go to sleep at sunset, but this particular bird sang and sang and sang all night long, and right outside my window, too. I couldn't exactly ignore his singing because it was really loud. And because it was in the middle of the night and there were no other sounds at all, his voice echoed against the rooftops and sounded really eerie. In fact, it sounded kind of spooky. I couldn't close the window because I would have sweltered in the summer heat. I couldn't chase the bird away because I would have made a lot of noise, and then my parents would have gotten angry at me for waking them up.'

'So what did you do?' asked Crow.

'Well, after hours of fighting it, I sort of resigned myself to the situation. But I felt very sorry for myself, because by this time it was almost 5 AM, and I hadn't slept a wink all night.'

I stopped for a moment, and listened to the ghostly echoes of the night bird.

Crow looked unconvinced. 'So that's it? That's the end of the story? There must be something else.'

I looked at Crow. He could see something I was overlooking, something I had forgotten. I let my memory dwell in those moments before the dawn, and gradually the darkness of the night faded from my mind.

Yes—I do remember something else.

'You are quite right, Crow,' I said. 'That is not the end of the story. Now I remember what happened. Yes, I resigned myself to the fact that this bird was there and that he was not going to fly away, and that I was going to be awake all night. But as I did this, I noticed that instead of staying angry at the bird, I started to pay attention to what he was singing.'

'Yes?' asked Crow quizzically. 'Go on.'

'Well, I noticed he was singing short, melodic phrases, and that he would repeat each phrase three times. After he repeated the tune, he would change his melody completely.'

'Really?' remarked Crow.

'Yes!' I replied, getting more animated. 'And after listening for a while, I found that the bird had a whole repertoire of tunes and voices. It was pretty amazing. Soon I found I simply couldn't stop listening to him, because I wanted to hear what song he would sing next. I became fascinated by his tunes. Some were cheerful and sweet, others screechy and harsh. Some were fast and staccato, others wide-ranging and rhapsodic. Like this—' And I attempted to imitate what I could only vaguely remember of that birdsong I had heard so many years earlier, so Crow could hear what I meant. I imagine I sounded pretty silly trying to sound like a bird.

'Remarkable!' exclaimed Crow. 'So what happened next?'

'Well, eventually, I realised that I had been awake all night long, not because of the noise, but because I simply couldn't pull myself away from listening. As the night ended, and the dawn started to come, all the other birds woke up and started singing, as birds do at dawn. And amazingly, the songs they sang were all the same songs the night bird had been singing throughout the night. It was as if—'

Suddenly I stopped.

'As if what?' Crow asked.

'I remember something else now,' I said.

'Yes?' asked Crow.

'I remember that the next day, I called the Audubon Society to find out what this odd nocturnal bird could be. I described his singing, and they told me he was a *mockingbird. Of course!* I thought. That would explain his vast array of melodies. He was imitating all the birds he had heard in the vicinity. I had never heard a mockingbird sing before. I didn't know anything about them. I didn't know they were nocturnal, and I surely didn't know they came to Long Island. I was really intrigued. I found myself wondering, *Does the mockingbird have a song of his own? Do mockingbirds pick up regional accents?* I became completely fascinated by the very idea of a mockingbird.'

And, while telling Crow about the mockingbird, another memory arose inside me.

With birdsong surrounding me like thick August butterscotch, I stepped into that dawn of the mockingbird. With wonder I beheld this pious nocturnal minstrel—his melodies a plaintive collection of hymns he had not himself composed, his chanting fervent like a solitary monk who had taken a vow to pray continuously throughout the night.

And then—

'Oh, my...I do remember now....'

And suddenly, words came to me that I had not heard in 40 years—

I heard a mockingbird last night...

'What do you remember?' asked Crow.

'I remember—'

He came and sat upon my tree
and sang a mist of miracles—

138

a litany
  a history
of time and space
  of everyplace...

'I wrote a poem about the mockingbird—'

In vigilance he prayed and prayed
  throughout the night while others slept
  mindlessly and unaware...

'I thought I had forgotten it completely—'

And at the break of day his voice
  then summoned forth the world to sing
  and melted to become a thousand
  other voices of the dawn

A symphony rising with the sun
  chasing fast the night away—
  and the mockingbird
  with it...

'The words are unclear, but I can still make out parts of it—'

Men—
  most fear the night, you know.
They sleep until the morning song
  and waken to those thousand voices
  knowing not from whence they came
  and knowing naught of mockingbirds

They see the sun ablaze
  at day
And dazed
  they wake
  but never dream

to hear
    the mockingbird at night.

I went silent for several moments. I suppose I started to look sad, because Crow seemed concerned for me.

'What's the matter?' asked Crow.

'I lost that poem years ago, and I can only remember these fragments of it. I know the original poem was much longer, but I cannot remember what I wrote. Even these words I just spoke are not precisely as I had written them in my youth.

'But even though I cannot remember it exactly, the essence of the poem is still here. The metaphors are here, even if the words are not. And I do know with certainty that I remember the first and final lines of the poem, just as I penned them when I was a young girl.'

The scattered words of my poem now echoed in my heart in much the same way as the voice of the mockingbird had echoed through my sleeping neighbourhood. Both were pieces of a puzzle that made an incomplete picture of reality, but that nonetheless spoke something of the inner reality of the poets who had composed them, decades earlier.

'And actually, Crow, I am not being completely honest with you. I didn't lose the poem. I discarded it. I tossed that poem away when I was 26 years old, along with hundreds of others, because I didn't believe anyone would ever like them. I just tossed them all away, like a piece of rotting fruit, believing they were imperfect things that had come from an imperfect 'me', and not seeing they had been sent to me as gifts. For years I felt like these poems had died. But you, Crow, have taken me back to the place of their birth. And even if I cannot remember every detail of *Mockingbird*, I feel really happy remembering that poem.'

'What is it that makes you so happy when you remember this particular poem?' Crow asked.

'The fact that this was the first poem I had ever written that had real substance. And not only that. This poem came to me without any effort. When I sat down to write it, the words just flowed out of my fountain pen in a single burst of inspiration.

'Through this poem, I inhaled my very first breath of the world around me. Instead of fighting against the world, I had allowed the world to come in. Instead of shutting the window, I let the song of the mockingbird enter me. I felt the mockingbird. I felt his life fill me and then I felt his life disperse into the dawn chorus across my garden, my town, the world. I allowed my whole self breathe in this seemingly insignificant dawn, and learn how to marvel at what was its truly unique significance. I had written many other poems before this one, but none of them had really come from this quiet place of reception, of acceptance, of joy, of life-breath.

'I had always believed this mockingbird had been sent to me so I could write this poem. But now, looking back, I see it is not just about a single poem. The mockingbird was sent to awaken the sleeping poet within me. I cannot believe I overlooked this before. What started as a sleepless night was actually a turning point in my life. It was the moment when I was shown who I was meant to be. It is so simple. Just thinking about this makes my heart swell up. The thought of this makes me so grateful to the mockingbird I feel like crying. How can I ever repay him?'

My throat choked up with heartfelt gratitude.

'So, I shall ask you again,' said Crow. 'What is here?'

I looked at Crow with wonder. I looked deep into his black eyes and into his knowing smile.

'For years,' I said, 'I mourned the loss of that poem. But now, Crow, I can see that the poem itself was not the most important thing about this dawn—it was the discovery of the poet within me.'

I looked at Crow and listened silently to the song of his Soul.

I heard my own Soul singing back.

My throat was so tight now it was hard to breathe, let alone speak.

'What else is here?' Crow prompted.

I shut my eyes and listened within. I heard the song of the mockingbird. I heard him and knew that he, throughout that night and into the dawn, was my herald into poetry.

But poetry was merely a manifestation. The mockingbird was much more than that—

He was the voice that called forth the voice of all the other birds.

He had called me to waken to the night,
    to the dream,
        to the silence,
            and to call me to waken others too.

The mockingbird was the voice that called forth my *own* voice.

'What is here,' I said, finally feeling the words burst forth from my throat, 'is Voice itself!'

I swung around to look at Crow. He stood there, face all very smirky and full of mischief. Suddenly, I had a random thought—

'The mockingbird, Crow—was it—*you?*' I asked him.

Crow didn't answer, but I almost felt as though he blushed a bit. He looked away, almost shyly, and said, 'Come on, we have other dawns to visit.'

With that, he whisked me away on a sea of black monsoon clouds. And as the drops of warm summer rain fell from their towering domes, I found myself falling with them. And as I fell, I heard the clouds rumbling in what sounded like a deep, resonant voice that was asking,

'What is the treasure?'

And just like the summer rain, I tumbled from the rumbling clouds, without any knowledge of where I would land...

*   *   *   *   *

...but when I did finally come back to Earth, I suddenly felt really strange.

'Push!' Crow ordered.

'What?!' I shouted.

I felt like I was in a fog. Suddenly I realised I was lying on my side and I felt really high. It was all pretty confusing.

'What the heck is going on, Crow?' I complained.

My eyes started to focus in the dull, pre-dawn light. Slowly, I started to recognise where I was. There is no way I could have forgotten this particular dawn. It was the month of May when I was 28 years old, and I was giving birth to my daughter, at our small apartment in Texas. I had gone into labour at midnight 29 hours before, just as I was going to bed after a very long day. I had wanted the birth to be completely natural, so I had decided I would not take any drugs, herbs or air at all during labour. I thought this would help me stay alert, but after the long, arduous process, I felt dull-brained and confused, and began to lose all sense of reality. Now, having been awake for the past 45 hours, all I wished I could do was go to sleep. Lack of sleep made everything seem surreal, and my slightly delusional mind started to believe I was trapped in some sort of twisted time-warp, that there was no baby, and that I was going to stay in this state of limbo for all eternity.

Then, around 4:30 AM, I remember that I sat on the floor, with my legs curled under me, ready to give yet another low groan as another contraction hit me. But instead, something suddenly made me sit up straight and say, 'Oh!'

The midwife asked, 'What's happening?'

'I don't know,' I said. 'All the pains have suddenly stopped. Something feels—different.'

The midwife examined me and said excitedly, 'The baby's dropped! You're ready to deliver—NOW!'

'Oh my God! Now?!'

I turned to look at the midwife, but all I saw was Crow wearing a white nurse's cap.

'Hey, wait a minute,' I said. I knew I wasn't so delusional that I was seeing giant crows dressed in nurses' uniforms. 'My midwife never wore a nurse's cap. And she certainly didn't have a beak or feathers. Just what are you playing at, Crow?'

'Push!' Midwife Crow ordered again.

This was clearly not the time to argue with Crow. I felt myself automatically going into 'push' mode.

I felt my whole self focus like a laser beam.

Suddenly, all the dullness I had been feeling disappeared and I became very sharp and lucid, and filled with an odd sense of power. I was aware of everything—every sensation, every sound, every touch, every breath. It was remarkable. I had never felt so alive before. I had complete control over my thoughts, my will and my body. I couldn't believe it.

'Ok, stop pushing!' I heard a voice say.

I stopped instantly. I held on to the urge to push like a sacrament, knowing that I could start and stop at exactly the right time. I was astounded at the fact that I felt such tremendous control in that moment. During pregnancy, I had worried that I might 'lose it' during delivery, that I would become totally incoherent, and this unexpected welling up of power and self-control was all a bit of a surprise. But it felt fantastic. I felt no fear whatsoever. I felt no panic or lack of faith. I felt like the most powerful person in the universe.

Hmm...or maybe it's just my body's natural endorphins, I thought...

'Ok, all we need now is just one last push,' the voice ordered.

I focussed. I felt all the energy of life entering me. I held onto that energy like a life raft, and felt myself go into action. Every vital drop of my consciousness was present in that fraction-of-a-fraction of a single moment, which was to come only once in the history of time.

I inhaled deeply—

And with that breath, my baby daughter was born. Every cell in my body had aligned to release her into the world, and I felt her tiny body wriggle on its own in the early morning air.

And then I finally let myself exhale, as my child took her first breath on that blushing morning in early May.

I hadn't had an ultrasound during the pregnancy, so I didn't know what the sex of my child would be. So when the midwives placed her on my abdomen, I felt a rush of surprise, thrill and delight to see my little baby girl. She was so perfect. She didn't cry—well, not really. She sort of picked her head up a tiny bit (I was surprised to see how strong she was) and squinted towards me and gave up the tiniest little whimper. 'Waa,' she said in a tiny, little voice. It reminded me of a little kitten mewing, and melted my heart completely. Then she put her little head back down on my abdomen and seemed quite content. It was as if she had been thinking, *Oh, yeah, that's right. I'm a baby. They're expecting me to cry,* and she whimpered just for the sake of establishing her official arrival into the world.

She was born at 4:43 AM, just before the dawn. In India, they say this is the most auspicious time of day.

I felt elated and full of energy after my daughter was born. Immediately, I jumped into the shower and then changed into fresh, clean clothes. I was so thrilled to be in my own home, and not at a hospital. Excitement and joy welled up in me. When I returned to my bedroom, I found the midwives had cleaned everything up, and the sun was just starting to light up the room. The Texas days were already quite warm at that time of year, so they had opened the windows to let in the cooler morning air. My first view of the room after I came out from the shower was life-changing. It felt like Life itself had taken birth in my room, along with my daughter. In those days, her dad and I were quite the hippies, and we slept on soft bedding on the floor rather than in a bed. And now I saw my tiny child lying asleep on a small yellow blanket on the floor next to my bedding. The sight of her made me feel as if the room had suddenly become filled with a sea of daffodils.

I stepped out of that moment now, so as to look at it better, and to relish it from a different perspective.

Crow came to stand next to me as I looked.

'What is here?' he asked.

'Perfection.' I said. 'Simplicity. Right now everything is perfect and simple. I am part of Life, and Life called upon me to bring more life into the world. And what that life will turn out to be is the great mystery and the miracle contained within this single moment. And that is all that Life is—the series of moments containing one miracle and mystery after another. We all make life so complicated, but right now I can see that it is all very simple.'

'What else is here?' Crow asked.

What else? I pondered.

Crow's question put me in a deeply reflective state, as I now watched myself lying next to that tiny, new life, swaddled in soft, yellow flannels.

Finally I found the words.

'It is here that first I learned how powerful we all can be,' I said.

Crow looked at me with raised eyebrows.

I looked at Crow. I nodded, understanding what he was implying.

'Yes, you are right, Crow,' I admitted to him. 'It is here that I learned that *I* am powerful.'

I reflected on this for a moment and then continued.

'My goodness, Crow, how many times would I forget this over the coming years? How many times would I resign myself to circumstance, feeling myself powerless to direct the course of my own life? Now, as I look at it and feel it once again, I can see that in this moment, my awareness of my own power was born. How could I have forgotten this essential lesson I learned on the dawn of my daughter's birth?

'This,' I added, 'was the moment the World gave me the gift of self-belief.'

And as I said this, I started to become aware of the many gifts the World had given me. In these two dawns alone, the World had given me the gifts of poetry and of power, of voice and self-belief. It had given me these gifts, but I had not fully received them. I had not really taken them in. It was as if I had let them brush against my cheeks, and then I put them away in a box. Forgetting that these wonderful gifts were within my reach at any given moment, I still tried to be more, do more, on my own without them.

But all that was before I had stepped into the world. That was when I was inside looking out, asleep in my bed. That was before I met Crow.

Crow stood silently, watching me. He could see I was processing all this. He didn't bother to ask me what I was thinking or feeling. He knew something was changing in me. Just as something had changed when my daughter dropped into the birth canal and was ready to be born, I had 'dropped' and was coming into the dawn of my own birth—my spiritual birth.

Then Crow whispered something in my ear:

'What is the treasure?'

I didn't answer, but the words sent a ripple through me like the magic charm of a hidden mountain stream. I let the sound of the words wash over me and through me. I felt the blood pulsing through my veins. I felt the air moving in and out of my lungs.

I felt myself breathing and my fingertips tingled with sensation.

Crow's voice was very soft now as he extended his feathery arm towards me and said, 'Come. Step into this dawn.'

Gently, he turned me 180 degrees to view the coming of another dawn, in the summertime nine years later.

This dawn, I remember well.

* * * * *

Crow and I stepped through a shadowy arch and entered a small bedroom in the darkest quarter of the night, about two hours before the sun was to rise in the heat of a very muggy Atlantic summer. The walls of this room were a pleasant peach colour. The floral pattern of the drapes on the windows matched the bedding on the queen-size, pecan-wood framed bed, and these perfectly offset the colour of the walls. There were subtle hints of blues, both navy and powder blue, teasing the eyes along with soft pinks, oranges and rust. There were cushions on the bed that pulled out these tones, and two watercolour pictures on the walls that enhanced the fusion of these colours even more. At one end of the room sat a lovely gold velvet chair that had a button-tufted back and an Italian cane-lattice wooden frame. There was nothing in this tidy room that had not been placed intentionally, for the purpose of creating an ambience that was both cosy and tasteful. On any given day, whenever the sunlight poured through those peach-coloured net curtains, the room was filled with colour, and everything looked rich and warm and cheerful, and perfectly dressed.

But this was not any given day.

Next to the lovely queen-sized bed was another bed. This one was not warm or cheerful or oversized or wooden framed. This bed was only large enough for a single person. It was heavy and metal-framed with mechanical devices for raising and lowering the back and legs. It had no colourful bedding, no duvets or lovely cushions. It was dressed in white sheets and white cotton blankets. And while it was impeccably clean, it was also cold and sterile.

This was a hospital bed, looking terribly out of place in this lovely peach-coloured room. In the bed lay the woman who, not very long before, had decorated this room with all these muted but pleasant shades of peach and navy blue, lovingly selecting each fabric, and each pattern, with the greatest of care. She loved to decorate her home. She loved to have others tell her how lovely her home was. But she was unable to enjoy any of this now. She could no longer see the pretty colours, nor curl up with the feather-soft cushions, nor wrap herself up in the comfort of her own bedding. She was in the final stages of cancer and was now in a deep coma. She was dying.

This woman was my mother.

This was the fifth night of a long vigil. I had arrived on Monday afternoon, and soon it would be passing from Friday into Saturday morning. But I was hardly aware of the time, or whether it was day or night, and the only colour I saw was a very dim amber glow that seemed to hang like a heavy veil over the entire scene. Since Tuesday, when she had gone completely into a comatose state and was no longer drifting in and out of consciousness, the hospital bed had been wheeled in by the hospice service. The bedroom draperies had been drawn and it now felt like one endless night. Even when a few rays of the hot summer sunlight would enter the room at midday, it seemed surreal and other-worldly in this lingering night.

But this was a night without the relief of sleep or the escape of dreams. I found it nearly impossible to sleep that week because I was afraid my mother might die while I was napping. And so I remained awake, and so became somewhat delirious as the days wore on. Once a day, I allowed my body half an hour's nap, but when doing so, I never felt fully capable of shutting off. Even if I dozed, my mind was conscious of my mother's comatose body only a few feet away, and of her laboured breathing. I would see images and impressions of the room even in my sleep. I would hear conversations that may or may not have been taking place. And as I napped, every change of tone or rhythm drew my attention and made me stir. I remembered how, when my daughter was a baby, the slightest rustle from her cot would cause me to wake. Now, my body entered this same state of alertness, as my mother lay dying a few feet away from me in that night that lasted one hundred hours.

I looked at her and thought how we all wanted to sleep—she, from the pain and suffering of the disease that was eating away her body, and we who were sitting sleeplessly in vigil waiting for the inevitable to happen.

I looked at the vestiges of my mother's frail body that lay breathing laboriously on the hospital bed. The cancer had eaten away so much of her that she was now little more than a breathing skeleton with a thin sheet of translucent skin wrapped loosely around her bones. It was impossible for me to imagine what she must have been feeling. Prior to that week, I hadn't seen my mother for about two years, so when I arrived on Monday it was a bit of a shock to see the toll the disease had had upon her. She had always been of very petite and slender build, but the cancer had reduced her to, I would estimate, about 65 or 70 pounds at most.

I do remember that my mother had called me about two weeks earlier, before I went to see her, and told me, 'These days, I look in the mirror and I think, *I can't believe it's me.*'

'That's because,' I replied softly to her, it's *not* you.'

I do not know whether my mother understood, accepted or appreciated my words, as she did not comment upon them. She was never open to talking about such things with me, or perhaps not with anyone. She never talked about life and death, or about what she believed in regards to them. But even though she offered no comment to my statement, her acute sadness was evident through her silence.

Crow, seeing how lost in reverie I was, stepped up next to me.

'Who is this person?' Crow asked very softly.

'This is my mother,' I told him.

'Who is this person?' Crow asked again without hesitation.

I looked at Crow quizzically. I took some time to consider this question before I answered, and my mind scanned the history of my relationship with my mother.

Throughout the 37 years she and I shared this planet, my mother and I argued a lot. There were countless power struggles and clashes of belief. By the time I was a teenager, I never shared the more private sides of myself with my mother, for I feared she would criticise them, or worse, reject them. And my fear was not mere paranoia; she had indeed shut me out many times over the decades, sometimes not speaking to me for years at a time. Invariably, all of our arguments revolved around her disapproval of my chosen lifestyle—my career, my friends, my education, my place of residence, my relationships, my philosophy, my clothes, my hairstyles, my religion. On top of this, my mother did not listen to music other than whatever popular artists were on the television, did not particularly like poetry and disliked speaking about things that were controversial or emotionally intense. This left little to talk about except the news, weather and television, and even that had to be dealt with cautiously.

And so my mother and I had a sort of mutual agreement that we would remain at a polite arm's length from one another, so that we did not shut each other out altogether. We became two-dimensional beings to each other, like paper dolls. And just like a paper doll, I myself felt flat and empty whenever I hung up the phone after speaking with her. Sometimes that emptiness lasted for days, only to rise again when I spoke to her the following week. I cannot know whether she felt the same, but I imagine she might well have. This was how we played our roles as mother and daughter. But in playing our roles so very well, we had along the way missed the opportunity to know each other as human beings.

Who is this person? I'm not sure how to answer that, Crow, I thought.

My mind came back to the scene before me, and I saw my mother on her deathbed.

During those last five days of her life, I had many opportunities to sit alone with my mother for hours at a time, as she lay without the ability to move or speak or react to me. My father and sister came and went, as there were a lot of other things that had to be attended to during that time, leaving my mother and me on our own in the house. I knew a coma did not necessarily mean unconsciousness. I knew it was likely my mother could hear everything that was being said. For this reason, I asked my father and sister to leave if they were talking about practical things, to give my mother some space, which they did. And in doing so, they unknowingly allowed my mother and me to transform our relationship into something it had never been.

During the first two days, I spoke to my mother in pretty much the same way I had always done, talking superficially about day-to-day events. But by the third day, I had run out of chit-chat. I didn't know what else to talk about. There were lots of other things I could have talked about, but I did not. All those other topics were in the unwritten code of things my mother and I never shared.

So I sat there with her saying nothing for a few minutes.

After a while, my mother made a low groaning sound, as if to ask me where I was. Instinctively, I knew she wanted me to keep talking.

'I'm still here, Mom,' I assured her. 'I've just run out of things to say, I guess.'

What can I say to her? I thought. *It's hard enough to talk to my mother, but it's even harder when she's not saying anything back. How do I know what she is thinking? There's a lot of stuff I could talk to her about, but...*

I started to consider the reasons why I was still withholding parts of myself from my mother, and I realised it was because I still feared her rejection of me. Throughout the years, I had learned to sidestep that possibility by withholding myself from her. After all, she could not reject what she did not know. My being distant had become a habit in all my dealings with her.

But now, here she lay, unable to speak, criticise or shut me out. What was I afraid of in this moment? What was I waiting for? Why was I still shutting *her* out? This was our final chance to know one another, and if I didn't do something about it right away, it would never happen.

'Hold on a minute, Mom, I'll be right back,' I said to her.

I got up and went into the bedroom next door where I kept my belongings, and I took a small book from my suitcase. Within a moment, I had returned to my mother's room.

I sat down in the gold velvet chair at the foot of her bed. I opened the book and began to chant a verse from the tenth chapter of the *Bhagavad Gita*—

> *aham sarvasya prabhavo*
> *mattah sarvam pravartate*
> *iti matva bhajante mam*
> *budha bhava-samanvitah*[1]

I paused for a moment. My mother was lying relatively still.

Encouraged, I continued to read the next three verses, chanting in the tuneful, traditional Sanskrit fashion I had learned over the years. The only sound other than my own voice was my mother's softly rhythmic, but laboured, breathing.

But then, quite alarmingly, just as I started to read the fourth verse, my mother suddenly gave a very loud cry, almost a shout, not at all like the low groan she had given off before. She didn't move or open her eyes, and her cry came completely without warning. Her cry startled me, even frightened me, and I quite literally jumped in my chair and dropped my book onto the floor.

Of course, I had no idea what this cry might have meant. Was she in pain? Was she reacting to my words? Was she saying, *'What is that you are reading?'* Was she saying, *'Stop that! You're scaring me!'*? Was she saying, *'That's really beautiful; please keep going'*? I had no way of knowing.

But instinctively, to me, her cry sounded like fear.

I picked up the book and placed it on the nightstand. I walked over to her and began to speak to her softly.

'I'm reading from a book called the *Bhagavad Gita,* Mom. It's an ancient scripture from India. The language is Sanskrit. I told you I had studied Sanskrit, didn't I? Well, really only a little bit. It's a pretty complex language. You know, I bet you'd be interested in it. I know how much you liked to study grammar when you were young. I remember how you told me about when you studied Latin. Sanskrit's a lot like Latin, actually.

'Anyway, what I was reading were four special verses. These four verses are supposed to contain all the wisdom of the rest of the *Bhagavad Gita* put together. Ancient tradition says that if someone hears these four verses, even if they don't know what they mean, the sound vibration from the verses is so powerful, it will liberate a soul from the cycle of birth, death and rebirth. Now, I know you don't believe in reincarnation or anything to do with eastern religions, but it doesn't really matter. I mean, if it is all just a lot of bunk, at least these verses are pretty to listen to. And if it's not a lot of bunk, I would be very upset with myself if I hadn't read them to you, just because I was afraid of what you would think of me. Now is not the time for us to worry about things like that.'

She was breathing much less laboriously now.

'You know, Mom, you and I always used to argue about my interest in Indian religion. I never told you much about it because I was always convinced you would freak out. But here's the irony of it. It was you who sent me off to Catholic school when I was a kid. That was when I became interested in philosophy and religion. When I felt the Church could take me no further, I just continued my journey somewhere else. So, like it or not, you're the one who got me interested in studying about spirituality in the first place. So if you don't like the fact that I practice an eastern religion, well, in a way it's kind of your fault, 'cause you're the one who started me on this journey. But you know what? I am grateful to you for that.'

My mother seemed completely settled, and her breathing was now soft and smooth.

But then, a sudden awareness came over me that went beyond my logical understanding, and intuitively I took my mother's frail, white hand in my own hand—and I started to sing to her.

I started singing sacred Sanskrit hymns, very simple ones, with simple tunes and simple rhymes. My philosopher's mind rationalised that these non-material vibrations would speak directly to my mother's heart.

But very shortly, much to my surprise, I found that my philosopher's mind was actually getting in the way of what was really important at that moment.

As I felt my mother's icy hand, and watched her steady breathing, I realised the most important thing at that moment was not the mantra, the tunes or the rhythms, but rather the soothing sound of my own singing. This was what my mother wanted. I could feel this coming from her.

I sang in simple lullaby tunes, making them up as I went along. They were not even real tunes, just a few notes really, simply rocking back and forth in a sing-song fashion. As I sat there singing to my mother, I could remember how I used to sing this same way when my daughter was an infant, as I rocked her to sleep. Now, I was stroking my mother's hand and arm, very lightly, so as not to hurt her, while singing these lullabies to her. I could feel that she was frightened. I could feel that she felt alone. I could feel that the thing she wanted most at that moment was for someone to be there with her, and to help her not to be afraid.

And so I sang her lullaby hymns for hours, for days. I sang and I sang. The daughter singing lullabies to the mother. Singing softly and repetitively and simply. Singing gently and reassuringly, as you would sing to a child who is afraid of the dark. This is all she wanted. I knew this now. She didn't need to tell me with words.

As I sang, I reflected upon the discussion I had had with my mother when I told her it was not she whose face was in the mirror. The face she saw was just the reflection of a body, which was now riddled with cancer. The 'me' she knew and wished to see was not bound by that body. The 'me' she wished to see did not have cancer. She was not the face in the mirror. That is what I was trying to tell her.

And now, the lullabies sang this truth to me as well.

As I sang to her, I came to understand that the person who lay in the bed was not my mother. Oh, yes, that person had indeed given birth to me, and had played the role of mother to me throughout my life. But what I knew as I stood watch over her as she struggled to shake off her tired body was that she did not belong to me. Or, at least, she did not belong to me in my limited role as daughter. How could I lay claim to her when she came into and was about to leave from this world without me? She belonged to the World, to the Universe.

She belonged to no one.

And she belonged to everyone.

We were two of the infinite number of souls passing through the corridors of time and space, who, by forces unknown to us, happened to cross paths. And in our crossing, we had made an undeniable impact upon one another. So, in that sense, we were eternally linked by the fact that our mutual impact could never be undone.

We had spent so many years arguing about things that would come and go, and had no permanence. Just as the face in the mirror was not who she was, those things that came and went were not reality either. All those events that come and go in life are not Truth. They are a deception—a distraction from Reality. But we humans spend so much time arguing about them nonetheless, believing them to be true.

Now, looking plainly at a single soul's imminent departure from the world, all the deception dissolved and I saw honesty at last. Here was Truth. And the Truth was this: we were just two tiny souls, trying the very best we could. We failed continuously. We kept going. And somehow or other, in spite of all our failures (or perhaps because of them) we found ourselves in that room together at the end of her time on Earth—me singing, her listening; me watching, her waiting.

I finally answered Crow's question.

'You asked me, Crow, 'Who is this person?''

'Yes?' prompted Crow.

'This person is the person who decorated this room,' I said. 'This person is the person who loved her home.

'This person is someone in great pain. This person is frightened and does not know what to expect. This person is someone who is grateful for the love and affection she is receiving in these moments. But above all, this person does not want to be alone.'

I looked at Crow, as the scene lingered in the background.

'Actually, Crow, since the time my mother died, a lot has changed. It was in the act of releasing her from being my mother that I finally allowed her influence to flow through me. These days, I look in the mirror and I see her eyes. I laugh or say a certain word, and I suddenly hear her voice. It's funny because I see and hear her much more now that she has been gone for sixteen years than I did when she was alive. I can feel her influence in how I do things. I doubt I would have been a writer or a musician if not for my mother. Surely, I would never have developed an interest in spirituality but for her. Ironically, we argued about every single one of those things when she was alive. But now, without the need to have her be my mother, but rather to see her as a spirit soul who shared with me some tiny part of her existence, I feel I know her, understand her and feel a gratitude that I cannot measure.'

'Listen to her breathing.' asked Crow.

Crow always startled me. *What did he mean?*

I could see now that I was once again looking at that final night of my mother's life on Earth.

My mother lay, breathing heavily, in her bed. Suddenly she bolted upright, flailing her arms wildly in terror. This made my own heart pound and I was petrified to see my mother so afraid. The home hospice nurse very flatly pronounced, 'Oh, that's just the cancer going into the brain.' She moved quickly to give my mother an anti-anxiety tablet, and my mother soon settled back down, returning to a steady, rhythmic breathing. My heart pounded quickly for several minutes, and I went into the next room for a little while to calm my nerves.

A few hours later, my mother's breathing began to make the most dreadful, ominous sound. Very matter-of-factly, the nurse said, 'Oh, that's called the "death rattle." It's when the lungs fill with fluid just before death. She doesn't have much longer now.' The coldness of her voice, coupled with the icy sound of the words, sent shivers up my spine, and I wanted to cry, but I didn't. The nurse quickly applied a decongestant patch to clear my mother's lungs. Soon, my mother's breathing ceased rattling, but it also grew dimmer and weaker. Nonetheless, she continued to breathe. I felt like I was looking at a breathing corpse. I couldn't understand the purpose for this elaborate demise. How much longer would this suffering continue?

When I had made my plane reservations to come see my mother, I had intended to fly home early on the morning of the sixth day. But now, that day was only a few hours away. It was close to 4 AM, and if I were to catch my scheduled flight, I would have to leave in less than three hours. But I simply couldn't see how I could leave my mother when she was so close to death. My father insisted I go home, no matter what, to take care of my daughter, who was only nine years old at the time. Indeed, my daughter missed me, and my father said there was really nothing more I could do by staying. I felt confused, emotional and unable to decide what I should do. Exhausted, and knowing there was no way I would be able to fly home in this state of mind, I lay on the bed next to my mother's, and tried my best to sleep for just a few minutes. But it was impossible. After ten minutes or so, I gave in completely to the anguish I was feeling. I sat up and burst into an uncontrollable flood of tears. It was the first time I had cried during the entire five-day vigil.

Piteously, I wailed loudly to my mother, 'How can I leave you like this?

'I don't know what to do,' I cried. 'If I am to catch my plane, I will have to leave for the airport in a few hours. I know I have to go back to my daughter. But what am I supposed to do? I cannot leave you now...not like this.'

I wept grievously for several minutes. I was nearly delirious from lack of sleep and near the point of breaking from watching my mother's suffering. I could not imagine how anyone could endure more than what she had already. Utterly depleted of my last reserves of physical and emotional energy, I started to drift into a foggy, semi-conscious dream. My father remained silent and motionless as he sat in the old cane-back, button-tufted, gold velvet chair that, in spite of the fact my mother had bought it nearly 30 years earlier, still looked brand new due to love and care. My sister stood silently by the hospital bed, holding our mother's right hand. It was as if time had stopped.

As I drifted away, I felt the same sense of surrealism I had during those pre-dawn hours when I was in labour with my daughter—an other-worldly thought that this moment of uncertainty would never change; a sense of disbelief that a new life was actually going to come into the world. In those hours, all I could feel was the pain of the transformation. It was as if I had fallen into another universe where pain was the state of reality, and that this state would last for the rest of eternity. It was only through faith that all was as it should be, that I could release my own fears and doubts, and allow Nature to be my guide.

Similarly, now, I was consumed with a sense of utter disbelief that this frail and fragile life I was watching as it ebbed away would ever depart, as all I could feel was the suffering of this moment. And just as I had released myself to Nature's wisdom in the timeless hours before my daughter was born, my heart now longed for Her to appear at this moment and let time flow once again.

Then, very subtly, only a few moments later, there was a slight change in the sound of the room. I sat up.

'How long has she been breathing like that?' I asked my sister. My mother's breathing had become nearly inaudible—barely a whisper of breath.

'She only just started,' my sister replied.

I got up and walked to my mother's left side. I watched as she took a slow and nearly silent breath. My sister and I waited a moment until our mother exhaled. I found myself sighing very quietly as I watched, fully aware these were the final breaths this little body would ever take.

My mother took one more breath. The breath lingered for a moment. Without awareness, I also held my breath and the air in the room was thick with a pregnant silence.

Then, effortlessly, the air came out of my mother's mouth, flowing and fluttering like ripples on a pond. Her tiny frame gave only the faintest of shudders as the soul shook off the body, as gently as you would shake droplets of water from your hair.

And as she exhaled, those droplets of her life dissolved into the coming dawn, and she left our vision.

The room then filled with a deeper silence. But this silence soon gave way to the breath of relief. And as I felt us all start to breathe again, I leaned over and whispered into my mother's left ear, 'Good job, Mom. And thank-you.'

I have to admit, I found myself baffled by my own choice of words at the time, which had come out of my mouth without premeditation. 'Good job?' Yes, I suppose this was what I had wanted to say. In her actions throughout her life, in her strength and endurance throughout her death—she had simply done as best she could. 'Yes, Mom,' I was saying, 'go without regret, knowing you did a good job. Be free.'

Crow stood just to my right, dressed in a smoky grey flannel waistcoat. We looked upon the shadowy scene, which was now giving way to the morning light.

'What is here?' he asked me.

I stood silent for a little while before answering.

'Here is detachment,' I told him.

I took this word in for a moment and then continued.

'Here is compassion. Here is acceptance. Here is the release of expectation. Here is forgiveness and appreciation.

'Here is letting go,' I said.

It was not until this moment when I had let my mother go, the moment when I no longer had a need for her to be for me and about me, the moment when I saw her as one tiny soul in the great expanse of Creation, who against all odds had crossed paths with me and made an impact upon me, that I had learned the essential lesson of detachment. It was only from this lesson that I realised how detachment is the golden key to unlock the doors to love in the World. I simply hadn't understood this before.

And what I would never have known without this lesson was that my mother would continue to live through me, with far more presence and power, long after she left the World, as a result of my having released her from my need for her to be my mother.

'What else is here?' asked Crow very softly.

I turned to my right to face Crow. His jet black eyes looked full of affection.

'Here, Crow, is unconditional love.'

The words caressed the scene before us, and it began to dissolve away into a gentle peachy hue.

Then Crow leaned towards me, and again whispered this question in my ear:

'What is the treasure?'

I heard these words echo over and over, as if through a vast stone palace, and I became aware of the faint scent of sandalwood, mingled with lotus blossoms, as I left that scene behind forever. Gradually, I could make out the distant sound of temple drums and brass hand cymbals pulsing in a steady beat, and gaining in intensity and volume. As the beat became louder and faster, I could make out the sound of people chanting with vigour, accompanied by the steady toll of a large temple bell. My feet felt slightly cool, and I looked down to find that my bare feet were stepping lightly upon a white marble floor. Soon, my pace picked up and I started to feel the heat from the bodies of hundreds of other people surrounding me, as I found myself being swept along in a circular procession.

The drums stopped suddenly and in the background, I could hear the rather bizarre din of traffic where the drivers were constantly honking their horns. And even behind that, a chorus of big raven-like crows cawed almost non-stop.

Night had already fallen, but the noise in this place was incessant.

I knew where I was. This was Calcutta.

*　*　*　*　*

'Crow, where are you?' I called through the crowd.

Crow turned to me and I noticed he was dressed in the saffron-coloured garb of a monk. He had a simple black umbrella in his hand instead of his walking stick.

I couldn't stop myself from laughing, as he looked pretty funny.

'What a sight—a big black crow dressed in a monk's outfit!' I said.

'Oh yeah? And what about you, dressed in that sari?' he retorted.

I looked down at my clothing. I was wearing a sagging cotton sari that was hanging out slightly around the waistline. *I never could get the hang of how to move in those things,* I thought. Even though I had spent so much time in India over the years, I was always tripping over my sari, stepping on the hem, and accidentally pulling out all the pleats. The shoulder piece would always fall off, and I absolutely never got the gist of how to use it to cover my head, as all the Indian ladies did so easily.

I had always prided myself on my respectful attitude towards other cultures whenever I travelled. And over the more than 20 years I had contact with the Vishnu temple in Calcutta, I had always adapted to what their cultural code dictated by wearing the clothes ladies were expected to wear in India. But while I made a show of adapting to the Indian culture, the honest truth is I never felt comfortable wearing Indian clothing. I never felt beautiful or feminine in a sari, even though all the Indian ladies seemed to flow with ease and grace when they wore them. I found the Punjabi-style trouser outfits that many of the women wore to be not much better of an option for my western body-shape. The ones off the shelf always hung weirdly on me, and to get ones that actually fit, you had to have a tailor make one for you, which was a luxury I rarely had when I was travelling around the country. So pretty much the whole time I lived in India, I walked around feeling like a 'sack of potatoes'.

'Ugh, Crow!' I complained. 'Why did you have to stick me in this frumpy brown sari? I gave that one away years ago.'

Crow did not answer, but he pointed to the temple hall.

'Hurry, the lecture is about to begin.' he said.

'Lecture?' I queried. I peeked into the temple hall and saw a large crowd had gathered there.

I entered and took my seat on the hard marble floor. I knew if there was going to be a lecture I was going to be sitting there a long time. While I enjoyed the lectures, I kind of dreaded them at the same time. The whole programme usually lasted a couple of hours or more, and sitting that long on a stone floor always hurt my ankles. Over the years, I had devised a way of taking the edge of my sari and crumpling it into a make-shift cushion to put under my feet as I sat there, but that didn't help terribly much. I also found it difficult to sit upright for such a long time, as it hurt my back, and I would lean to the left or right, from one hand to the other, to relieve it. But no matter what I did, my feet would invariably fall asleep, and go numb. This would make me fidget and shift around a lot throughout the programme. I always felt self-conscious about this, as very few of the Indian people, or the seasoned westerners, seemed to be as uncomfortable as I was. Sometimes, just to avoid embarrassment, I would stay frozen in one uncomfortable position for long periods of time, so as not to appear to be a 'novice'. Of course, when I did that, my feet would lose circulation completely. I can remember more than one occasion when I forgot to get up slowly at the end of the programme, and my dead feet simply caved in underneath me altogether, causing me to fall down right in the middle of the temple crowd. People were nice about helping me up, and I got used to being laughed at. But it never ceased to be embarrassing.

You might have thought I would have gotten more comfortable with the cultural divide over the years. But the truth was just the opposite. When I first went to India, my primary concern was to blend in and show respect. But the novelty of being in India wore off after maybe my fourth or fifth trip there. Instead of getting more culturally acclimated, I actually experienced more and more culture shock every time I went. It wasn't just the clothes, or the sitting on the floor—it was my whole person. After a while, I felt as though my western body was somehow hopelessly unfit for this environment. It was like trying to live on Mars, knowing you will never be able to walk in the atmosphere without a spacesuit. And so, even though I had affection for a great many people there, I could never really feel at home.

'Crow, I had forgotten how foreign I felt here,' I said to him, as I tried to massage the pins and needles from my feet.

'Shhh!' said Crow. 'Gurudeva is starting his prayers!'

I cast my attention to the elderly priest who sat on the podium at the front of the hall. I knew this person. He had been my spiritual mentor for nearly half my life. I met him when I was 26 years old, when I had come through the university to study music in Calcutta. My husband and I had met Gurudeva through a series of 'divine accidents' that had become the fabric of many a colourful tale we told to friends and family over the years. But all tales aside, the authenticity of Gurudeva had immediately struck me when we met him. He was the head of a large collection of Vishnu temples throughout India, and had hundreds of Indian followers. He was both kind and gentle, both inspirational and powerful—a genuine guru—and within a few months I became his first western disciple. I was given a spiritual name, and was known by that name for the two decades to follow. For years, I immersed myself in the devotional practices of the Vedic tradition, studying the scriptures in great detail. I even became one of the leaders amongst the western community, helping to promote my guru's teachings. I created a website and transcribed his lectures into books. I helped coordinate world tours, and was one of the founders of an international organisation for the dissemination of the tradition in the west. Gurudeva had gone global. He spoke everywhere from Oxford Street in London, to a Magician's Circle atop a desert mountain in Arizona. Everyone in the temple knew who I was.

Or at least, everyone knew who I was pretending to be.

In spite of all my seeming contact with my guru, throughout those years I never felt completely connected to him, to the rest of the temple, to the religion or to myself. Yes, I found it beautiful and inspiring, but something was always missing for me, which I could not put my finger on. It appealed greatly to my intellect and to some degree my senses, but something was lacking for me at a heart level. I wasn't sure why or how this was so. The philosophy was all about divine, mystical love. Theoretically, divine love is boundless. But for some reason, that boundless love never entered my life through my devotional practice.

But something even more basic was unfed in all my dealings with the temple—my essential need to feel fully seen. And as a westerner in a woman's body, I never could figure out how to get what I so deeply craved.

In spite of how actively involved I was, the cultural barriers for a woman within the temple structure were immutable. As a woman, my only 'ticket' into the company of my guru and other elders was through my husband. It was nothing personal, of course. This was simply the way Indian temples had operated for centuries. The elders were all celibate monks, and if you were a woman, you had no access to having a private audience with them, except under extreme circumstances. Women were expected to be happy enough to associate with other women. The problem for me was that most of the Indian women did not speak much (if any) English, and my own language skills in either Hindi or Bengali were also not very good. But even amongst those women who could speak English well, most were not particularly interested in speaking about philosophy, or even about 'real life'. Most seemed quite happy just to sit and chant on their prayer beads, to attend the temple rituals and to help out with chores like cooking. While I had nothing against these things, I deeply craved an intellectual and social outlet, but could find none. The men were the only people who spoke English well, and who would engage in interesting conversation. But I had only limited access to their company, and could only ever speak to them if my husband was with me. Thus, it was culturally impossible for me to have an individual friendship with any of them. I was, and always would be, my husband's wife to them. After years of this experience, I ended up feeling like I was some sort of germ that would infect the purity of their austerity simply by my presence. This is why, instead of becoming more comfortable and tolerant in India after so many years, I actually became more irritable, resentful and intolerant.

But what really drove the nail into the coffin for me was when that alienation caused my faith in the religious path itself to erode. It wasn't even the 'high philosophy' of the path I had a problem with. I still found the high philosophy of devotion to be beautiful. What had happened to me was that I could no longer see the integrity of the first and most basic tenet of the religious teachings of the temple—*You are not this body.*

From day one, every temple devotee is been taught, *You are not this body; you are a spiritual being.*

Ok, in theory, that sounded really good to me when I first came to the temple. But over the decades, I found this fundamental principle increasingly ironic in actual practice. If you say I am not my body, why do I need to play the 'role' of a woman? If you say I am not my body, why does it matter if I wear a sari or western clothes? If you say I am a spiritual being, why do celibate monks need to avoid me? If you say we are from the spiritual realm, why are we so wrapped up with all this cultural protocol?

Why should any of this matter?

Actually, the only message I ever get around here from people is that I AM my body. There's a hole in this bucket, and it simply no longer holds water for me.

That was the overwhelming conclusion I had come to, after half a lifetime of sitting on the marble floor and having my feet go numb. And the fact that I was carrying all of these questions around with me on a daily basis only made me feel even more isolated. How could I possibly voice this to anyone? I thought, *Everyone else around here at least appears to be completely comfortable, so how could they possibly understand what I am feeling?* So, I adopted a mode of behaviour where I pretended everything was just fine. Day and night, my life was a walking, talking lie.

Eventually, I simply vanished and became a shell of a person, donning the spiritual name I had been given.

But I felt I was not the only liar amidst this environment; much of the world around me seemed to be encased within a tightly cloaked veil of self-deception of its own. The whole reason why I had come to this temple in the first place was to find the Truth, but I was finding less and less of it as the years went on. Privately, behind a thin veneer of social acceptability, I was diving inwards, deep within an empty void, where my heart prayed that I might somehow receive at least a hint of what

Truth actually was. I longed to receive a glimmer of divine love, a flicker of divine ecstasy, a glimpse of the face of God, and a feeling of belonging that could only come from spiritual awakening, which had none of these cultural trappings or limitations.

'Wake up!' chastised Crow. 'You are daydreaming. I brought you to hear the lecture, and your mind has gone somewhere else. Take a look at this scene. Do you remember this night?'

I shook off my reverie and looked around me. Night had now fallen and it was very dark outside. Gurudeva started chanting a long litany of sombre mantras, as he always did before starting any lecture, paying his sincere respects to the lineage of gurus that had come before him, so they would give him the divine wisdom to speak the Truth.

'Yes, Crow, I do remember this night. This is about eight years ago. Five of us, including my husband and daughter, had just arrived here by train after being on a pilgrimage for several weeks through the Punjab and Rajasthan. We came to Calcutta to attend the big Janmashtami Festival. If this is the night we arrived, it is two days before the big celebration. I remember my body was totally exhausted and I had not been feeling very well for a couple of days. I also remember I had a bad stomach ache the afternoon before.'

'Ok, shush, now,' Crow beckoned, 'the lecture is starting.'

Gurudeva had now completed his prayers and began his lecture for the evening. He always gave wonderful lectures. I loved to hear him speak. He used to complain that he felt his English was not very good. But whilst his use of the English language may have been simple, his words always had a very direct and profound impact upon me.

As expected, Gurudeva spoke that night about the coming festival—

In two days time, we will celebrate Janmashtami. What is the meaning of Janmashtami? It is the birthday of Sri Krishna. We are celebrating that day when God made his appearance in our world thousands of years ago. We celebrate it once a year, in this month, at midnight of the eighth day after the full moon. We celebrate that single moment of a single day of the year on which we say that God has taken his birth in our world. And just like any other birth, we are preparing for it. We clean the temple and we gather together. We chant and we read the sacred scriptures. We are getting ready to welcome Krishna to this planet on this special day. It is a very joyful time of year. Everyone is happy at this time.

But this is only the apparent meaning of Janmashtami. This is not the absolute meaning. God is absolute, infinite and eternal. His creation is therefore absolute, infinite and eternal. There are infinite universes, unlimited universes. There are unlimited planets, unlimited moons. And there is also eternal time. In some corner of the universe or other, there is a full moon at any given moment. At any time, somewhere in the unlimited universes, you will be able to find a midnight after the eighth day after the full moon. At every moment there is a Janmashtami, somewhere or other. So, Janmashtami is not taking place on a specific moment in time. That is only how it appears to our limited vision. It is occurring at every moment.

Actually, God's appearance is not an event at all. It is continuously happening. It is God's 'lila'—His eternal pastime. He takes birth continually and eternally for His own pleasure. Krishna is unlimited. He is not bound by time and space. So, in this way, you can understand how Krishna displays His eternal pastime of taking birth, by appearing throughout unlimited creation at every moment, eternally. This is a deeper meaning of Janmashtami.

But still, this is also not the actual and complete meaning of Janmashtami.

Just as there are unlimited universes, unlimited planets, there are also unlimited spirit souls. And within those spirit souls, there are unlimited hearts. And just as Krishna takes His apparent birth at every moment, somewhere within the universe, He is also taking His actual birth at every moment within the heart of one of the countless and unlimited spirit souls throughout creation. At every moment, Krishna takes birth in the heart of one of His dear devotees.

And for this birth, we must also prepare. We have cleaned the temple to prepare for Janmashtami. We have placed beautiful flowers on the altar, and we have put on new clothes, so we can be ready to welcome Krishna nicely when He comes.

But ultimately, if we are to welcome Krishna, we must prepare our hearts first. We must make room within the chamber of our hearts. If you fill up a chamber with so much furniture that it fills the room completely, you cannot move around inside it. It is full of sofas and chairs and tables. It is so full that they go all the way up to the door. If you try to open the door, you cannot get in or out because the furniture is blocking it. Like this, we also fill up our hearts with so many useless things that keep it blocked.

Tonight, you are calling Krishna. You are chanting His holy name. You are saying, 'Krishna, come! Come!' And Krishna does come. He comes to you. He has heard you, and He comes knocking on the door of your heart. He tries to open it, but finds that your heart is so cluttered with other things that He cannot even open that door. What will He do? He will go away, feeling disappointed. He is your dearest Friend. He has come to visit you, wishing to share your company, but you have left no space for Him. How can He come in? You have called Him, and He has answered you, but He cannot enter. And because you are locked inside that room, you do not see that He has already answered your call, and you come to believe that Krishna has forgotten you.

We must clear a place within the chamber of our hearts if Krishna is to arrive. Only when our hearts are clear, and we have made room for Him to come, then Krishna will appear. Then, when you call His holy name, and He comes *knocking on the door of your heart, He can enter. Then He can take birth in your heart—the heart of His most dear friend.*

So the question then is this—'In whose heart will Krishna take birth tonight?'

And that is the true meaning—the actual meaning—of Janmashtami.

'Oh Crow, I am really pleased you brought me here,' I said. 'I hadn't realised that I could still remember so much of it. I may not remember all of the exact words, but I know this was the essence. I remember how lost I was feeling, and how much that lecture helped to bring me back to myself. It was like a gift sent to me.'

'And then?' asked Crow.

'And then?' I echoed. 'And then what?'

'And then, this—' he said. And the scene changed instantly.

It was now late in the evening. Everyone had gone off to bed, and the temple was quiet. I was lying in my bed in the dark, still very much awake.

'Oh, yes, Crow,' I said. 'I remember all of it now. That was the night everything changed.'

I could not get my mind off the lecture Gurudeva had given that night. I had become absolutely captivated by it. I repeated his words over and over again in my mind. I tried to picture unlimited universes and how God appeared continuously throughout them. I let my mind drift through visions of infinity and eternity. I allowed myself to feel delight over the idea of what 'eternal pastimes' meant. And then finally, I meditated on what I found to be the most profound idea of the lecture—the idea of God taking birth in the human heart. Over and over, I could hear Gurudeva's final question:

'In whose heart will Krishna take birth tonight?'

For at least an hour, I meditated upon this question. I kept asking it again and again in my mind. And each time I asked the question, I heard myself say,

'Me! Let it be me tonight!'

What an absolutely cool thought, I mused. *I mean, sometimes I wonder if I am just in love with all the pretty words. But this time, what if this—this one thing—were really possible? What if, out of all the unlimited spirit souls in all the unlimited universes, I was the person in whose heart Krishna would appear tonight?*

And then, I found myself having a conversation with God.

'*God, I have tried to figure out how to find you my entire life. I have wished and wished for you. I have prayed and chanted and studied and listened and hoped. I have eliminated all kinds of material things in my life. But still I feel like You are a million miles away. I guess it's like Gurudeva said. My heart is so full of rubbish that it's small wonder why you haven't come before. I'm so full of all kinds of mixed up emotions, that I just haven't left any space for You to come in. But is it really just a matter of clearing my heart and calling You? Is it really this easy? Yes, I believe it. I do. It makes so much sense. Truth must be this easy.*

'*But how, God, do I clear my heart? Oh, please, can't you just come and clear my heart out for me? Just come and throw out all the crap for me. It seems pretty obvious that I sure don't know how to do it myself.*

'*I need You to help me! Please! Let it be me tonight!*'

After my conversation, I started to rationalise my feelings to myself.

Well, why should I think it isn't possible? Why can't God take birth in my heart tonight? I mean, I always say I believe in God. Well do I or not? If I do, why should anything be impossible? It isn't really such a crazy idea. After all, it's just logical. If there are countless spirit souls, eventually God will take birth in every single heart. Well, sooner or later, He's got to get around to me. So why not now? Who's to say that it won't be tonight?

And then, I started to drift into a dream—

Wow. I wonder what it feels like...

I took note of the time. It had just struck midnight. I knew I should try to get some sleep because I would need to rise before dawn for the morning temple rituals. But I couldn't sleep. I couldn't stop thinking about this delicious thought of God— whoever or whatever that meant—coming to you. I thought about how it must feel to let God take birth in your heart, and how different everything would be when He did. I tried to imagine the indescribable sensation of spiritual transformation.

And as I let my imagination run wild, I started to feel the hair on the back of my neck stand upright.

Mmm...that feels really sweet, I thought.

Then, I felt a cool chill flutter lightly over my arms and back. This was nothing terribly unusual. I had felt similarly many times before, when absorbed in deep spiritual thought.

But then the fluttery chill started to turn into a cold shiver.

Soon the shivery cold spread across my abdomen and legs and I felt slightly delirious.

Gosh, this is weird, I thought. *Is this what spiritual ecstasy feels like?*

But then, I started to tremble uncontrollably from an icy cold that gripped my entire body. I felt as though I had been hurled stark naked into a snowstorm, even though I was in India in the middle of summer. I became confused and completely disoriented.

Wait a minute—this can't be right, I thought. *This is not spiritual ecstasy. I'm ill! I have a raging fever. I just can't stop shaking.*

And then, I suddenly realised I was in extreme pain across my abdomen. I began to moan loudly in agony.

Oh God help me. This is the worst pain I've ever felt in my entire life. What is wrong with me?

'Crow, this is horrible. Do I really have to relive this?' I pleaded.

As I spoke to him, my teeth chattered from the cold, and I could hardly speak the words. There was a violently sharp pain that spread right across the solar plexus and I was utterly delirious from the fever. I couldn't think.

'What is here?' Crow asked.

The room started to swirl. I heard the siren of an ambulance and voices of people all around me. I couldn't make out anything.

'Here?' I repeated. 'Where? Where am I going? What's going on? Who are all these people?'

'Ok,' I said, 'I think I am in a hospital now. Yes, I can just about make it out. My body isn't working. I cannot eat anything. There is a drip in my arm. It burns like fire. Somebody sticks it in wrong and I start shouting but no one understands English. I can't figure out what's going on and I have no idea what's wrong with me. I yank out the drip from my arm. Days go by. I am not even sure of how many days. I get weaker and weaker every day. I remember saying over and over, "If you don't get me out of this place, I will die". Then, I am in another hospital, still very delirious. I still don't know what is going on. I cannot even quite comprehend that I am in a hospital. For some strange reason, I keep imagining that I am on the deck of a big cruise liner. I imagine the nurses are members of the crew. I can't figure out where we are going. All I know for sure is that my body isn't working and that I cannot eat or even move.'

'Crow, please let me step away from this,' I begged.

I took a step away from my hospital bed so I could see myself more clearly. I looked so weak lying there, so completely helpless.

'The doctors told me I had pancreatitis,' I said to Crow. 'I had never heard of it before. A very large gallstone had gotten lodged in my pancreas. I nearly died from it. After I went back to England, I had to have surgery to remove my gall bladder.'

'So what is here?' Crow repeated.

I stopped to consider Crow's question. I could tell he wanted me to look beneath the surface of these events.

What was here?

I surveyed my private hospital room. I saw myself lying there, awake but unable to do much more than listen, with the drip in my arm. On the sofa on the other side of the room sat my husband, reading a magazine. I felt myself sigh.

'Here is disconnection,' I replied. 'It makes me sad to look at this.' And I watched silently for a few moments. Then I remembered many things I had not looked at for many years.

'I can remember that on that day, all I could think about was how I was feeling. I was critically ill. I was in pain. I was unhappy. I was frightened. I felt really needy. All I wanted was for my husband to come and pick me up, hold me close and let me tell him how scared and alone I felt. But this didn't happen. I wanted to cry in his arms. I was longing for him to come to me, really come to me, but he didn't. During that period of my life, I was extremely resentful towards my husband. We had had a long, turbulent marriage with a lot of physical violence. I was already feeling unloved and unsupported, but this single scene at the hospital told me that someday our marriage would have to end. On that day, for the first time, I knew that he and I would not be 'until death us do part'. I wasn't sure how or when it would happen, but I knew it was inevitable. I distinctly remember thinking, *I know I am starting to recover, but what if I hadn't? What is going to happen when I am actually on my death bed? Will he be reading a magazine then?*

'I felt very bitter towards him,' I told Crow. 'And I justified my bitterness for a very long time by holding onto the mental image of him reading a magazine while I lay there. Even after the divorce, I held that image vividly in my heart.

'But, Crow,' I added, 'there is something else here— something really important—something I didn't see back then.'

'Oh?' he said quizzically. 'So what else is here?' he asked.

'What else is here, is Gurudeva's lecture. He said when we call God, but our heart is too cluttered for Him to come in, God comes to us, but He goes away, disappointed that He cannot enter.

'And what is God but Love itself?' I asked. 'When we call out for Love to come, our hearts must be uncluttered. Otherwise, it will not be able to get into the chamber of our hearts.

'I had convinced myself that I was calling out to Love,' I continued, 'but my heart was so full of anger and resentment there was no room for Love to enter. I wasn't ready to receive Love; I was bolting the door and shutting it out. I wasn't calling Love; I was challenging it.'

I stood there for a moment. I looked at myself lying in the bed. I looked at my husband flipping through the magazine. I began to wonder whether or not, had my husband put down the magazine and let me cry in his arms, I would have made room for him in my heart. Would I have accepted his love fully, or would I have held on to the resentment, and not been able to let Love enter?

'Gurudeva was right,' I said. 'In order to receive Love, we have to make room for it in our hearts. How can Love come in if the heart is full of anger? It has no space to enter, to be, to grow. But when we clear the heart of all that rubbish, and make a place in which Love can dwell, then we can receive it.'

Suddenly I felt myself astounded.

'Wow, Crow. Truth actually *is* that simple. How amazing.'

I went silent for a few minutes, absorbed in this new realisation.

Then Crow asked quietly, 'Who is this person lying on the bed?'

I looked at him in surprise. 'What do you mean, who is it? It's me of course,' I said.

'Who is this person?' Crow asked again without wavering.

I looked into his deep black eyes. They shone like two onyx globes, and I could see my reflection in them.

'Oh my goodness,' I said, feeling stunned by a sudden vision I beheld within those jet-black spheres. 'Yes, I can see exactly who this person is.

'This person is someone who feels like she is split in half,' I said. 'This person is someone who desperately wants to heal all these sides of herself and become a whole person at long last.'

LESSONS FROM THE IRIS

'Crow, it's so obvious I don't know how I missed it before. The pain from the pancreatitis actually made me feel as if my body had been split into two halves. It felt like a big stone axe had severed me across the middle of my body. It was a very profound sensation, and I kept telling everyone I felt like I had been split in two. And that *is* exactly how I felt back then—not just in my body, but in my whole life. I felt severed. My life felt like it was split in two. I was always leading two lives, but I felt present in neither of them.'

'How so?' Crow queried

'Oh, there were many splits, Crow,' I said. 'There was of course the whole east-west thing. There was the split between my religious life and my musician life. And there was the split between my married life and my parents. But even these things were not the most painful way in which I was split. The biggest split in my life was inside of *me*. I was split because throughout my 22-year marriage, I hid the fact that I was miserable from everyone I knew. There were so many secrets I kept from everyone. I didn't want anyone to see or know what was really going on behind closed doors. That was the real split. I was split between what was actually going on in my life, and the person everyone else thought I was. And somewhere in between, the real "me" got lost completely.'

I went silent for a moment. I wasn't ready to tell Crow all of the details. Even though it was such an old story, I was somehow not ready to let go of it completely.

Crow bent his head slightly to the side and looked at me quizzically.

'So you were split into two pieces. The outside you and the inside you,' he said.

'Yes,' I said, sadly.

'Hmm...before you stepped out from your bedroom window this morning, you were very wary of the gap between the inside and the outside,' Crow said matter-of-factly.

'Oh my goodness,' I said. 'Yes, Crow. You are quite right. That is exactly it. Back then, all I ever felt was that I was either inside myself looking out on the world, or living on the outside looking in. And I stayed in that pattern for most of my life. This lesson is not at all about the disconnection between my husband and me. That's just the symbol of a much greater thing. This is about the complete lack of connection *within* me. I was simply disconnected. My pancreas was probably just trying to get my attention.'

'So what do you think it was trying to tell you?' Crow asked.

'Ha!' I exclaimed, 'It was probably trying to tell me to pull myself together!'

Crow laughed.

'Actually, Crow, that is indeed what it was trying to tell me. I was only ever two halves of a person. And in this case, two halves did not make a whole. But that moment, that day when I was lying there, the seeds of change in me started to grow. A few months afterwards, I had surgery to remove the gall bladder. After that, I changed my lifestyle completely. I started eating much more healthfully and my body healed of so many ailments. I started clearing out all the things in my life that didn't feel right. I left my marriage. I actually left the temple, too. And that is the biggest irony, because as a result of hearing that lecture by Gurudeva, and being so moved by it, I also knew it was inevitable I would soon need to leave his company if I was ever to become a whole person.

'That night, I prayed that God would take birth in my heart,' I said. 'I knew there was something special about that evening, but I never thought my prayer was answered.'

'And now?' prompted Crow.

'When a child is just born,' I said, 'he doesn't just stand up and change the world right away. He takes birth. He has to be nurtured. He has to grow. Like this, something very rare took its birth in my heart that night. It was so subtle I didn't even notice it come in. But I have cultivated that subtle thing over the years, and it has grown. Now, I can see it. Looking back, I can see that on that very night, at midnight, in the darkest hour of the day, when my body became completely broken in two, and my mind became enchanted with wonder and awe, the innermost prayer of my heart of hearts was indeed answered—

Love took birth in my heart that night. In spite of my heart being cluttered with so many things, in spite of not at all being prepared to receive it, Love came to me anyway. It was a gift of grace; it was given to me not because I was enlightened or special in any way. It came solely because my heartfelt request was sincere, and because I fully believed it was possible.'

Crow smiled at me with mellowness. As he did so, I could see Gurudeva's eyes. And in that moment I knew that, even though I had left the temple and given up that spiritual practice, I had not left Gurudeva. There is only one Guru, and I was looking at him now.

The dark night melted into a pale blue mist. The gold-pink hues of early morning spread out from beneath my feet, and boundaries ceased to exist. I began to float above the scene upon a white satin sheet that wafted in the breeze. Crow flew high above my head and I could just about make out his words when he called out to me, asking:

'What is the treasure?'

I had no time to answer, as the air began to fill with the intoxicating scent of orange blossoms. I felt nearly drunk from its perfume, until I became aware that Crow and I were now surrounded by a blanket of creamy clouds, and we were floating high above the world as if in a hot-air balloon.

But, wait a minute—we actually *were* in a hot-air balloon...or something like it.

'Wow! Crow, what's going on?' I exclaimed.

I looked around to find we were standing in a wicker basket held by satin ribbons connected to a multicoloured bubble, sailing us along the landscape. Along to—where?

I felt the air moving in and out of my lungs.

I felt myself breathing—with a thrill that I had not known before.

* * * * *

'Hmmm...' murmured Crow. I looked around to find him scrutinising a map that he had spread out on the floor of the basket of our floating ship.

Wondering what was going on in that beaky brain, I asked, 'So, what's up with the balloon?'

'Hmmm...very funny,' Crow scowled. I hadn't meant it as a pun.

Abruptly and without explanation, Crow folded up the map and put it back into the left pocket of his waistcoat. Then he stood up and pulled a tiny golden telescope from his right pocket. He expanded it and surveyed the horizon.

'Ah, yes. That's it over there,' he said. 'Have a look.'

'What am I supposed to be looking for?' I asked. And then I looked through his telescope and saw the long ridge in the distance. Excitedly, I looked down over the edge of the balloon and saw a dramatic landscape beneath us that looked as if someone had etched it out with the fine blade of a sculptor's knife.

'Oh, Crow!' I exclaimed jubilantly. 'That's the Little Grand Canyon down there. We are flying over the Navajo Nation in Arizona. What an incredible sight. It doesn't look real.'

'We've got to hurry before it gets too dark,' said Crow.

'Where are we going?' I asked. And, just as you would move in a dream, I saw the landscape swirl beneath me, past visions of the Painted Desert to the east as we sailed further and further north, until at last we reached the Grand Canyon. Then, in one fell swoop, we were no longer in the air. We had come back down to earth, in the middle of a scrubby looking forest. It was sunset on a summer evening and the mountain air was cool and fresh. I remembered this place. It was the Kaibab National Forest. I came here with my family and some friends two years after my mother died.

'Come on,' said Crow. 'We've got to get the tent up before there is no light left.'

Of course, when I turned to look, the tent was already there, and this was just one of Crow's ways of jogging my memory. Shortly after, the sun set in the west, and the moon rapidly took its place to illuminate the darkness. We were in the middle of nowhere. This was not an actual campsite. There was no one around for miles and miles and there was not the faintest hint of manmade light coming from surrounding areas. We were at an elevation of 7000 feet, about 30 miles outside the South Rim of the Grand Canyon. This odd-looking forest was comprised of small, scruffy little pine trees loosely strewn along, as if thrown randomly against the landscape. In fact, if I remember correctly, in some Native American language, the word 'Kaibab' meant 'trees that had fallen down'. It was a humble and perhaps forlorn-looking place, in sharp contrast to the magnificent Whispering Pines of the Grand Canyon itself.

I stepped into the tent and the darkness was immediately profound. The sense of isolation from the rest of the world was only broken by the intermittent sound of coyotes crying eerily to one another across the expanse. Their high-pitched voices carried spookily in this vast openness. It was difficult not to feel a bit fearful, even though I knew there was no one around for miles. It is funny how we imagine monsters in the dark, even when we know fully there are none.

Suddenly, Crow popped his head through the flaps of the tent.

'Come on, get ready,' he said. 'We've got to get going if we want to see the sunrise.'

'Sunrise?' I asked. 'But it's still the middle of the night...'

I poked my head outside the flaps of the tent and was immediately stopped in my tracks by what lay before me. The moon had set. We were now in total darkness, a hundred miles from anyone, and more than a mile in elevation. The air was thin and free of smog. Awestruck and speechless, I stepped out of the tent, and felt as though I had stepped into the vastness of space—

I had stepped into the Universe.

What I saw was at once both captivating and disorienting. I could see neither trees, nor land, nor Crow, nor even my own hand in front of my face. What I did see, however, was the Milky Way and its billion, billion stars stretched almost vertically in

180

front of me. I saw nebulae and swirls of cosmic dust. I saw clouds of pink and spirals of green amidst a blanket of uncountable pinpricks of silver and red and yellow and blue lights that twinkled like ornaments along this gateway to the heavens.

There was no up or down or here or there. It was simply everything, simply all there was.

And in that moment, I knew I was a traveller within this unique and complex galaxy, and that I was one of a billion, billion unique passengers throughout its unique journey amidst all the other billion, billion unique galaxies. We were experiencing it all together, this time, this space. I was not sitting inside of the four corners of my own self looking out at it; I was part and parcel of it. And oddly, in spite of the awesomeness of this moment, I did not feel small or lost. Rather, I felt the galaxy wrap me up into its milky arms and I was embraced by its life-giving mystery. I felt loved. I felt I had meaning within this unknowable, yet familiar, celestial soup.

I felt I was home.

I literally shouted for joy at the sight of it. I stretched my arms outwards to take it in, and to let it take me. I couldn't take my eyes away from this sight, and I felt myself, as author Fredric Brown once said, *'whirling with it; whirling through time and space to an unknown destination.'*[2]

And in that moment, I found myself crying out, 'Oh, Crow— you have taken my breath away!'

And with those words, we found ourselves now in a different place. The stars were gone and the sky was no longer black, but rather a pale indigo. Dawn was approaching. I recognised this place. It was Shoshone Point, a remote spot on the South Rim of the Grand Canyon. It is not one of the usual sites for tourists, as it is quite a slender sliver of earth, with a flat top and almost vertical sides. It is like a fjord without water that juts out as a lone tower high above the floor of the Canyon. Even at its widest point, it is already quite narrow and, if you dare to walk out on it, it becomes narrower and narrower, ending in a sharp point barely large enough for one person. I say 'if you dare' because if you peer over the edge of this towering plateau, all you will see is the mile-long drop from where you are standing to the rocky floor of the Canyon below. Perhaps to a seasoned climber this is not such a big deal, but really it is difficult to fathom what the sight of an unprotected mile-long vertical drop feels like until you have stood in such a remote place, with no one else around, holding on to the rocks to steady yourself against the strong windy updrafts without the benefit of guard rails. It is, in fact, quite a dangerous place, and it was probably mad for us to be there, but someone in our party had insisted this was the best place to view the sunrise, so there we were.

As I looked around me in the dim light, I cast my vision eastwards. The view in that direction extended unobstructed from this point for what I would think was—what? Fifty miles? A hundred miles? I really don't know, but the elevation of our vantage point and the sheer dropping away of the earth in front of us created a vast horizon the likes of which I had never seen before, nor have ever seen again since that morning at Shoshone Point.

Gingerly, I walked to a point where the width of the plateau was not so extremely narrow as to make me feel too afraid, and I sat down very close to the edge, and faced the east. It was difficult not to let myself be overwhelmed by the idea that just a few inches away from where I sat was a gulf of air that went a mile down. At an intellectual level, compared to what I had seen of the seemingly limitless Milky Way just an hour earlier, a single mile seems barely worth mentioning, but I must confess that within my earth-bound body, ruled by the laws of gravity, my heart pounded more than a little as I dared to peer over the edge of the cliff. My daughter and her friend, both 11 years old at the time, were (understandably) absolutely terrified, and sat a bit further behind me, so as not to be in the line of vision of the vertigo-inducing drop.

When we had been standing up, the sensation was that the winds could knock you over and hurl you over the edge. Once seated, I started to relax a bit. Now able to breathe more easily,

I gazed towards the eastern horizon in the distance and could see the faint glow of morning light as it began to give colour to the scene. I had a clear view of the Painted Desert, and at once knew how its amazing shades of purples and blues and golds and maroons had given it its special name. The hint of light was just enough now to enable me to make out some of the landmarks across this part of the Canyon. I saw the rock formation known as the 'Vishnu Temple', so-called for its conical shape, as Vishnu temples in India were. I reflected upon this, and considered how I had come to be sitting there at that particular moment.

The friend amongst us who had brought us to Shoshone Point was now pointing out and naming several other natural landmarks that had been given similarly exotic names. This made me wonder what it must have been like to be those first European explorers who had named these naturally formed monuments just a few hundred years earlier. They came here to make knowable the unknown, just as they might have navigated through the jungles along the Amazon, or hunted for lost cities of antiquity. But then, I started thinking about the centuries of lost generations of Native Americans who had lived in this region, and who knew well all these monuments long before any European had ever set foot in this place, and undoubtedly had their own names for them. Then my mind went back even further and I found myself wondering what in the world had happened to create these incredible stone monuments millions of years before any human being had ever come to explore the Grand Canyon.

What had the Earth seen that none of us would ever know?

By now the light had grown from the dull indigo to a shy blue, but the sun had not yet actually risen. As I continued to gaze eastwards, I saw something truly remarkable. The great solar disc began to show itself, first like the tip of a gleaming golden knife blade piercing the soft blue cover of daybreak. As it rose, I found I could actually make out a visible line between night and day that ran from north to south. It was stunning. Imagine a line, the length of the earth itself; on one side is night, on the other, day. The line is continuously moving westwards, sweeping away the night as easily as a child might knock down a row of toy soldiers with his arm in a single, nonchalant movement.

As I watched, this line moved rapidly towards me from the east, as the shadow of night was brushed aside by the light of the sun. From this perspective, sitting on a ledge one mile above the ground, with nothing blocking my line of vision, I could see this north-south line sweep across the countryside, as if the sun were simply lifting a blanket from the land, at a breakneck speed of 1000 miles an hour. And as I watched this blanket of darkness lift, I saw the line between night and day zoom visibly across the expanse until it swept over us as well, moving ever westwards. I had never seen such a sight before. When you are on the ground, or in the middle of a dotted landscape in the city, you cannot see this. Removing the obstacles that obscure our vision, the reality of dawn is visible. And after that blanket of night was lifted from my vision, the dawn kept going ever onwards, never stopping, never slowing down.

As I felt the dawn sweep over my head, I became even more aware of my point in time and space, sensing how I was travelling along with this colourful planet that was whirling through the universe, ever dancing with the sun to the rhythm of the days and nights, and to the tunes of the ever-changing seasons. I became keenly aware that everything was in constant motion and constant change, but also that within the constancy of that change was a continuity and wholeness in which nothing actually ever changed.

I could feel myself breathing softly and peacefully as I saw with clarity how everything that had ever been, or ever would be, was knowable from any point in time or space. Within any given moment is contained all of Eternity.

There is no time except Eternal Time.

Dawn is not here or there or then or now. Dawn is everywhere and always.

And as we are part and parcel of this cosmic dance, we also are everywhere and always.

Transfixed and amazed by this inner vision, I saw a crow fly over my head. It was one of those massive grackles so common in the south-western part of the United States. These noisy birds are much more aggressive than the gentle raven-like crows in Britain. The grackle circled back, and again flew barely a few feet above my head. From where I sat, he seemed to be flying very low for a crow, but then he took a sudden nosedive down into the Canyon. As my eyes lost sight of him, I realised he was actually flying very high for a crow—a mile high, to be exact.

The crow then changed direction, and sailed upwards with outstretched wings on the updraft of the open air. As he glided just a few feet in front of me, he turned to me and winked. I knew then that it was Crow—my Crow.

'What is here?' Crow called out.

'Oh, Crow!' I sang. 'What is *not* here?'

'Ok. So what is it?' queried Crow.

'I came to the Grand Canyon years before I had heard Gurudeva's lecture. I had never heard about infinite worlds with infinite midnights, or about how God's eternal pastimes are continually happening at every moment. But although I had not yet heard this message with my ears, that message had been revealed to me years before—right here at the Grand Canyon. Here is the place where I could see these Truths with my own two eyes. There is nothing theoretical about Truth in this place, nothing intellectual. Truth was staring me right in the face. It was all there right in front of me. It had always been there. All I ever needed to do to see this Truth was to rise above my ground-level perspective. All I had to do was to fly above it so that nothing blocked my view.'

I sat without speaking for a moment and then a flash of insight illuminated my understanding.

'Oh, Crow! This must be what is meant by clearing out the heart—to clear your spiritual vision of obstructions so you can see forever. It is so simple!' I exclaimed.

185

'From this place, I can see Dawn is both racing towards us as well as racing ever onwards, as one never-ending Dawn. In all directions, there are endless, continuous and immeasurable beginnings at every moment—continual night turning into continual day. Dawn is forever; it is not a moment. Dawn is not an occurrence; it is a relationship, a marriage. It is the never-ending kiss of Earth, Sky and Light. It is always Dawn.'

Crow seemed pleased and he sailed jubilantly even higher in the sky.

'What else is here?' he called out, with even more vigour.

I reflected upon his question for a moment. I considered how odd it was that we humans always seem to need to relate everything to our own reference point in time and space, and thus cannot see how much the world is giving us at any given moment. I remembered all the times I had sat inside of the four corners of myself looking out into a world from which I feel hopelessly separate.

And then I considered how easy it had been to change that, simply by taking that step out my window, and into the Dawn.

I watched Crow's silhouette dance against the light of morning sun, as he swooped with joy and abandon through the open air, and I felt a smile emerge from within my being.

'What is here, Crow,' I said, 'is belonging.'

'We are travellers with this Earth,' I continued. 'We are part of it. We belong to it. We are the children in this marriage between Earth, Sky and Light.'

I looked out across the expanse of that marriage stretched before me.

And then I looked into the expanse of Self that lay within me.

And from this view, I felt the marriage, the harmony, the union of all that lived at that time, at that moment—and at all times, at all moments.

I inhaled and felt all of those moments enter me. And then, in a single exhalation, I released those moments back into the unlimited space surrounding me.

'Here, Crow,' I said finally, 'is Home! From this place, I can see that I am always and everywhere Home!'

Crow sailed higher and higher and my gaze followed up, up the rugged cliffs, up into the sky, to take his place next to Apollo, as his seven horses drew the chariot of the morning light into the blazing brilliance of daylight.

He cawed to me in a loud voice, calling me forth, asking once again:

'What is the treasure?'

I felt myself irresistibly swept up, as I flew with Crow to the heights of the heavens. I rode with him through cloudy canyons upon the chariot of the Dawn. I felt my lungs fill with life. I felt my soul dance in ecstasy. I felt poetry, power and unconditional love enter me as simply as breathing it in. Effortlessly these gifts filled me, and I drank them in like a clay vessel being filled with the cool waters of a mountain stream. Effortlessly, I felt that unending stream of gifts fill me, flooding my lungs with the cool, clear breath of Eternity.

Breathing is never-ending.

Dawn is never-ending.

I became full with the Breath of Dawn.

At last, I could answer Crow's question.

'Oh, Crow, the treasure is Breath itself.'

*   *   *   *   *

This morning I was awakened by a crow.

The call of Crow had had a remarkable effect upon me. As I rose from the softness of my bed, I felt the arms of the summer dawn caress my face, my arms, my shoulders. I opened my eyes and felt myself step from the four walls of my room and into the Dawn. I had stepped into the Dawn of Possibilities, of Being, of Life itself.

Today, I step into this Dawn.

I step into this Dawn and life looks very different to me. I listen to the birds and feel that I now live in a world where I am surrounded by angels who laugh, sing and crow at my window to waken me. In turn, I must also laugh, sing and waken others.

I step into this Dawn and feel grateful for every breath I take, for every thought I think, for every drop of light that enters into my eyes. I intend this day to taste the morning as it enters my portals, to allow it to fill my room with its gentle cooling and its private calm, and to feel its loving whisper against my aging and sensitive skin.

I step into this Dawn and I can touch Time. I can touch the Dawn of every morning that has ever been.

And in the day to follow, is the promise of everything that every Dawn calls forth—for to walk, to live and to breathe fully in the daylight is to walk in the world of angels.

From this perspective, I am no longer alone.

From this perspective, everyone and everything is my home. There is no place I could go that is not where I live.

From this perspective, the very concept of being alone simply does not exist.

From this perspective, all that I could possibly want or need appears coyly at my fingertips.

Life becomes effortless and easy.

Even as I write this, you are only at arm's length from me, reachable by a short flight of memory, a gentle call at your window, or a whisper in your ear, at any chosen moment. For we breathe the very same air, you and I. There is nothing that can come between us.

And to breathe is really very simple: breathe in; breathe out. And just don't stop.

Breathe and breathe and breathe—
and become so full
that you have no choice
but to give yourself away.

Then, know with certainty when the Angel-Crow alights on your windowsill at Dawn that he has come there to call you to step into Creation, and to fly to the heights of the Dawn of Possibilities. Then you too must alight on every windowsill you see—and announce to everyone the coming of the morning light.

*　*　*　*　*

REVISITING THE IRIS

The sudden burst of thunder woke me with a jolt half an hour before my alarm was due to ring that morning.

Almost instantly I heard the torrential sheets of rain pounding on my rooftop. I leapt from my bed and drew the blinds on my window, to see the weighty black clouds hovering low over the eastern horizon, the dawn sun piercing through them like white-hot sabres of light that spread unendingly into the heavens.

Then, suddenly, I had the urge to run out into the storm.

I have to hurry, I told myself, *or I might miss it.*

I grabbed a shiny red mackinaw and threw it over my head without taking any care to comb my hair. I hastily jumped into my bright blue wellies and ran into the Garden as fast as I could. It occurred to me that I must look a bit like Paddington Bear the way I was dressed.

Such an alluring flower, this Iris, I thought. *I find the very thought of being with her, of sharing a moment with her, irresistible. With her, even the smallest moment feels as large as the entire universe.*

Soon, I once again found the tiny grotto in which the Iris lived. She stood there like a hidden treasure, a saintly hermit amidst the craggy blackness of the cave. I felt my heart pounding as I neared her. And then, I also heard it pounding, as my awareness became filled with a subtle sound from all directions.

I slowed down my pace to nearly a standstill, and simply breathed for several moments, allowing the rain to stream down my clothes, my hair and my face. The moment tickled me like a naked kiss in the woods, and gave me a chill of ecstatic pleasure. I took in the sound, the temperature, the texture and the taste of it all. I became quieter and quieter until the space before me was so vast that the entire world of possibilities was able to fit within just the tiniest corner of totality. I fell deeper and deeper into the microcosm of that moment, and felt myself become awestruck with how far I could travel within and into its essence. And then, just when I thought the moment could get no smaller, I looked around me, and could see the space in between the spaces—and the spaces in between those as well—and ever inwards and outwards, all at once.

'It goes on forever,' I heard the words escape my lips.

I stood there and simply watched, simply sensed, simply listened. And the more I stood there simply watching, sensing and listening, the more I found there was to see, feel and hear.

Transfixed, I watched as, almost imperceptibly, the light shifted in colour and intensity from the faint, non-descript purple hues to bright pinks and golds, darkened and made ever richer by the blackness of the morning thundercloud.

I felt the Earth move—and my body pulsed with the inconceivably gigantic wave that sent ripples throughout the solar system as this gentle planet, ever beneath our feet, whirled faithfully around the Sun. And I felt myself move with it—feet and toes reaching deep into the Earth, and arms completely weightless, tossing effortlessly upon the breeze like the branches of a stately chestnut tree.

But most of all, I heard the Earth sing—not with any human ears, but with the subtle ears of my intangible and immeasurable essence. And with that song I heard all the harmony and dissonance of the seasons, the planets, the cosmos and the micro-cosmos. All of it was singing as I stood there and simply listened.

Then I heard her say, 'Oh, good! I was wishing for you to come. You always come just in time! Come sit with me. I want us to watch this miracle together.'

I stepped delicately into the cave and took my place next to the Iris, sitting upon a soft tuft of crimson autumn leaves.

'You look very still this morning,' she praised. 'I can barely hear your breathing, even though I know you ran all the way here.'

The Iris had a way of reading into me like no other being could.

We sat without words for several moments, and gazed eastwards at the emerging prism of colours arching through the black storm clouds.

The Iris held her breath. I did too. Then I heard her whisper, almost inaudibly—

'Ah—here it comes.'

And then we saw it.

The rainbow spread its colours from one side of the Earth to the other until it formed a perfect bridge across the sky.

Time passed. I don't know how much. Perhaps it was only a few moments, but it could just as easily have been epochs of time. There was a sense of timelessness in this moment. In this moment were all moments in time; in this moment, there was no time at all.

Together we sat and listened to the counterpoint of the raindrops falling upon the rocks, the moss and the treetops. We heard the rolling echoes of the thunder across the hills as it travelled further and further from us, until at last we could hear it no longer. The rain stopped, the light returned, the density of the air shifted, and our ears became filled with the early morning birdsong that now rose into a symphonic splendour.

And then, the rainbow melted into the light and vanished.

Without a word, the Iris exhaled a sigh of deep delight, and turned to face me, with dreamy, half-closed eyes.

'Tell me what you have seen since we last spoke,' she requested.

I told her the story 'Learning to Breathe'. I told her about the Grand Canyon, the mockingbird, my baby daughter and my mother's peach-coloured bedroom. I told her about Gurudeva's lecture, my prayers and the birth of Love. I told her all about the people, places and things in the story. And, of course, I told her about Crow.

Then the Iris asked—

'Most gentle and elegant friend! What have you learned about the Principle of Receiving?'

I sat and shut my eyes, so as to feel the Principle enter me. Then, feeling it fully, I opened my eyes and spoke with clarity.

'I have learned about the true nature of Time and Space,' I said, much to my own astonishment.

'Oh, I would also very much like to know the Truth about Time and Space.' she said simply. 'What can you tell me?'

'Well,' I began, struggling to put what I could feel intuitively into words, 'Space... hmm... Space is Here. And Time is... well...Time is Now.'

The Iris was delighted, and her purple petals deepened to a rich, royal velveteen.

'Oh, how wonderful!' she applauded. 'That sounds both simple and mysterious. Please tell me more!'

I took a moment to dive into Endless Time and Endless Space. I let my senses expand and allowed that expansiveness to enter my lungs.

'Well,' I explained, 'until I met Crow, I did not understand Space at all. I used to think there was a here and a there, an inside and an outside. And for most of my life I felt like I was stuck on the wrong side of that Space. I was either looking out at the world from the inner world of my own limited awareness, or I was looking into the world from the outside, feeling destined to remain an outsider to it forever. Either way, regardless of whether I was on the outside looking in, or the inside looking out, I saw people, places and things as something other than myself. And because I saw them as other, all I ever felt was the distance between me and the rest of the world. And living within that distance, I always felt alone, in both the vastness and the smallness of Space.

'Feeling alone and separate from the world, it was not possible for me to Receive. Or at least, I wasn't aware of it. I wasn't breathing. I wasn't taking the world into my lungs, my heart, my mind or my soul. There was no way for life to enter me. How could anything enter me when I saw it all as separate? How could I take in a world that I believed was "over there"?

'But ever since Crow came to my window, I can understand that all my conceptions of Space had been illusory. There is no distance within Space. There is no inside or outside. There is no here or there. Everything is here. And here is everywhere.

'And because here is everywhere, it means I am always home. Everything and everyone in creation is connected to me. I am a part of them and they are a part of me. There is no separation. And because there is no separation, the entire universe fills me from all directions. I can see, hear, and touch all within that unlimited Space. And through seeing, hearing, touching, experiencing, I am receiving it—unlimitedly, continuously, rapturously. Just like the dawn that is happening at every moment, I am receiving the world at every moment. I become filled with Space.

'Just the simple act of thinking about this fills me with awe, wonder and amazement,' I concluded.

The Iris made a gentle, wordless, cooing sound of pleasure upon hearing these words.

'What you say about Space takes my breath away,' she said softly. 'I scarcely know whether I have room in me to hear what you will say about Time. But still, I'd like to know, if you will tell me.'

I breathed in the Spaciousness, and let Time fill me up. Then I spoke.

'Until I met Crow,' I continued, 'I did not understand Time either. I used to think Time was fleeting and that I had to run after it, to capture it. I couldn't savour anything because as soon as I became aware of it, I felt it pass over me and leave me. When we believe dawn to be a single moment, we wait and wait for it, and then we lose it as soon as it happens. Like that, I led my life always waiting for the next moment to occur. I was always waiting for something to come to me. Life was filled with vast amounts of waiting for moments that never seemed to last. And because I was always waiting for the next moment, or reliving the fleeting moments of the past, I never felt the wealth contained within the moment in which I was actually living.

'Without being able to feel the wealth contained within the moment in which I lived, I felt empty. I felt like a pauper wandering penniless through the story of my own life. I had no knowledge of how to Receive what was already there before my eyes. I could not see my own wealth.

'But now I know that all my conceptions of Time had been illusory. Dawn is not a point in Time. It is merely a microscopic perspective within Endless Time. Dawn is ever-present. Dawn is contained within any moment. I can hear the music of the mockingbird at any moment, if I listen. I can see and touch the soul of another human being when I let go of my limited vision of who that person is. I can feel the birth of Love within my heart simply by looking with clear vision to see that it is already there. I can Receive anything the moment I allow myself to breathe it in.

'Every time is Now. And Now is Always.

'And because Now is Always, I need wait for nothing. Now is not a single, tiny point; it is every point simultaneously. And because Now is every point simultaneously, I can delight and relish the sheer pleasure of totality at every moment within that Unlimited Time. Now is delicious—and still more and more delicious at every moment.'

The Iris gave a sensuous little shiver.

'So tell me,' she whispered, 'what is the great *secret* you have discovered about the Principle of Receiving?'

I looked at her and took a moment to consider how utterly beautiful she was in that moment. The lingering humidity of the recent storm had left pearls of perspiration upon my brow, and drops of dew upon her soft petals.

'The great secret of Receiving,' I replied, 'is that it is both Infinite and Eternal. Receiving is Everywhere and Always. And because it is Everywhere and Always, we are continuously Receiving at all times and all places. There is no moment when we are not Receiving, and no limit to what we Receive. There is no end to the abundance of the universe. It cannot run out. And it is filling me up at every moment.'

We sat together silently, simply feeling the moment. After some time, perhaps a few seconds, perhaps centuries, the Iris spoke again.

'So, if the secret of the Principle of Receiving is that it is Everywhere and Always, what is the *power* of this Principle?'

'The power?' I asked, stopping to reflect upon her question.

'Why, the power of Receiving—is that it is the *key* to Giving!' I cried in great surprise.

'When I do not Receive, I view myself as a pauper. I am poor in spirit. I feel I have nothing to Give. But when I Receive— really Receive—all that is there to Receive, my wealth knows no bounds. I am full beyond measure. I am uncontainable. And feeling wealthy beyond bounds, my very soul feels the urge to spill over into the universe—

'And you *"become so full that you have no choice but to give yourself away"?'* the Iris offered.

'Yes! Yes!' I said. 'When we are young, we are taught it is better to give than to receive. But actually it is when I do not Receive that I am the miser, the skin-flint, the Scrooge, because without Receiving, there is nothing I can possibly Give to anyone or anything. It is by Receiving that I become at once both grateful and generous.

'In fact,' I said, getting even more animated, 'I cannot actually see where Giving ends and Receiving begins. It is only our perception that makes them seem like opposites. They are inseparable parts of the same, endless, timeless, beautiful state of flow between all conscious beings. The flow between Give and Receive is a never-ending wave that weaves together the fabric of existence itself.'

I went silent and simply took in the Time and Space that was present.

We looked at each other, and felt no distance or difference between us. We forgot the time of day. We knew only each other, and saw each other clearly now. I felt a stirring within my life force, and could feel the flow of Giving and Receiving, and of Receiving and Giving, moving gracefully through my lungs, into the world, back into my lungs...

I felt her breath enter into mine, and mine into hers, without distinction. It required no thought, no effort to breathe, to Receive, to Give, to Receive...

197

Then after some time, the Iris spoke again.

'I told you there was much you already knew!' she whispered lovingly.

'So now,' she asked, 'what will you do next?'

I stood up and walked to the opening of the cave. Looking out across the wide open expanse of Earth and Sky before me, I could feel the rays of the sun upon my face as the storm clouds had now departed completely.

Then, I turned towards her and gave her my sincere promise.

'I will walk daily through the Garden of my own Soul.

'I will nurture it and tend to the weeds that spring up within its flowerbeds.

'I will learn more and more about the Principle of Receiving from the simple stories of my own life.

'And,' I concluded, 'I will tell all I meet about the Treasure they will find when they do the same.'

* * * * *

Section Three:
Lessons from the Daffodil

The Principle of Becoming

Characteristics and Attributes:

joy, curiosity, playfulness, creativity,
laughter, fun, growth, spontaneity, silliness,
discovery, imagination, youth, play, freshness,
delight, exploration, innovation, inspiration,
rebirth, regeneration, newness, eccentricity,
blissful surrender to all that unfolds,
awareness of creation within every moment

Guides:

bumblebee, locust, catfish, tree,
dreams, make-believe, backyard, swings,
father, husband, childhood, mid-life,
flight, falling, letting go, being caught

SONG of THE Daffodil: THE SCENT of THE EARTH

Asleep—
I'm walking
   through the wood

Dreamless—
but longing
   so for dreams

Climbing—
I reach
   a vast plateau

A tundra—
cold and barren
   beneath my feet

I pause—
I wonder what dreams may lie
   beneath this black and formless soil
that cracks beneath my frostbitten toes
   but does not buckle or give way
      to the weight of my own dreamlessness

It holds me—
   this emptiness

It keeps me from falling
   whilst sleeping
      walking
         watching
            and wondering

A dewdrop falls—
   just one

It lands upon my sleeping form
and melts the ice within my heart
and nestles deep within my soul

The earth now turns from black to brown
and colour starts to claim its space
in this colourless and sleeping place

Another drop of dew—
just two

The earth begins to crack
And then
I see it start to crumble too
and become rich with the treasure of its own moisture

And in that moist and muddy place
a scent arises—
the scent of the earth

It lilts and dances in the air
and caresses my sleepwalking form
with lacelike arms that tickle me
and stir me from my emptiness

My eyelids open—
The tundra is gone
the soil is fertile
and little green patches
just barely green
and barely seen
and still quite unclear as to what they will become
are dotted everywhere I look

But become, indeed, I know they will.

A fragrance thick as honeyed sunshine permeates the air

a sweet liquor bidding me to drink deeply
of its nectar

And I find can no longer resist.

I shut my eyes again
   but now

Abandoning all fear, I fall—
deep into the earthy womb
   to take root
      within its warm and welcoming embrace

Her scent fills me up—
   my lungs
      my mind
         my heart
            my trust

My imagination runs wild.

And I know now
   it is spring!

* * * * *

The Daffodil – The Principle of Becoming

E aster Sunday fell very early that year—only two days after the spring equinox.

I woke very early in the morning and noticed there was frost on my windows. I got up and looked out my bedroom window to find it had snowed during the night, and there was a blanket of pure white spread out in all directions across my Garden. The rest of the world was still asleep on this chilly holiday morning, and there was not a soul in sight. I wiped the frosty condensation from my window so I could see better, and noticed the only colour amidst the sea of pristine whiteness came from eccentrically strewn patches of yellow daffodils scattered hither and thither.

What unexpected weather for Easter, I thought.

I felt a slight chill and then decided to go back to bed for a while. I curled up under the duvet and fell back into a slumber, with an odd but pleasant dream where I was picking up and embracing a very tiny child who was trying to get out from a miniature pond in my Garden. The child was only about two hands' width in length, much smaller than any baby in real life, and she could talk like an adult. I cannot recall everything we talked about, but I do remember watching her as she had some difficulty climbing out of the pond. Bundling her up in a blanket, I told her she really needed to be more careful when she went swimming next time.

Soon after, I awoke from my dreams, half-imagining someone was coming to serve me breakfast in bed on a finely lacquered tray laden with French toast, orange juice and freshly brewed coffee.

No such luck, I realised as I opened my eyes. I had really slept a long time, and it was almost noon.

I finally got up for the day, and looked outside again. The snow had all melted now and my Garden was once again an expanse of green. The daffodils now seemed curiously less conspicuous than they had been amidst the snow.

This seemed like such an odd day that I decided I should go for a walk in my Garden, just to see what would turn up next. So I bundled up and made my way out, tromping through muddy patches of black earth, through overgrown stretches of green grass that had been untended throughout the winter, until I came to the river. I stopped for a while to watch a group of male mallards, their iridescent heads changing colour in the sun as they swam—now green, now blue, now indigo, now green again—like some sort of psychedelic lightshow.

I was starting to feel the unseasonably cold air against my skin and I wrapped my chenille scarf tighter around my neck. This was really unexpected weather. Nonetheless, there was something delightful about it, something unique about it. I looked up at the sky to see clumps of blackened clouds here and there, lingering ominously amidst the brilliant sunshine.

I walked along the river, through Gardens of different shapes and styles. The Earth had not yet fully awakened, and the tips of the leaves from the tulips and hyacinths were only just starting to show. Following nothing but my own whim, I turned down a pathway I had not explored before and found myself in a small abandoned churchyard—an odd thing to discover in my Garden. Within its gates, there were dozens of gravestones. Some were so old I could not even make out the date of the departure of the person who lay beneath the earth. I found myself reflecting upon these departed souls. Although I had never met them, I somehow felt they had had a hand in leading me to this place, to this time. I stopped for a moment and could smell the scent emanating from the moist black soil, which had drunk deeply from the morning snowfall. Inhaling deeply, I took in the essence of these unknown ancestors, whose remains were feeding this patch of earth upon which I now stood. Their fragrance filled me, and I found myself saying, 'Bless you, all of you.'

I walked past these long-forgotten graves—so old even they who had erected them were also now long forgotten—and reflected upon this very strange afternoon. I hadn't celebrated Easter since I was a child. I tried to remember what it felt like back then, and slowly I stared to feel a very curious sensation— the tingle of regeneration was entering into my lungs and the pores of my skin.

It is all about rebirth, I said to myself.

And most amazingly, the skies suddenly opened up and started snowing again. This was completely unexpected, and the sun was still full and yellow. Nonetheless, I found myself pelted with tiny snowflakes—more like little crystal pellets than flakes—and they bounced merrily on my nose, my head, my duffle coat. I found myself laughing at how they tickled me.

How utterly random! I said to myself. *It is as if the Sky had read my thoughts, and was putting a punctuation mark on them.*

The snow pellets became heavier and heavier, and bouncier and bouncier. It was as if the clouds were just in the mood to be playful. It was fun, but it also was getting a bit cold, so I looked for someplace to duck until the clouds had finished their game. I saw a small sylvan patch of fir trees and decided to seek shelter there.

I reached the wood, and instantly felt the embrace of the feathery spruce and wispy pine trees, as their low branches brushed against my face and arms. The earthy aroma was captivating and I found myself forgetting completely about the cold. I wandered along a dirt path that swerved first this way, then that, and eventually allowed myself to get rather lost, but without a care in the world. I started spinning around in circles, my arms in the air.

'What a wonderful hiding place!' I said aloud, without thinking.

And then I heard a hundred voices call out to me in a thunderous bubble of excitement, 'Hello! Hello! Hello! Hello!'

I nearly jumped out of my duffle coat.

I stopped spinning and looked around to find I was surrounded by a sea of yellow Daffodils, swaying and waving at me.

The Daffodils called to me in a silly voice. 'Come play with us!' they cried together, all a-giggle.

They twittered and tossed their pretty little heads wildly, as my eyes tried to take them in. They flashed like lightning in all directions amidst the dark green wood, poking their bright yellow bonnets through the cold, muddy earth.

'You look funny!' they laughed. 'Your feet are all muddy and your hair is all wet from the snow!'

They were a most delightful presence, these Daffodils. For all their playfulness, their petals were so full of strength against the snow and the cold. They stood like an army of springtime against the slumber of winter, standing boldly against the elements when no other flowers dared yet to show their faces. They seemed ready for the unexpected, ready for anything to happen. The air was so filled with expectation I could not resist coming closer to them.

The Daffodils stood winking at me and wiggling their little bodies in a silly dance. Some of them stuck out their tongues, teasing me to come and play. They were so inviting I simply could not resist. For several hours we saw castles in the clouds and played make-believe. I stomped through the mud puddles and we all played Prince and Princess with the mighty fir trees. All the while, the cheery little Flowers sang the joyful (and sometimes silly) song of the Daffodil—the song of Becoming. We laughed and laughed and laughed so hard together that the Daffodils started to toot from their petals like trumpets, like elephants, like choo-choo trains. My sides ached with laughter and I could not stop myself from rolling on the ground with tears streaming down my face into the cold, dark earth.

We played and played all afternoon, until we all became quite tired out. I sat down in the middle of them, as we exhaled a great sigh of satisfaction together. As I caught my breath, I gazed around me and surveyed my Daffodil playmates. How unexpectedly strong they were. While they were full of play and silliness, there was a vitality and power within their humour and joy that had made me impervious to the elements, and unmindful of the time of day. In their presence, I felt no limits to the imagination or to what was possible.

These Daffodils were very different from both the Rose and the Iris. They were undeniably social creatures, who delighted in the implausible and the unexpected, and who were open to all that came their way. And in this way, in spite of being the most childlike of the Flowers I had met so far, they also seemed, in some inexplicable way, to be the most fearless. They braved the snow, the cold, the darkness. They didn't need thorns. They didn't need solitude. They didn't need warmth. They simply played with whatever was there. They welcomed everything into their playing field as a new experience, a new creation, and were full of delight.

I sat amidst the Daffodils, silently feeling their joyfulness as my breathing slowed down until it moved with the pulse of the Earth itself. I smiled at the sight of their pertly upturned petals that looked like little golden trumpets, heralding the coming of spring. It seemed as though they were ready to burst with all that was ever-fresh and ever-new, and I smiled as I felt a wave of gentle warmth—not too warm, but not too cold—fill me up. These Daffodils were like sunshine amidst little cotton puffs of clouds, and I could not imagine or remember anything that could possibly be wrong in the world. I felt like dancing, like singing, like hopping on one leg.

Tasting the flavour of their inimitable yellowness, I eventually found the words I wished to say to the Daffodils. And as I knew with certainty these Daffodils had much to teach me, I asked them—

'Most playful, joyful, and inspirational Daffodils! Oh souls of my imagination! What can I learn from you?'

The Daffodils crossed their eyes and stuck their tongues out at me, making me laugh out loud.

For a few moments, the Daffodils settled blissfully into the flavour of my question, sighing dreamily with a lovely, 'Ahhhhh!' Then gently, and with sweet affection, their petals tingled with a tinkling, musical response and they told me what they could teach me.

'From us,' they replied teasingly, 'you can learn the Principle of Becoming,'

'What is the Principle of Becoming?' I asked them. 'Does it mean I have to change? Does it mean I am not enough? Does it mean I have to work hard to become something else?'

The Daffodils twittered like munchkins at my lack of understanding, as if to say, 'Oh, we are going to have a lot of fun with you! I'd love to give your cheeks a nice, big pinch!' The sun, which was now starting to move towards the west, had changed from a bright yellow to a pale white, making the Daffodils stand out like beacons in the darkening wood.

Then the Daffodils chimed altogether in a sing-song, like children, as if simple words were utterly incapable of expressing of what they wished to say.

'The Principle of Becoming is joy, spontaneity and delight,' they said together.

'It is silliness, play, laughter and fun,' said one Daffodil.

'It is curiosity, discovery and exploration,' said another.

'It is innovation, inspiration and creativity,' said a third.

And one after another they continued.

'It is birth, growth, rebirth and regeneration.'

'It is freshness, youth and newness.'

'It is eccentricity and unpredictability.'

'It is the blissful surrender to all that unfolds.'

'It is acute awareness of creation within every moment.'

'It is living every moment with wide-eyed wonder and faith.'

'It is overflowing possibilities!' a patch of them cried out in unison.

Then, one very tall Daffodil, nearest me, sang for all of them.

> It is a necklace upon a string
> with beads of now and now and now
> Each now has something new to bring
> if everything you will allow
>
> Release the need to know what is
> and dance with wonder of what could be
> Then feel the tingle before the surprise
> and fly and soar unlimitedly!

'In short,' they all chimed together, 'the Principle of Becoming is Freedom!'

The child in me began to rebel. This sounded like an awful lot to learn! I didn't want to work. I wanted to play. These funny Daffodils had suddenly become pretty enigmatic now, and I felt a bit self-conscious as I sat with them in my muddy boots and wet hair. I just wanted to make mud-pies and dig for buried treasure. But I was also getting tired. I began to feel like I did when I was a little girl after spending all day outdoors at play. At some point, somewhat reluctantly, you know you have to stop playing and return home.

The Daffodils could sense my tiredness, and they turned in all directions, as if to light up every possible corner of the Garden with their yellow sunshine. I felt my weariness lift just enough to express my concern to them, as I looked plaintively at the Daffodils.

'Joyful friends, how can I learn all that you know?' I asked them in a piteous voice. 'I don't know how to fly. Even now, I find myself crashing back down to Earth, wondering how to get home. I think I must be afraid of flying. And creativity? So often, my creativity gets swallowed up by practical things. My mind gets cluttered and my feet get stuck in the mud. How can I possibly learn how to dance in the moment without care?'

'Oh, but there is much you already know!' they giggled in unison.

The laughter of the Daffodils uplifted me. I became curious to find out what I might already know about the Principle of Becoming.

'Me? What could I possibly know already? Where have I learned it?' I asked.

'Come on, now! You already know the answer to that question!' they chided, rolling their eyes at me. 'Just take a walk through your own Garden to see what is already there.'

They were right. I knew from my lessons with the Rose and the Iris that all the answers to the teachings of the Flowers were to be found in my own Garden.

'Oh playful Daffodils,' I asked, 'where in my Garden shall I look to find the Principle of Becoming?'

The Daffodils shook their perky little forms and, dancing more merrily than ever, said, '*Be joyful, my forever friend—*

In all directions are your Guides
and endless journeys you will fly.
Locust, Fish and Bumblebee
will show you what you're meant to be

I did not at all understand what the Daffodils meant, but I had by now learned to trust without question whatever the Flowers told me.

Weary from play, I stood up to get ready to leave. Seeing I was squinting to find the route back to my house in the darkening wood, the Daffodils perked up their yellow heads like footlights along the earthen pathway, escorting me out of the woods and back into the Garden. When I made my way into the open air, I was delighted to feel the touch of the brilliant late-afternoon sun, and to see the last of the dark purple snow clouds vanishing over the eastern horizon.

It was much too chilly that night to sleep with my window open, but my day of laughter and play with the Daffodils had tired me so much I fell asleep quite easily. In my dreams, I could see and remember so much of my life that had been full of what the Daffodils had spoken about. I could see laughter and play and make-believe. I saw fear of flying and letting go. I saw birth, rebirth and regeneration.

The next day, when I awoke from those nostalgic dreams, I found that, in much the same way that I had learned from the Rose and the Iris, I could indeed recall many simple stories from my life that had been lessons from the Daffodil, but I hadn't recognised them as such. I could remember times when the sheer joy of creation filled my heart, and when I struggled to create anything. I could remember when I longed so much to fly, but did not know how to get off the ground. I could remember the joy of finally letting go of the chains that bound me to the Earth, to sail freely upon the winds of my own imagination. I could remember countless dreams that had been lessons from the Daffodil, inviting me to take flight into the freedom of unlimited possibilities.

It was all there—all that the Daffodils had described.

The Daffodils' teachings were indeed, as they had said, all to be found within the Garden of my Soul, within the simple stories of my own life. And as I reflected upon these stories, I understood more and more how the Principle of Becoming is sometimes brilliantly visible, and sometimes slow to appear, and how much delight can be found within the delicate interplay between the light and the shadow of our own experiences.

And so, I felt the desire to write some of these stories down within these pages...

* * * * *

Fly Away

I am standing at the foot of the scaffold.
My body feels a faint sense of something I cannot quite understand. A slight buzzing in my head. A vague flutter in my stomach.

I can hear Manuel talking to me, with his delightfully honeyed Spanish accent, but I am not completely conscious of what is about to happen. Somehow my brain has gone numb and I am not taking this in fully. It is as if I am not inside myself, and I am simply going through the motions because my will has told me to do it. But, in this moment, I am not sure of where I really am.

Manuel asks me whether I want to practise and I nod somewhat nervously. I place my hands on alternate shoulders, criss-crossing my arms on my chest, not unlike the way a corpse is posed inside a coffin. I make my body rigid.

I fall backwards, just a few inches. It seems like such a simple thing.

I know what I am supposed to do. There are only a few steps to the top of the scaffold—maybe five or six...

*   *   *   *   *

I cannot remember ever having met Karen.

Karen was someone who had just always been 'there' in my life. My mother sometimes would tell me about the time when Karen was born—a year-and-a-half after I was—and how her mother strolled proudly up and down the street with the pram to show off her brand-new baby girl to all the neighbours. I cannot remember that day, of course, as I was only a toddler myself, but I do remember the pram. It was a lovely, old-fashioned wooden carriage with pink trim. When we were little girls, Karen's mother used to let us play with it so we could push our baby dolls in it, up and down the sidewalk on our suburban street.

Our Long Island neighbourhood was one of hundreds in the US that had been created to accommodate the post-war Baby Boom in the 1950s. I think back to those times and realise that such a time period would be very difficult to recreate today. The adult population in our little town was comprised almost completely of either immigrants or first-generation Americans. My own father was born in a part of Austria that is actually now a part of Italy; in fact, it was the Italians moving into their Tyrolean territory that prompted their move to the US back in the 1920s, when he was very young. My mother was a first-generation Irish American. All the parents on our street, including Karen's, came from similar backgrounds, the vast majority being Roman Catholic, and of Italian, Irish or Polish descent. A community of Jewish immigrants was a mile or so across the turnpike, and a small pocket of Black families sat only a few streets away across the boulevard. In contrast, there was the very wealthy White neighbourhood of Garden City, comprised of people, probably much less likely to be recent immigrants of any kind, which was positioned literally 'on the other side of the tracks' from us, as the Long Island Railroad served as the dividing line between our two towns. My neighbourhood playmates and I, living in our modest, post-war, 'Cape Cod style' housing development, would sometimes sigh as we looked out the car window when our parents would drive by the mansion-like estates in Garden City. As a child, I imagined these were the types of citizens who considered themselves to be 'real' Americans, unlike immigrant families like us, who lived across the tracks. The irony, of course, was that the families in the Black community, who were largely ignored by the Whites in those post-war days, could probably trace their American roots back further than anyone else in the area.

But as children in the 1950s, each of our respective neighbourhoods was completely sheltered and socially segregated from the others, and we were largely unaware of what lay beyond the tracks, the boulevard or the turnpike. We lived in isolation in our middle-class ghettos, and stuck to our own 'kind'. As we grew a little bit older, we became vaguely aware that there were other neighbourhoods, not so very far away, that 'felt' different from our own. But we didn't dare to venture out much, and our universe had a radius of perhaps less than a quarter of a mile.

But during the first ten years or so of our lives, a quarter-mile seemed perfectly adequate to us first-generation kids. For, as the progeny of the post-war era, our suburban streets were literally bursting at the seams with children in all directions. In those days, Catholics were especially prolific breeders, and to find a playmate, you only had to look out your front door. There was always someone outside who was ready to play. Everyone played with everyone else. Girls, boys, younger, older—it didn't matter. We would even play with kids we didn't particularly like. As long as they came from our neighbourhood, they were fair game. That was pretty much the code of ethics amongst us. And in this way, we knew everyone and everyone knew us—at least, inasmuch as any of us could know anything about anyone else. In short, we lived and played and stayed within a world that we told ourselves was both safe and familiar.

To understand this microcosm in which we children lived, you need to know something about New York in the Baby Boom era, which was, or at least it seemed to me, a society still trying to balance itself—to find itself. In the 50 years prior, New York had experienced the influx of unprecedented numbers of immigrants around the turn of the century, followed shortly after by the Great Depression. My parents, like most of the other parents in the neighbourhood, had grown up in abject poverty. Many of them had to go out to work when they were still, by all accounts, children themselves. My own father started to work when he was only 8 years old; my mother left school to go to work at age 13 or 14. Things like property ownership, education and financial security were distant dreams that had to be pushed to the background because sheer survival was the primary concern. Escapism was, naturally, sought in the form of the cinema, radio, cigarettes, alcohol and a unique sense of romanticism that characterised the era.

The Great Depression was, by all the accounts I heard from people in my parents' generation, only finally alleviated by the coming of World War II. The war, although fought on distant shores, created several ripples within American society. First, it instilled a mood of nationalism that brought the country together in the face of adversity. Secondly, it sent thousands of young men into combat, changing both the social and economic balance at home. Young couples hastily married, prodded by a fear (often well founded) that the young man may never return to his young bride, except in a plain wooden coffin. This, in turn, created a romantic notion of the faithful wife, or the 'girl back home', working diligently during the day in factories or government offices, and sitting patiently at night with the light in the window, waiting for her man to come home. Whether or not this notion was actually true in fact is not the point. The point is that this is how people imagined life to be. My own parents were not immune to this romantic nationalism surrounding the war, and they married in May 1943 at my father's army base in Texas in between his assignments in the Pacific War with Japan.

But perhaps the most pervading and lasting knock-on effect of the war was in how people in my parents' generation found an odd kind of identity with the war era itself. The verbal pictures my parents and their friends painted of the war would indicate that they felt it had actually saved them from all the suffering of the past. Twenty, thirty, forty and even fifty years after the war was over, they would still be talking about those times with a profound sense of nostalgia. The war itself became an icon that represented a complex set of values, within which lived the elusive notion of the 'American Dream'. And that dream included all the things that had been absent during the Great Depression. In short, World War II had become the saviour of the American people and the progenitor of a new economic ideology far more powerful to them than any of the cultures from which these immigrant peoples had originally come.

And therein lay another irony, because many immigrants, such as my father's family, had originally come to America in order to retain their indigenous cultures, and to escape oppression, whether political, religious or economic, that threatened to wipe them out. They wanted to be able to speak their own languages, practise their own religions and retain their own social customs. So, they landed on Ellis Island or other points of entry seeking the freedom offered by the promise of the great American Dream. But what they did not realise at the time was that, within that very dream they sought, there was actually no room for their native cultures. To live the dream fully, one had to embrace it, to surrender to it. And to a great extent, the measure of how well you were living the dream was in how far away you had moved from your cultural origins. Very few children in my generation, myself included, could either speak or understand the mother tongue of their parents. We had become 'Americans'.

But even as a child, it was clear to me there were definitely some very dark shadows lurking behind the brilliance of this American Dream. The inevitable sinister flipside of nationalism is that it can quite easily become a candy-coated version of intolerance in disguise. When people are rallied around an 'us', there must also be a 'them' that is different from 'us'. Wars are, by definition, battles between 'us' and 'them', regardless of what side you are on. The problem is that when this type of thinking becomes the foundation for your identity, you actually have little, if any, concept of your own self, except by way of comparison with someone or something else. In such a dualistic cosmology, our view of ourselves must fit neatly within the definitions of what 'us' is, lest we stray dangerously across the lines towards becoming 'them.' If we allow ourselves to do that, we lose ourselves.

And in the grips of this most tenuous concept of self, the only thing that keeps us feeling safe is the tight-knit cloak of segregation, woven together by the woolly threads of bigotry and fear. In this way, we become imprisoned by our own ignorance, which leaves us barren and without any real identity.

I grew up in both a household and a society that kept itself safe by these boundaries of segregation. Bigotry, as I grew up, was rife, if not a socially acceptable way of thinking. I heard it at home, I heard it at the neighbours' homes, I heard it at my relatives' homes, I heard it at school. And I also heard it at church. But bigotry at church was very subtle. Heaven, we were told, was something exclusively attainable only to people like 'us'. And the more we praised the glories of 'us', the more we could be justified in rejecting, ignoring or even condemning 'them'—whoever 'them' were.

And since we were justified in rejecting 'them', it meant we gave ourselves permission not to know them, or anything about them.

In those days, the people in my environment seemed to feel quite comfortable about openly using racist labels to refer to anyone who was 'not us'. You know all the words I mean. They are the kinds of words that still shock us if we hear them in a film or television. They would use these words quite unabashedly, as if they were the norm. Such words are like daggers that sever society, and help to keep it segregated by fear and hatred. I would never allow myself to utter such ugly words, and when I was young, I spent a good deal of time arguing with people who did. Someone would say that he hated 'those' people—whatever 'them' it was he hated at the time. But if I ever asked him, 'Really? You hate them? So tell me, how many of them have you known?' he would very simply reply, 'Are you kidding? I don't know any of them. Why would I *want* to? I hate them, get it?'

The truth is, while walking in the comfortable shadow of the American Dream, society in the Baby Boom era had given itself the permission to remain ignorant. And that blanket-like ignorance was a way of life that both protected and isolated everyone under its cover.

But it did not merely protect us from the 'others'; it protected us from *each other*—friends, family and neighbours alike. When I was growing up, there was a sanctity taught to each one of us about protecting the 'image' of the family. We children were taught we had to 'look good' to everyone else. If there was anything unsavoury going on in the household, it was the rule that we were not to disclose this to anyone. The most horrible thing that could possibly happen to a family would be for someone outside to find out what was *really* going on behind closed doors. So to speak publicly would be the ultimate betrayal, and it would bring disgrace and shame to the household.

And because we were so pre-occupied with spending all of our energy on preserving and upholding this shadow of a dream in the eyes of others, we built taller and taller hedges between our homes, and lived in an ever-shrinking universe of isolation where nobody ever really knew anyone at all. We might have listened to a message of 'Love thy neighbour' on Sundays, but the real message we heard on a day-to-day basis was 'What would the neighbours think?'

We gave lip service to worshipping an all-merciful Supreme Being, but we were actually worshippers of the unmerciful and unloving status quo.

But the really frightening thing about the darkness in that all-pervading, unrelenting shadow of ignorance was that it spread not just between ethnic groups, not just between neighbourhoods, not just between our homes, but also *within* our own homes as well. Because the truth is, the 'unsavoury-ness' of our lives was not even permitted to be discussed within our own four walls amongst the family. We learned how to deny the presence of anything unseemly, and to pretend to live lives that simply did not exist.

And so, we children born in the 1950s grew up learning how to survive within an unspoken code of isolation, where no one ever said anything that could possibly reveal anything about themselves that might be construed to be a flaw, a weakness, a fear or something not quite 'normal'.

And therein lay the ultimate irony, because that shadow of ignorance that lay behind the illusion of the perfect American Dream—deemed by its adherents to be the foundation of stability and normalcy—was itself flawed, weak, fearful and utterly abnormal.

But from within that shadow, one sunny ray of light was my friend Karen, who was there from the very beginning of it all.

*   *   *   *   *

'Team ready?' I call out.

'Ready!' is the affirmative response I hear from 20 disembodied voices.

As I ascend the steps of the wooden scaffold to the top of the platform, my mind abandons me and starts to drift randomly to very strange places, leaving my poor body alone in this unfamiliar place. I am aware of a growing sense of anticipation in the air, and things start to get quiet—quiet enough for me to hear the sound of my own footsteps creaking on the wooden stairs.

In this descending quiet, my mind runs unexpectedly and bizarrely to the memory of the passage in 'A Tale of Two Cities' where Charles Dickens describes the sheer terror of the condemned as they await their turn to go to the guillotine. 'What an incredible writer,' I think for a fleeting moment. Then, equally bizarre, my mind connects this image to the ominously blaring sounds of the execution scene of Berlioz's 'Symphonie Fantastique'.

All this makes me laugh to myself, because it is all so ridiculous. This is no guillotine. I am not on my way to die. But what am I on the way to?

My mind starts to come back to me, and it returns to my body, to the moment.

As I near the top of my ascent, my skin starts to tingle as I become aware that two dozen pairs of eyes are now looking only at me. I turn my back to them.

I know what I am supposed to do when I get to the top of the platform. But I am not really sure what will happen...

* * * * *

When I was growing up, Karen was almost always at our house. Unlike most of the stay-at-home moms on the street, Karen's mother worked during the day, so she wasn't home for Karen until late in the afternoon. My mother frequently used to point this out to me, saying how unfortunate Karen was not to have her mother around. But underlying her concern for Karen, I always sensed an encoded message coming from my mother that we were ever so much better off than Karen's family because my father made enough money to support us without my mother 'needing' to go to work. The American Dream of the post-war era was one of single-income families with stay-at-home moms whose sole responsibility was to take care of the kids and the household duties. The fact that our family had this lifestyle was a measure of our success.

But, as a child, none of that mattered to me. As far as I was concerned, it was no problem that Karen's mother wasn't around. We didn't pay much attention to our mothers during the day while we were playing anyway. Oh, yes, it was good to have them around in case we got hurt or hungry, but other than that, we kids kept to ourselves. The most important thing was that Karen and I had each other. And Karen and I played together, either alone or with other kids, nearly every day, rain or shine.

Of all my neighbourhood friends, Karen had a special place in my life as my partner in 'make-believe'. To us, making believe was the magic door to colourful lands where anything that could be imagined was possible. Making believe was having an unlimited supply of storybooks, costumes and characters. Making believe was a bottomless treasure chest full of dreams. To us, there was nothing quite as exciting as the moment when we had finished playing some other game, and one of us would say—'I know! Let's make believe!'

We used whatever we had at our disposal to create new worlds for ourselves. Sometimes, all it took was the weather to inspire us. During thunderstorms, we loved to go into my basement and turn off all the lights. Then we would put on my parents' recording of Duke Ellington's *Caravan*. During the eerie verses, we would walk through the dark with our eyes shut and arms outstretched in front of us, pretending to be sleepwalking ghosts to the backdrop of the sound of the rain and thunder outside. Then when the upbeat chorus kicked in, we would jump around madly like vaudevillian jazz dancers, wagging our fingers wildly in the air until the verse came back, and we suddenly became ghosts again, walking blindly to the haunting and exotic melody. It felt spooky, and we would laugh until our bellies hurt, filled with the delicious feeling of being scared by our own imaginations.

In the cold winter days before Christmas, there was always one day every year when we would help my father put up the Christmas lights outside the house. On that day, my dad would bring out a plate of chunks of parmesan cheese—he regularly bought a huge wheel of this delicacy in Brooklyn—and Karen and I would prance around pretending to be Santa's reindeer, handing my father different coloured light bulbs, and coming to nibble at the cheese every now and again. Sometimes, it would start to snow and we would prance out into the front yard, still as reindeer at the North Pole, and dance under the gossamer net of the falling sky. We would hop from foot to foot, with our little pink tongues outstretched to catch the snowflakes, and feel them turn from icy jewels to melted water in our mouths. We imagined this is what Santa's reindeer would do whenever they wanted a drink. Life seemed perfect as a reindeer.

But on sunny days, at any time of year, our favourite place for make-believe was on the swings in my own backyard.

When I was very little, perhaps three years old, my father had set up this swing set against a shrubby, but very full, hazelnut tree. There were three swings and a glider that could carry two more children. There were also cross-bars from which you could hang upside down by your knees. Our swings were the very best in the entire neighbourhood, and children in all directions would come to my backyard for a chance to swing on them. Karen and another little girl named Laura would always come over to play on our swings. If we just wanted to swing, we would face away from the hazelnut tree, towards the wide open area of the garden, so we could swing freely into the air. We played all kinds of games while swinging. Sometimes we would jump from the swings and fly through the air to land across the other side of the garden. We liked to pretend we actually could fly and that someday we would be able to keep on flying if we just kept practising. We imagined we could fly over the houses and over the town and wherever we wanted. It was that wonder, that question that asked, 'Do you think it could really happen?' that made flying on the swings so exciting to us. The thrilling possibility that 'One day, one day, we will fly away' made our hearts flutter inside our tiny chests.

Then, one day when I was eight years old, I was playing on the swings on the warm Sunday afternoon when I made my First Holy Communion in the lovely month of May. I was feeling extremely happy that day. I had gotten to wear a pretty white dress with a bridal veil and carry a bouquet of pink and white flowers. A professional photographer even took a photo of me in my outfit. I loved it all because it was just like making believe I was getting married. The weather was sunny and warm, and the beautiful ceremony at the church, where hundreds of us had taken our First Communion that day, had been a very moving experience for me. Then, my cousins and aunts and uncles came all the way from New Jersey just to celebrate with us. I got lots of presents and got to eat cake and ice cream. My mother gave me a gorgeous green flowered dress to wear to my party. I can still see the pattern and the colours in my mind. I think it was made of rayon, but I pretended it was made of rare Chinese silk. All in all, the day was nearly perfect and I felt high on life. The only thing that could have made it even better was to go for a wonderful ride on the swings in my back garden. So, I grabbed my two girl cousins, and we three spent hours and hours sailing away in the warm spring air.

And so there I was, swinging away, quite deliriously absorbed in a gush of blissful freedom, and chatting merrily away with my cousins, when suddenly, a very large bumblebee came buzzing right next to my face just as I was at the height of my swinging. He was huge! I was so startled and frightened by the bee that I impulsively, and unthinkingly, let go of the chains of the swing and flew high up into the air. I was absolutely terrified. I had never jumped off the swing from this height before and I had no idea what would happen. For the first time in my life, I felt the rush of adrenaline zinging right through my body. I heard myself scream as I flew across the garden, feeling weightless, petrified and thrilled all at the same time.

Within a second or two, although it seemed much longer to me, I landed on the ground, a few feet from the end of our back porch, next to the peony bush, which was in full bloom with top-heavy plum-coloured blossoms. I could not believe I had flown so far across the yard. I was also quite amazed I had not broken my leg from the fall. In fact, I had landed quite gracefully, and the worst part of the experience was the effort I had made to keep my pretty little flowered dress from billowing up in the air to show my underpants.

After I landed, I started to take in the fact that I would never have tried this daring stunt if the bumblebee hadn't startled me. It was as if the bee had come to push me into the air, saying, '*Try it out! You'll like it!*' And he would have been right. Flying through the air had been magnificent. It was scary, but it was also free and daring. The sensation of being able to fly—fly away on those swings—was sheer exhilaration.

The world of possibilities had just become that much larger, and more possible.

After that experience, I got braver and braver. I started taking more risks when jumping off the swings. The next time I saw Karen and Laura, I told them about my high-flying experience and announced that I wanted to recreate it. It took a little practice, but eventually I could fly as high as I wanted whenever I wanted to. With time, Karen and Laura, who were both younger than I was, got braver and braver as well. Soon, we were all flying across the garden. No longer just a wishful dream, we now really and truly believed that someday, if we kept on trying, we would indeed be able to keep going and fly right out of our garden and into the sky. We wouldn't fall back to earth. We would simply let go of the chains on the swing, and keep on flying as high and as far and as long as we wanted.

'I can fly!' 7-year-old Karen would cry out in childlike ecstasy. 'I want to fly away on those swings!'

Of course, I had to be sure my mother wasn't looking out the kitchen window, because she would probably have had a heart attack to see all of these little girls leaping off the swings from such a height.

The bumblebee had taught us how to fly higher than we had ever gone before. But sometimes, our flights were flights of imagination rather than of body. And in those flights, we could indeed defy the laws of gravity and fly as high and as far as we wished. On those journeys, we would turn around to face the other direction while sitting on the swings. No longer facing the openness of my backyard, our swinging would fly us into the dense foliage of the hazelnut tree, and we would sail directly into the dark canopy of its leaves. This became a delightful source of make-believe for us, and we would pretend we were in a spaceship flying through the Milky Way. Indeed, we thought the very name 'Milky Way' sounded extremely exotic. We would jokingly say, 'Let's go to the Milky Way and get a drink of milk!' This always made us laugh. I do remember that whenever we said this, I could distinctly experience the cold sensation and taste of a glass of milk in my mouth. I think all three of us felt this, as we all used to go 'Mmmm...' every time we stopped off at the Milky Way.

On these journeys, it was always my role to pretend to be a very clever parrot named Polly (of course), who was the navigator on the spaceship, guiding the crew of humans on their explorations. 'Peter' (played by Laura) was the captain and his girlfriend 'Penny' (played by Karen) always fed me magic crackers, which gave me my very 'un-parrot-like' powers. This scenario and cast of characters became a favourite make-believe game of ours for several years throughout our childhood, until adolescence started to kick in, first for me, then for Karen, and then Laura. But until I was perhaps eleven years old, the three of us would fly together every now and again throughout the galaxy to discover new worlds—uncountable worlds—all found within the green canopy of a hazelnut tree.

We children had no motives, no analytical thoughts, and no pre-conceived notions of what we were playing, how we should play or why we were playing like this. Our world of make-believe served no function other than the sheer pleasure of play. We had no care about the lack of feasibility of what we were pretending. We knew it was probably unlikely you could get a glass of milk from the Milky Way. We knew it was probably unlikely you could feed magic crackers to a talking parrot who would guide you to unknown planets. We knew it was probably unlikely you could, with practice, simply leap into the air without any kind of apparatus and start to fly—and keep flying—up, up, up and away.

We knew all these things were probably unlikely, but likelihood was not one of the rules of make-believe. In fact, likelihood was positively against the rules. In make-believe, the only rule was that you believed in what you were making up. In make-believe, we really *could* fly away—far, far beyond the quarter-mile universe.

Logic has no place in the universe of make-believe; make-believe is the place of unlimited possibilities.

It was only many years later that I would realise to what degree we were all creating worlds that served us far better than the world in which we actually lived.

* * * * *

'This is easy,' I tell myself. 'You're only six feet off the ground. Don't think about it. Don't think.'

My body and mind are now struggling to stay with each other. In this moment, each really needs the other to cooperate.

I know what I am supposed to do now that I am at the top of the platform. I take refuge in the instructions Manuel had given me earlier. Mechanically I begin to go through them. 'Go to the edge of the platform and turn backwards. Let the heels of your feet extend a few inches beyond the edge. Keep your arms crossed. Keep your body straight and rigid...'

I take a deep breath and then call out the request.

'Lynn fall?' I call out.

'Fall, Lynn!' comes the thunderous reply of the team.

But I don't fall.

Instead, a rush comes over my body and I am gripped by an unexpected wave of terror. I feel my knees wobble and I teeter just a bit at the edge of the platform, my back to the people behind me.

'Oh, God!' I cry out to the trees in the surrounding forest. I am trembling.

My arms are still criss-crossed across my chest. I suddenly feel immobilised by fear.

*   *   *   *   *

'Come here,' my father calls to me. 'I want to show you something.'

I am 8 years old. It is now mid-summer, and my father and I are walking in my grandparents' garden on a Sunday afternoon. They live in a semi-rural part of New Jersey and they have a small but operational wine vineyard behind their house. As usual, there are a lot of scary black wasps and other insects flying about, lured by the thick, heavy scent of the pungent purple grapes.

I walk over to my father. As I approach, I notice he is holding a small locust in the open palm of his left hand. The docile little creature is sitting passively, and I can see its soft brown furry body and its big bulging eyes. It looks very pretty in an awkward sort of way. I want to stroke it, but am afraid I will scare it off.

Then my father says, 'Watch this.'

Without hesitation, my father takes his right hand and quite impulsively snaps off the head of the locust, with one quick, unthinking motion.

It happens so suddenly that my mind can hardly register what is going on.

Casually, my father tosses the severed head of the locust into the cold, dead ashes of a rubbish burner my grandfather keeps in the garden. Then, he shows me the body of the locust, turning it so I can see inside the cavity of its abdomen.

'You see?' my father says. 'No central nervous system. It feels nothing. It's just a machine.'

I am in complete shock, and cannot move or speak a single word.

Then, before I have time to gather my wits and react to what just happened, my father hurls the headless body of the locust into the air above our heads, and it flies dizzyingly across the garden and away out of view.

My father says nothing more to me, and simply starts walking back to my grandparents' house, as it is time for lunch. He never explains why he wanted to show me this. I begin to make up possible reasons in my 8-year-old head. *Does he think I am too sensitive? Is he trying to make me tough? Does he want me to become cruel? Does he think this will make me a stronger person? Is he trying to protect me in some weird way?*

Or, I ask myself, *does he simply find it amusing to snap off the head of a locust, and he actually has no real purpose for doing it at all?* I find this to be the scariest possibility.

I shake off these uncomfortable thoughts and break into a run in the direction of my father. Soon, I catch up with him and we walk side-by-side. My father says nothing to me. I say nothing to him. But although I do not say the words, even at 8 years old, I am not at all convinced the locust felt nothing.

But I am also not convinced about my father. *He is the one who seems to feel nothing. But how can that be?*

Does my father have a central nervous system? I ask myself.

As we enter my grandparents' kitchen together, I realise I am both confused and frightened by a question that would continue to haunt me for many years to come—

Who is this person who is my father?

* * * * *

I am 22 years old, and on a camping trip along the Colorado River in Texas. I am walking along the river with a friend and notice some chains dangling from the riverbank into the water. Not knowing what they are, I ask my friend, and she tells me they are 'stringers.' She explains that fishermen catch fish during the day, but leave them, still alive, at the end of the hook, swimming in the water, so as to keep them fresh until they are ready to kill them. This is something completely foreign to me, never having been a country girl, and being very new to the American southwest.

The next afternoon, I am walking along the same stretch of river. This time, a burly fisherman who, apparently, had set the stringers the day before is there. He has now come to haul in his catch and prepare his dinner for the evening. I watch him as he draws up one of the stringers from the muddy brown waters of the Colorado, and as he pulls his prize to the surface, I see it is a massive catfish, at least two-and-a-half feet long, and probably about fifteen inches in diameter around the gills. All in all, he is a magnificent fish, a grandfather amongst catfish, and very much full of life.

As I stand there, a young woman from the suburbs of New York who has never fished before, I realise I have some pre-conceived notions that a fish, once out of water, will die pretty much immediately due to drowning in the oxygen-rich air. But to my surprise, this fish does not die when he comes out of the water. Instead, he gasps and writhes before my eyes, as the fisherman now places him in a metal clamp to hold him in place and keep him from slithering back to his watery home.

Bound by the clamp, the fish is now flapping and gulping in complete distress. But the fisherman is unperturbed. Coolly, he picks up one of his knives from his kit and begins to saw through the large girth of the fish's neck, to try to cut off his head. The fish starts to bleed. The fisherman continues to saw away, unmindful of the fish's struggling.

By now the fish is flailing madly, gasping even more frantically and bleeding profusely, with his head partially sawn off. There is a gash perhaps two inches deep cut into his flesh, running six or eight inches in length around his neck.

After several minutes, the fisherman gets frustrated because his knife is not strong enough to cut all the way through the thick neck of this grandfather catfish. So he gives up on the idea of slicing off the fish's head and tosses his knife onto the ground. He stands squarely in front of the fish and puts both hands on either side of the fish's face. Then, I watch him as he actually tries to wrench off the head of this fish with his bare hands. Back and forth he twists the head, trying to snap the neck and break it off from the backbone.

An image flashes back in my mind, and I find myself remembering my father and the locust. I become just as speechless.

The fish's neck is simply too massive, and eventually the fisherman gives up on that tactic too. He stops for a moment to contemplate what his next course of action should be. The fish's terror, pain and anguish are obvious to me. I find myself stunned that a fish could live so long out of water, let alone survive such physical torture all the while suffocating in the air.

Finally, the fisherman decides his next, and final, course of action. Thoughtfully, he picks up his knife again. Then, I watch in complete horror as he begins to flay this fish alive.

I now look into the eyes of the catfish. I feel at my core that if this fish only had a voice, his piteous screams would curdle the blood of anyone who might hear them.

And I do hear them—not with my ears, but with my heart. This fish cannot speak for himself, but something in his eyes creates a stir within my own throat. And almost beyond my control, I find myself starting to shout loudly at this unknown fisherman—

'For God's sake, it's bad enough you are killing that fish, but why do you need to torture him like this?! Can you just end this right now?'

But the fisherman seems unconcerned. Perhaps he thinks I am just an ignorant city girl. Without so much as a flinch in his concentration, he answers me without any emotion, saying, quite matter-of-factly...

'If you don't filet it when it's fresh, the meat is tough.'

'Fresh?' I say incredulously. 'But this fish is *still alive*.'

The fisherman ignores me, and continues his task without responding. I get the feeling he thinks I'm pretty nosy for telling him what to do. I start to imagine what he might be thinking. *This is* my *fish, lady. I caught it. Who are you to tell me how to kill it?*

Feeling powerless, I watch the fisherman slice strips of pink flesh from the fish's living body. I feel my eyes well up as I look into the face of the fish, his body barely having the strength to struggle anymore, his mouth still vainly gulping for air, his whole body bleeding profusely.

And then, with half of his body sliced away from his bones, the fish's eyes finally roll upwards into his head and, mercifully, he gives up his life, to suffer no more.

The writhing stops and the body is motionless. There is no more resistance and the fisherman now completes his task without effort.

Packing up his knife and his freshly filleted dinner, the fisherman seems very happy with his catch. Nonchalantly, he tosses the mangled parts of the fish's body that are now valueless to him—including the fish's head—back into the river, to be caught in the current. I watch the head float downstream, seeing the fish's now lifeless eyes staring vacantly into nothingness. My mind drifts along with it, back in time to my childhood, and I find myself wondering how long the headless body of the locust had lived after my father had released it, and how it could possibly know where it was going as it flew madly away into the next yard.

Well, Dad, I think, *I do have a central nervous system. And I cannot live my life without feeling something.*

At that very moment, I decide I will become a vegetarian. *The world has enough violence in it without my help,'* I think, *'I do not wish to add to it.'*

It would take some time before I would be brave enough to stand up to my father about my choice to stop eating meat and fish. He would challenge and ridicule my vegetarianism whenever we sat down to a meal together for many years to come. Perhaps he felt I was a disappointing student, not having understood what he had wanted me to learn from his lesson with the locust.

*   *   *   *   *

It is 6:25 PM. I can hear the whistle from my father's train arriving at the station a few blocks away. In three minutes, he will walk through the door, as he does every weekday evening.

My mother, being a model housewife of the 1960s, has dinner ready just as she does every other evening.

My father arrives home. Before sitting down to dinner, he goes down into our finished basement for 15 or 20 minutes, where he keeps a stash of my grandfather's horrible homemade wine. He slugs down just enough of the sickly-smelling potion to get reasonably drunk. Then he comes back upstairs and takes his place at the dinner table, his ears and nose swollen to a deep shade of purple. I think to myself how this colour is the same colour as the grapes from my grandfather's vineyard.

My father starts to eat. If he is in a good mood, he compliments the dinner. If he's in not so good a mood, he calls it 'slop', throws his napkin onto the plate, and refuses to eat.

He then starts to talk about something he saw on his commute that day, or something in the news. He starts to become agitated as he complains about the 'dregs' of society.

He expresses his hatred of Blacks, Hispanics, Italians and Jews, calling them 'Niggers', 'Spicks', 'Guineas' and 'Kikes'.

He hates Asians of all kinds, and considers them so low he doesn't even bother to discriminate between the Asiatic races. Whoever isn't a 'Chink' or a 'Jap' is simply a 'Gook'.

He equally hates people who are poor or homeless, calling them 'scum,' 'derelicts' and 'parasites'.

And he absolutely hates single mothers and their children, calling the women 'whores' and their children 'bastards'.

In the late 1960s, he hates hippies, of course, and has all kinds of creative names for them. I can't even remember them all. He even hates my own friends who seem like hippies to him, even though they are model students who don't do drugs. He accuses me of smoking pot when he gets a whiff of my sweet-smelling cherry bark incense. He calls me 'Buffalo Bill' when I come home one day with a $21 fringed faux-suede jacket, which I had saved for many weeks to buy.

As the 1960s draw to a close, and the 1970s brings in a new era of social reform, my father adds more people to his hate-list. Now he can also hate homosexuals and feminists (gay or not), calling them 'faggots', 'queers' and 'dykes'.

And now he also hates 'bleeding heart liberals' who are in political power in New York at the time, and who, he says, are ruining society.

But most of all, and in any decade, my father hates God.

Several times a week, he openly challenges God to strike him dead on the spot. I always find it amusing how he puts so much energy into challenging something he says he doesn't believe exists. To my adolescent thinking, it seems contradictory.

But my father does not only hate God; he also hates anyone who *believes* in God. I find myself wondering why he had ever agreed to let my mother send me to a Catholic school when I was younger. My mother always called herself a Catholic, so I start to wonder whether he hates my mother. And I wonder whether he hates me too.

Every night, my father spews his messages of hate all around the dinner table, like poison. As he speaks, the food becomes toxic and tasteless and none of us can eat any longer. Eventually, my mother simply cannot take it anymore. She explodes in a rage, and a screaming row ensues. Then, after winding everybody else up, my father inevitably leaves the room, muttering and sputtering. He retires to the basement, slamming the door behind him, to drink more of my grandfather's sickly wine, and leaving my mother upstairs to scream blindly at the walls for another half hour until everyone is completely worn out.

Around 7:15, my father resurfaces. He stumbles upstairs and falls asleep in front of the television, snoring loudly. My mother tidies up the kitchen, puts away the remnants of the evening meal, and says no more about the incident. Around 8 PM she takes her place in front of the television. She stays up until 1 AM watching *The Tonight Show Starring Johnny Carson*. She turns off the TV and goes to bed alone, leaving my father asleep on the sofa. He wakes at 5 AM and leaves for work before anyone else is out of bed.

The next night at 6:25 PM, it happens all over again.

And again the next night.

And every night to follow.

And also at Sunday afternoon dinners, especially if we have company.

Life never changes for better or worse.

But then, one day when I am about 13 years old, the stories begin...

* * * * *

My father came home that night at 6:25 PM just like all the other nights.

But on that night, after he had completed his nightly ritual of wine drinking in the basement, he took his place very calmly at the dinner table, with a very smug look on his face. At first he didn't talk at all. He tore at the meat on his plate, making growling sounds that he seemed to find very funny. He made some offhanded comment about us all being animals. He said something about life being all about survival of the fittest. This kind of talk was nothing unusual. He had spoken like this many times before.

But all this was just a warm-up for what he was going to say next.

'Well, today I feel really proud of myself,' he said, focussing his gaze on the food on his plate, 'because today I helped to cleanse society.'

I wasn't sure I wanted to enter into a dialogue with him, but my curiosity got the better of me.

'So what does that mean?' I asked, apprehensively.

Seeing I was 'hooked', my father now had a slight smile on his face.

'Yeah, you really shoulda been there. I tell you—it was a work of art,' he said, continuing to chew away at his steak, not missing a beat.

'What are you talking about?' I asked him, unwittingly playing directly into his game.

My father didn't answer right away. Instead, he seemed to change the subject.

'There's been a repairmen strike this week,' he said.

My father was an electrical engineer. Whenever there was a labour strike, all the engineers, who were 'white collar workers', had to go out into the field and do the repairs themselves until the repairmen, who were union members, returned from the strike. On those weeks, my father had to carry around a repairman's toolkit all day. These kind of strikes happened about once a year. We were used to them.

'Yeah, I know about the strike,' I said. 'So?'

He continued his tale, 'So today I had to ride the subway all day to make the repair calls.'

'Uh-huh,' I said, not knowing where this was leading.

My father kept eating.

'So anyway,' he continued as he chewed, 'after my last call on the lower east side, I was on the subway heading back uptown to Penn Station. The subway was packed and lots of people were standing. When I got in the train, I saw this stinking drunken derelict in the same car with me.'

I started to feel uneasy, but said nothing at this point.

'So, anyway, I sat there watching. Nobody noticed. I watched this disgusting scumbag from across the car. He was staggering and stumbling over other people every time the subway car swerved.

'And then...' my father paused a second to swallow his steak before continuing, '...the subway car jolted as we stopped at one of the stations, and d'ya know what happened? That creep *fell* right on top of me! Can you believe it? His whole body landed right in my lap, his face nose-to-nose with mine.

'That piece of shit was so close to me I actually could smell the stench of liquor on his breath, and the disgusting stink of his own filth. I felt like vomiting right on top of him.'

My father made a deep guttural sound as if he were vomiting. I have no spelling for it. Something like, 'Blech!'

'Scum,' he said. 'He's not even human. Just a *peoch*.'

(That's Tyrolean slang for 'flea'... I have no idea how to spell it).

My father sneered and rubbed his thumb and forefinger together, in a motion I had seen him do many times before, metaphorically indicating that he was crushing and smearing a flea between his fingers. In his family, this was a manual gesture of utter contempt for someone, indicating they were the lowest of the low.

'No,' he said, wiping his hand on the leg of his trousers, as if wiping away the human being he had just crushed between his fingers. 'He's not even a *peoch*. Not even. He's nothing. Nothing. Blech!'

My father cut his meat and shovelled a couple of bites into his mouth. I found I could no longer eat, nor even look at my father as he spoke. Whenever my father spoke like this, his face became extremely ugly and I found it difficult to look at him, as I would feel physically nauseous. But I was too nervous around him to divert my eyes altogether, so I adopted a kind of frozen stare into space directly in front of me. Out of the corner of my eye, I was continually wary of my father's cool, if not inhumanly cold, facial expressions.

My father continued his story.

'So, when he fell on me, instinctively, like an animal, I took both my hands and hurled that piece of shit off me with all my force. I threw him so hard he fell on the ground way on the other side of the car. Ha! Boy, was he stunned! He just lay their mumbling. Disgusting piece of scum.'

Of course, I found it ironic that my father told this tale while he himself was quite drunk. There was a smugness here that didn't seem to work, and I challenged him.

'So, you're saying you helped to cleanse society by pushing a drunk off you on the subway today?' I asked sarcastically.

'Oh, no, no,' he said. 'I'm just telling you the background so you can appreciate the beauty of the whole story,' he said with a slight sneering in his voice.

I didn't know what he meant by that cryptic remark, but I remained silent, as did my mother, as my father, knowing fully that we were a captive audience, continued his story.

'So, anyway, after the drunk landed on the ground, he got up and staggered a little way down the car. But I watched him very carefully, out of the corner of my eye. I wanted to know where he was planning to get off the train. After a few stops, he got up and started moving towards the door to the left of me, like he was getting ready to get off at the next station. So then, I knew it was time for me to make my move, and I also got up. And I timed it just perfectly.'

I started to feel nervous now as my father went on.

'When I saw him going towards the door, I got up and positioned myself just to the side of him, just a little bit behind his line of vision, pretending not to be paying him any attention. Then slowly, without anyone noticing me, I slid my hand inside my toolbox, nice and casually, and felt around for just the right object.

'As we pulled into the next station, I pushed my way through the crowd so I was near the door. Then, the train screeched to a halt and the doors opened. Immediately I shoved everyone else out of my way until I was standing directly in front of the drunk. But I didn't get off the train at first. Instead I just stood in the doorway, blocking the doors, without moving, trying to sense when it was almost time for the doors to shut. You know, it was really something. I timed it just right.'

I could feel my breathing getting heavier and hotter. 'What do you mean, "I timed it just right"?' I asked.

'Well now, see, that's the beauty of it. Just at the last moment, the *right* moment, I stepped off the train and onto the platform. Then, quickly, I turned back around to face the open doors, and came face to face with the drunk. And then—and here's the art—I pulled out a sledgehammer from my toolbox.

'It was so fast, it was beautiful. All it took was one smooth motion, one single tap in just the *right* place. Ha!

'And I smashed that piece of shit right across the bridge of his nose!

My father howled in a kind of sinister delight that frightened me terribly.

'It all happened in an instant. The drunk was so shocked he actually fell backwards into the train. He couldn't even say anything. He just grabbed his face, and the doors to the subway car shut in front of him. And through the window, I could see all the blood gushing from his face as the train pulled away. And let me tell you, it was really gushing. His face was covered in blood. Ha! And the beauty of it was that no one noticed me. No one knew what happened, not even the drunk. No one could have stopped it. It was so perfect.

'Like I said,' my father gloated, his voice cool and callous, 'You really should've seen it. It was a work of art.'

As I heard my father finish his story, I could see the headless body of the locust flying blindly away in my mind's eye.

I could hear years and years of arguments and racist dinner conversations echoing in my ears.

I could feel years of fear and confusion that had compelled me to remain silent whenever my father spoke.

But on this day, finally, finally, after years of my father trying to provoke a reaction in me, something finally did react within me. And I exploded.

'What are you saying? How can this be true?

'If it's true, what kind of a man are you?

'Are you telling me that my own father is capable of smashing the face of a complete stranger in cold blood?

'Is this really who my father is?

'And if it's not true, what kind of a man can make up such disgusting, elaborate lies?

'And if these are lies, what would possibly compel you to say such things to your own daughter?

'What do you want me to do with this?

'You are either some kind of deranged criminal or you are completely insane.

'I am not sure which frightens me more.

'Why are you always trying to frighten me?

'Why are you saying all this?

'Why are you doing this?

'Tell me!

'Why?

'WHY?

'Who ARE you?'

I had become absolutely enraged. I could hear the sound of my voice, almost as if disembodied from my being, screaming at the top of my lungs with a kind of fierce power I had never felt before. It was as if the shouting came from someone else, something else. I couldn't really comprehend where it was coming from, even though I knew it must be coming from me. It was like I was being controlled by a voice, an emotion, a rage that had just suddenly appeared without warning or forethought. I felt completely in control and completely out of control at the same time. After years of silence, the sound of my own screaming was even more frightening to me than my father's story.

My father did not answer. Quite coolly, as if satisfied in some way, he left the room as usual, and went down into the basement to get even drunker. Later, he came upstairs and fell asleep in front of the television, snoring loudly as always, as if nothing had happened.

I went into my bedroom and shut the door. I turned up the volume of the top-40 station on my AM radio, flopped onto my bed, and stared blankly at the ceiling, my heart still pounding and my own words still echoing in my brain, until I could no longer restrain the hot tears that wanted to gush from my eyes.

As I cried, I asked myself over and over, *Who is this man I call my father?*

And then I asked myself, *What the hell just happened to me out there? What am I turning into? Who am I becoming?*

Nobody talked about the incident afterwards. And because our family code was that whatever went on within our four walls had to remain within those four walls, nobody talked to anyone outside the house about what was going on inside, either.

This was just the first of many such stories my father would tell over the years during my adolescence. A new, even more outlandish and detailed story would appear every few months or so. Before long, my father was giving elaborate descriptions on how to murder people with your bare hands, giving graphic examples of how he had done this.

And as the stories grew in size and extremity, my displays of rage towards my father also got bigger and bigger, as I gradually took on an active role in the nightly drama that had originally been between my mother and father only. And after every performance, I would retreat to my room and slam the door.

In the beginning, I would cry for hours. I always cried when I was angry or afraid. But because everyone else in the house was just as imprisoned within their own isolated little worlds as I was, no one would bother to comfort me when I cried. They just left me alone to cry myself out. The only 'person' who would come to my room was our soft-natured calico cat, Wilma. If she saw me upset, she would sit at the side of my bed, and reach up to tap my face with her paw, making consoling little cat sounds as if to say, 'There, there.' I was always impressed with how sensitive a cat could be. As far as human beings were concerned, I just learned how to be alone with my emotions over the years.

But, over time, crying became exhausting. After being broken repeatedly, my heart eventually became so shattered I felt it could break no more. When that happened, numbness came in to replace the pain. And as the numbness grew, the crying lessened until it eventually stopped completely. Numbness seemed to be the only remedy for the complex bundle of emotions that gripped me on a daily basis. It was a way not to feel anything.

I had finally grown the same protective shell around me that my parents had grown around themselves. I had become just as numb as my father. I found it very difficult to feel my central nervous system.

And so, within my quarter-mile universe I stayed within a much smaller universe of four walls, and within those four walls was an ever-shrinking universe of isolation, in which I, still really a child, felt I was becoming ever smaller and smaller as I started to implode. Life became a lonely void where one neither spoke, nor was spoken to, neither within the house nor outside it.

I learned to live alone in my tiny bedroom, with my thoughts, my AM radio—and my pen and paper. For it was around that time that I started to write. Writing became the only way to speak.

No fewer than 200 poems and a handful of semi-finished stories streamed from me between the ages of 12 and 25. I kept them in a folder and showed them to no one except the occasional close friend. Mostly, I wrote about numbness, isolation and longing.

Then, I threw them all away in my late twenties, when the numbness had consumed me fully in my marriage. By that time, I had finally given up trying to speak.

* * * * *

'I thought I knew what I was supposed to do, but I hadn't expected this to happen,' I think. 'It seems like such an easy thing. All you have to do is fall. How difficult could it be?'

I take a few breaths as my body and mind start to feel each other again.

I am standing atop a six-foot platform in a beautiful forest near the north coast of Spain. I look out and see a vast expanse of rolling green terrain. I take a breath of this remarkable air.

'What are you holding on to?' I ask myself. And then my mind becomes more lucid.

'Think about it,' I tell myself. 'What is going to happen to you at the moment of death, when you have no choice but to let go completely? Are you going to resist like this? Look at you. Here you are clinging to this platform in sheer terror over something you can see is completely safe. Imagine if you could not let go when it was actually time to let yourself fall into the unknown. That would be the ultimate failure in life.

'Come on. This is easy,' I tell myself. 'All you have to do is let go.'

*   *   *   *   *

When I was a child, it was only when I went to play with Karen and we escaped to the land of make-believe that I ever really felt like myself. But even as childhood departed and adolescence took its place, we never really stopped pretending, although the things we chose to make up for ourselves changed. Around the age of 12 or 13, we no longer made believe we were talking parrots or ghosts; instead we started making believe we had boyfriends. We pretended that boys we knew, or movie stars, or pop musicians, were madly in love with us.

But apart from Karen, I had become quite isolated amongst my peers over the years. Isolation was something I had gotten very good at, both at home and at school. Although I had played violin since the age of 9, most of my classmates didn't know about it, as I feared their ridicule, as playing violin was something 'squares' did. I was always at the top of my class, and I knew several of the more aggressive students in my class didn't appreciate that either. I used to hate being so 'smart', and throughout my childhood I felt like my intelligence was something of a curse. I went to great measures not to stand out in any way, so as not to be bullied. I tried to be quiet, and for a long time I never smiled or made eye contact at school. I tried like crazy to avoid praise or recognition from the teachers. But this didn't do me much good, because the teachers would always choose me, the 'responsible kid', to do this or that task for them, and I stood out anyway. Because the teachers seemed to regard me as their pet, there were always a few clever bullies who were determined to 'get' me in the schoolyard, no matter what. And throughout my younger years, I was truly an easy target, and the bullies knew they could reduce me to tears without much effort on their part.

But as I got older, and my numbness increased, these bullies found they could not provoke me so easily. By the age of 13 I discovered that, instead of being a curse, my brain came in quite handy, as I developed the ability to be quite witty in public, and to make others laugh. This new skill felt good, and I used it to my advantage as an effective way of deflecting the class bullies. I remember the first time I tried out my wit on one girl bully, and her 'assistant' bully started to laugh, causing the 'boss' bully to back down and walk away in embarrassment. After she left, the assistant bully and the other kids asked me to say more funny stuff. I did, and they laughed even more. And so, I started to adopt a new role—the role of the 'entertainer'. Very soon, kids that previously had avoided me actually wanted to be around me. I told myself it was simply because they thought I was amusing. I started getting invited to parties, and I became part of the 'in' crowd, of which I had never been part before.

But even though this persona seemed to serve me, inside I was very nervous about my new role as the entertainer. What if

I wasn't so funny one day? What if my mind went blank and I couldn't think of anything entertaining to say? What if I had a sad day? Would the 'in crowd' reject me? Would I still get invited to parties? What if they found out who I really was?

So, to ensure my ticket to these social circles, I thought it best to give myself some added value. I started to buy the latest records, and brought them along whenever there was a social event. When I was 14, I had the biggest and best record collection in our class. This made me even more popular. No one would think of having a party without inviting me. And everyone wanted to come to the parties I gave, too.

But as I became more popular, I also became increasingly unsettled and inwardly fearful that it would all simply fall apart, and I would be 'exposed' as a fraud. As far as anyone could tell, I had effectively become my role. Pretending had now become a permanent part of my life. No one, not even I, knew who I really was.

Then, one night, when I was 14, I had a dream...

*   *   *   *   *

I was standing in the living room of a male friend of mine— no one I knew in waking life. We were getting ready to go to a party. I looked at myself in the mirror to admire the lovely moss-green shift I had designed and sewn myself. I smiled at the sight of this sleeveless mini-dress, with its soft-woven fabric and empire-cut bodice, thinking it looked quite 'mod' and was very much in line with current styles for 1969. Around my neck I wore a long strand of bright yellow love beads, made of various sizes of crystal-cut plastic baubles that reflected the light. I wore bright yellow fishnet stockings to compliment the ensemble, and a little pair of yellow princess-heeled pumps. I was really pleased with how I looked and couldn't wait to go to the party.

I turned to my right and saw my friend sitting there on his flowered sofa. I asked him when we were going to leave for the party. Instead of answering me, he suddenly leapt off the sofa and started to tear the seat cushions off it.

'What the heck are you doing?' I queried.

'This is how we *get* to the party,' he said, pointing to a small round hole beneath where the cushions had been sitting.

I came over to the sofa and looked inside. To my amazement, I saw a tiny entrance to a passageway...like a vertical tunnel to the floor below. Without a word, my friend proceeded to crawl headfirst down the tunnel until I saw his feet disappear behind him. This made me think of Alice going down the rabbit hole, and then I noticed I could hear the haunting strains of the song *White Rabbit* by Jefferson Airplane being played somewhere in the distance.

As my friend disappeared into the sofa, he gripped the sides of the tunnel and swung himself around like a gymnast, landing upright on a concrete floor below. Perplexed, I looked down the shaft to see him standing on a circular platform about ten feet below me.

'Come on,' he said, looking up through the hole in the sofa at me. 'We're going to be late if you don't get going.'

Curioser and curioser, I thought, remembering Alice and the March Hare.

I decided the best way to get down the tunnel would be feet first, so I could jump down onto the platform upright. So I lowered myself through the sofa and slid downwards until I was brave enough to let go and jump the short distance to the landing. My friend and I could hear music being played in the next room. We opened the big, wooden door that led from the landing to the party and looked in to see a finished basement full of young teenagers dancing freely to *Incense and Peppermints* by Strawberry Alarm Clock. The room was filled with ambient lighting in different colours and everyone was dressed the part. It looked like a great party.

But, all at once, the music stopped abruptly and everyone in the room halted to look at us standing there. After a short hush in the crowd, they started to cry out, refusing us admission to the party. 'How dare you show up to the party dressed like that?' they challenged. 'Bright green and yellow? Are you kidding? Go away!'

I stood on the platform bewildered by their reaction, but the scene immediately faded and I was now outdoors, across the street from my parents' home. It was a late afternoon in November. I was with exactly the same group of people who were at the party, but this time everyone was dressed in street clothes, instead of party frocks. Suddenly, a girl named Genevieve, who was the most popular girl in the clique, stood up and announced they were going to have a bicycle race. She got up on her bicycle and took off down the street. All of the others followed suit, grabbing their bicycles and pedalling rapidly after her. I looked around and found a bicycle. I got on, but found that the pedals, for some reason, would not move. I fought with the bicycle for some time, in frustration.

Now the cyclists were passing me, as they were on their second lap around the block.

'Wait! Please!' I cried out in desperation. 'I can't get my bicycle going...'

*   *   *   *   *

Feeling oddly shaken, I am standing still at the edge of the scaffold for a moment to compose myself. I feel my heart as it is starting to return to normal after racing very quickly.

Slowly, I am becoming aware of my body again. Yup, fingers... toes...lungs. Right. Ok, I'm back now.

I'm wiggling my fingers. Actually, I'm amazed I can move my left hand at all. Only yesterday, my hand was sore and swollen from a bee sting. It healed pretty fast.

Hmm....Now that was a pretty bizarre event. There I was just standing around minding my own business and a tiny yellow bee just flies into my brown suede glove, stings me and then flies away. No provocation whatsoever. He just came and stung me. Wonder what that was all about?

It's so funny. I'd never been stung by a bee before. How weird that it should happen with no provocation. Even more amazing is that the pain and swelling are completely gone today. It's almost as if the bee had been trying to get my attention—to tell me that something important was about to happen.

Something important...

I feel the kiss of the warm Mediterranean breezes against my face and remember the big fat bumblebee that brushed against that same cheek on my Communion Day back when I was 8 years old.

I can't help but smile...

*   *   *   *   *

Sitting on my bicycle, I became more and more frustrated, as I tried like crazy to move the pedals, but my foot kept slipping off again and again. The cyclists were gaining speed and they were now on their third, and then fourth lap around me. They continued to whiz by me like a blur, and I started to panic, feeling I was now hopelessly behind.

In a state of utter desperation, I jumped on the pedal with the entire weight of my body. Then—something finally changed.

Suddenly, I could feel my bicycle rivet into action. But something wasn't quite right, and I realised I was no longer seated on a bicycle—it had turned into a motorcycle.

The motorcycle lurched forward and started to zoom down the street beyond my control. I had to hold on for dear life as I passed the other cyclists at breakneck speed. I started to shout, and had no idea of what I was supposed to do now. I was just 14—I had no idea how to manage a motorcycle!

Suddenly, I saw something that made me fear for my life. Directly in front of me, at the junction of two streets, was a huge tree that stood perhaps 300 feet in height. In reality no such tree existed in my neighbourhood, but it looked completely normal in my dream, as it sat on the edge of one of my neighbours' lawns. The motorcycle continued to gain in velocity and was aiming directly for this gigantic tree. Any moment now, I knew it was going to crash right into it.

'No! I can't look!' I cried.

But then, just as I got to the tree, something completely unexpected happened. I didn't crash at all, but rather, the motorcycle turned nose upwards and started to rise vertically, right up the side of the trunk of the tree. This, of course, was completely illogical and I didn't know what to make of it. But now my view was directly upwards, and I could see this massive tree, and could feel myself going up... up... up... into the sky.

After a few moments, the motorcycle slipped away and flew off almost unnoticeably into space, but I continued to rise up this tree, becoming increasingly fearful of what was to happen next. My breathing became more laboured as I moved more and more slowly towards the top of the tree. The higher I rose, the more I could feel the pull of gravity slowing me down, and a gripping fear took hold of my heart, my mind and my breath.

With terror, I realised that very soon would come a moment, an instant perhaps, where I would be neither flying nor falling, but standing still in the air, at the exact point where velocity and gravity converged with equal force. And I dreaded that singular fraction of a second before my almost assuredly fatal fall back to earth would begin.

And then, that moment came. I reached the top of the tree, and I felt myself suspended in air, neither rising nor falling, for a singular, pregnant moment in time. I surveyed the landscape within that moment. All I could see around me was the leafy treetop, but I was aware that I was at least 300 feet off the ground. Knowing that this meant I was about 30 storeys up, I found myself standing in mid-air and thinking—

This is it. The fall will definitely kill me!

* * * * *

Ok.

My breathing is soft now. I have returned to myself and the fear is starting to melt away.

My eyes also become soft in focus as they gaze out across the green terrain to see a line of tree-covered mountains on the Spanish horizon. My vision becomes dreamlike and the distant peaks take on hues of soft violets and mauves as the sunlight catches them at different angles. They look like a painting of pastel chalks. How very beautiful it all is! How amazing that I am standing here, right now!

I remember the bumblebee.

My soul now whispers to both my body and my mind— 'Just let go.'

My body sighs like a young girl who has finally been kissed by the one she has loved for so long.

My mind remembers what I am supposed to do and again it calls out the request to the team.

'Lynn fall?'

'Fall, Lynn!'

And this time, I fall.

* * * * *

Standing motionless just above the top of the tree, I was prepared to meet my doom. The only way down from here was to fall.

But then, a most unexpected thing happened.

Instinctively, I reached out my right hand and grabbed a delicate branch of the tree, near the top of its canopy. To my complete surprise, the branch bent like a bow and gently swooped me down about ten or fifteen feet. I had butterflies in my stomach from this buoyant motion, the way you do when you are falling on a rollercoaster. I was amazed to find I wasn't plummeting to my death.

When the branch had bent as far as it would go, I reached my left hand out for another, and it also bent flexibly to carry me another bit of the way down the tree. I did this over and over again, hand over hand, and the falling sensation turned to a kind of euphoria as I felt myself floating effortlessly, supported by this tree all the way down. Then, to my utter amazement, I eventually landed ever so softly in a large wheat field, with no injuries whatsoever.

I looked around me and could no longer see my Long Island hometown. I was in the middle of farmland and the tree, now looking much smaller, was perhaps 50 feet behind me at the end of the field. Everything was peaceful and welcoming.

A short distance away, I could make out two figures coming towards me. As they got closer, I saw that it was an old farmer accompanied by a young boy, presumably his grandson.

The farmer spoke to me. 'Are you all right?' he asked. 'We saw you falling from over there.'

'Yes,' I said. 'I'm fine. Well, actually, I'm in a bit of shock. I mean... when I stopped flying and got to the top of the tree, I was positive I was going to die...' I stopped for a moment to gather my thoughts.

'But actually,' I said, 'what's so weird is that it was the going up that was the hard part. Coming down was really simple.'

'Yes,' the farmer said quite matter-of-factly, as he helped me up, and motioned to come along to his home. 'A lot of people fall over that tree.'

I woke from the dream, knowing that the voice of my own wisdom had been speaking to me. I knew it was trying to tell me this shell I had built around myself would only get worse the more I tried to build it up. I knew it was telling me there was no danger in letting down my defences, and that my holding on was due only to my fear of falling into an unknown. I knew it was telling me to let go and become myself.

I knew exactly what I had to do.

But unfortunately, at that tender age, I didn't have the courage to listen to the voice of my own wisdom.

*　*　*　*　*

I fall.

And within the sweet surrender of that fall is a magical abyss of not knowing and not needing to know, and I am suddenly overcome with the chill of an all-embracing ecstasy that sends shivers up my spine.

'I am not falling,' I hear myself say. 'I am flying.'

And then—

I am caught.

* * * * *

My father.

He was the ultimate paradox, this man who was my father.

He claimed to hate God-believers of all kinds, yet he drove me to and from church every Sunday. And when he picked me up, he always had a thermos full of hot soup and a bagful of grilled-cheese sandwiches wrapped up in aluminium foil and tea towels to keep them warm for me.

My father chauffeured me everywhere when I was young. He drove me hundreds and hundreds of miles every week to make sure I got to my violin lessons, orchestra concerts and rehearsals, or just to my friend's houses for socialising. On those journeys, he and I would talk for hours. Once away from home, he would frequently confide his thoughts, his feelings and his troubles to me, especially as I got older.

My father was a highly respected design engineer, and he invented all kinds of telecommunications gadgets. When I was eleven, he let me help him in his experiments as he was developing the first telephone device for the deaf and deaf/blind in 1966. A photographer even took a picture of me working alongside him at his workbench. The telephone company put a photo of him holding the new device in a full-page advert in *The New York Times*. My father always seemed very proud of this achievement. I still believe it was not only because it was a technological success, but also because it had opened up communication to people who were otherwise cut off from the rest of the world, in that era before the dawn of the Internet. People even wrote to him from other countries, thanking him for making his marvellous invention.

On weekends, my father meticulously tended to our garden, which was the pride of the neighbourhood year-round. My mother took great pleasure in telling people it had been carefully designed so that something was in bloom from February through October. My father gave much care to the red and pink geraniums that filled the flowerboxes beneath the front windows. He trimmed the long privet hedges that lined either side of the property. He cared for the gorgeous red maple tree that went from being a twig to a massive shade tree through his care. He transplanted our white-blossomed dogwood tree several times over the years, upon my mother's request. He trimmed back the yew bushes so they did not obscure the other plants and he kept the driveway lined with a perfectly maintained strip of purple-blue periwinkles. In the summer, he painted the wrought iron banister that ran up the steps to the front door with a thick black gloss. Every few years, he would repaint the house, and put a new coat of clean white enamel on the faux-shutters that framed the front windows.

And I always felt he did these things solely for my mother, regardless of how distant their relationship had become over the years. My father may well have fought with my mother on a nightly basis, but he never missed a single birthday, anniversary, or holiday. Every Christmas he brought home a bottle of expensive French perfume or jewellery for my mother. Every Valentine's Day, he came home with a huge box of chocolates in a red, heart-shaped box, and an armful of red roses for her. And so that his daughters were not forgotten, he would also bring two smaller heart-shaped boxes for my sister and me. In some strange way, he was very romantic, even though he and my mother had no apparent physical relationship whatsoever.

And my mother was not the only woman my father cared for. He was like a second son to his mother's sister, who never really learned how to speak English, and was widowed and childless after her own son had died. Every week he took her shopping, and kept her company. When she became paralysed on the right side of her body from a stroke, he used his engineering skills to invent all kinds of little devices for her to use around the house that were left-handed and required only one hand to operate.

And, indeed, by all accounts my father was also a generous man who gave his money away to many people, for no apparent reason. I have seen him give thousands and thousands of dollars away to others, and not just to family. Perhaps most paradoxically, in spite of all the stories he told me about 'derelicts' or 'scum' that he had killed or injured, with my own eyes I have seen my father give money to drunken beggars in the streets of New York City. Nearly every time we drove along the very rundown area of Canal Street on the way to the Holland Tunnel, he would see homeless drunks along the street and call one of them over to the car window to give him a dollar bill. And whenever he did, he would say with sarcasm, 'Yeah, that's me after I retire.'

None of this was consistent with the image he projected of himself, and I grew up very confused about my father. Living in the same house with him was a continual battle between the image he forced upon me and the image I saw, and wished to hold in my heart.

The truth is I loved my father. I could see through all the horrible things he said and did and could see the decent, loving person behind them. But living under the same roof with him kept me locked within a tense and bewildering environment where everyone was constantly screaming, but no one was really talking. Because of this, no amount of love was going to be able to prevent me from getting as far away as possible from my childhood home as soon as I was old enough to leave.

* * * * *

'Fly away!' Karen had said. 'I want to fly away on those swings.'

I flew away, or at least I tried, somehow believing that the mere act of leaving Long Island would bring me to another world, another life, to escape the one in which I had been living.

I wanted to live beyond the quarter-mile universe. So, I attempted to enlarge my world through travel, study and experiencing everything I possibly could—the stranger, the more unusual, the more outlandish, the better. I left home at 18 and floated around somewhat aimlessly for many years. To get away from my parents, I married for a year or so and divorced almost as quickly. Thereafter, I became something of a collector of esoteric experiences, travelling to foreign lands, learning lots of exotic languages, voraciously studying every religion, folk tradition and philosophy I could find, engaging in many risky love affairs with men of different ages and from cultures far removed from my own, and learning how to play music from all over the world. I wanted to taste everything I could.

Finally, at age 25 when I was a graduate student in Texas, I was given a grant to go to Calcutta to study music for a semester, thinking I might find some vital link in my path towards enlightenment there. *Surely this will finally make my world big enough,* I believed.

But while all of that was fascinating, none of it made me happy. Yes, the world was now bigger, but I only felt smaller in comparison. After I returned to the US, I found my stay in India had radically impacted my worldview. Coming home to colour television and wall-to-wall carpet seemed surreal and decadent in comparison to the sights of poverty and disease I had seen in the streets of Calcutta. I now found myself nearing the long-awaited end of my Master's degree in world music, living alone with no partner, no real career direction, no life purpose and absolutely no passion for anything I was doing anymore. I wanted to find my true love. I wanted to find my life's path. I wanted to find Truth.

One afternoon, totally disillusioned, I stormed into my graduate advisor's office and had a long debate with him on the pointlessness of absolutely everything. I told him I saw no ultimate usefulness in what I was studying. I told him we were never going to stop wars or end world poverty or feed the starving by sitting in an ivory tower studying about other cultures.

I remember asking him, 'How can you justify what we are doing here, when the very people we are studying in our air-conditioned lecture halls are starving in the streets?'

He said, 'I do what I do because I enjoy it. I feel no need for further justification.'

Bluntly, I told him, 'Well, I am happy that your conscience is clear. But enjoyment is no longer enough of a reason for me to stay on this path.'

I left his office, knowing I had just set the stage for another change of scene in my life.

I was just about ready to throw in the towel on my life altogether and join the Peace Corps. I sat at home that evening browsing through their pamphlet, which I had picked up from a recruiter outside the main concourse at the university. I started to imagine what it would be like to toss all of this away and just live in South America or Africa for a few years, digging fresh water wells...

And then the phone rang.

At the other end of the line was the man who, unbeknownst to me, was to become my husband. He had just moved to Texas from California and was looking for someone with whom he could play Indian music. A friend of a friend had given him my number. We met a few days later, and I felt as though I recognised him from another lifetime. I soon fell in love with this very good-looking 27-year-old man. Here was someone with whom I could finally share my musical interests and create new music together. Here was someone with whom I could talk intellectually about all the esoteric things I enjoyed. He was also a vegetarian. I had been dabbling with vegetarianism for years, but my courage to declare it openly faltered whenever I came head to head with my parents. Now I finally had an ally in my desire to stop eating meat completely. But the real showstopper was that this man was a practicing initiate of a bona fide Indian religion, a religion that taught *bhakti yoga*, devotion to God, and a religion with which I had no familiarity at all. This meant

I now had a whole range of new and exciting things to study. Life was suddenly all new and shiny. It seemed as though all my wishes had come true. Suddenly, I had found a life partner, a new burst of enthusiasm, a new life path, and a new path to Truth, all rolled into one.

As a couple, who were both musical partners and marriage partners, I always felt my husband and I projected a public image of being a passionate and colourful duo who had a kind of special charisma that followed us everywhere we went. People commonly said they thought we were 'made for each other'. We often said that we believed we were 'soul mates'. And together we created a kind of romantic mythology around our relationship that made us look, possibly, more magic than we actually were.

But as attractive as the image of our newfound love was, day by day, in the heat of its passion, I found myself getting burnt. Because in those early days, I was not simply being courted by my husband; I was also being wooed by a new religion and a new musical lifestyle. And all of these three suitors quite rapturously swept me off my feet—and swept me away—with equal force, like a scorching summer wildfire.

In that hot and steamy summer of 1981, within a few months of our meeting, my husband agreed to go back to India with me, so we could study music in Calcutta together. One evening around sunset, about a month after we arrived, we were walking along a street in Calcutta in a very light rain. My husband stopped suddenly and said, 'Can you hear that?'

I tried to hear what he was hearing, but didn't at first.

'No listen,' he said. 'It's temple drums. Let's go find them'

We followed the sound of the drums and eventually came upon a tiny little Hindu temple, with maybe a dozen men and women chanting hymns. They invited us to come in and chant with them, which we did. Oddly, one of them handed my husband a drum to play, which was a very strange thing to have done, because my husband was a westerner, but he actually did know how to play this drum a bit. The people were extremely impressed that he could play and they became very friendly towards us. One of the young boys was a very good drummer, so my husband asked whether he could come back and study with him. The boy said we should come back the next day, because his own teacher would be there, and he could teach my husband himself. This was extremely exciting, and we went home that night feeling really happy.

The next day, around noon, my husband went back to the Hindu temple for his drum lesson. But this time, the sun was blazing brightly and there was a lot of traffic. He went back to the exact spot where the Hindu temple had stood the night before, but to his bewilderment, it simply wasn't there. Scratching his head, he walked up and down the street, over and over, trying to find the temple. It was as if it had simply vanished.

Then suddenly he looked down the street and saw a monk, perhaps in his mid-forties, walking towards him. The monk was dressed in the orange robes of a worshipper of Vishnu.

My husband stopped the monk and asked, 'Do you know where the temple is around here?'

The monk said, 'Yes, I will take you to the temple. I just have to do some shopping first. Follow me.'

My husband followed this monk through New Market, as he bought bags of fruits and vegetables and flowers. As he shopped, the two of them chatted about many things, and made friends with each other. Although he was enjoying this monk's company, my husband could not help but look at his watch, slightly worried that he was going to be late for his drum lesson. Sensitive to my husband's concerns, the monk said he was finished shopping and was heading back to the temple. Together, they went down winding streets here and there until they came to a street that was off the beaten path. The sound of traffic was not nearly as loud on this street. My husband quickly realised he was not on the same street as the Hindu temple had been. Then, he saw a cluster of spires in the distance that designated a temple of Vishnu. He was astounded.

'Wait a minute,' my husband said. 'This is not the temple I was trying to find.'

'No,' said the monk. 'But this is where you want to go.'

It was that afternoon that my husband met my Gurudeva for the first time. It was a rare privilege, as Gurudeva spent most of his time travelling, and there were no other westerners who came to this temple in those days. They spoke for some time, and my husband promised to return the next day, and this time he would bring me with him. Remarkably, later that day on his way home, he actually found the Hindu temple he had originally tried to find, at the exact spot on the main street where he had been looking earlier. When he entered the tiny temple, he found the boy's teacher sitting there waiting patiently for him to arrive, and my husband took his first drum lesson, with many more to follow.

Why had the little Hindu temple not been visible to my husband's eyes earlier that day? Some have said that my husband's vision had been clouded by divine forces, because we were destined to meet my Gurudeva that day. Regardless of whether you accept this cosmic explanation or not, the incidents described within the story itself are all factual.

I tell this story here not just because it is charming, but also because it became a kind of folkloric tale over the years, told again and again to everyone who met us. And as the story became a kind of legend, so did our relationship. For more than 20 years, this story firmly established a mystical connection between our marriage and our relationship with the Vishnu temple, and provided a kind of legendary validation of the marriage itself. And when your marriage becomes the stuff that legends are made of, it becomes extremely hard for people to see it as it really is, even if there are problems within it.

This legend became the defining link between our marriage and the temple. But it was not the only one. The very fact that I had met my husband and my Gurudeva within a few short months of each other meshed my marriage and my new religion together in my mind somehow. Sometimes, if not most of the time, I found it difficult to draw the line between my religion and my marriage. They seemed to be one and the same, and I soon found myself dissolving into both of them without distinction.

But in my mind, there was also a very blurry line between music and my marriage as well. Within a very short period of time after meeting my husband, I no longer played music independently, but rather, exclusively with him. And while over the years we unquestionably made some wonderful music together, both literally and figuratively, the truth is I found it difficult to determine the boundaries between music and our marriage, and these two also fused together in my mind.

So basically, our marriage seemed to have melted into two very odd and very different kinds of soup called 'religion-marriage' and 'music-marriage', but 'marriage' as an independent concept seemed not to exist. And as confusing as that was for me, the really frustrating thing was that I felt these two soups never seemed to be able to coexist peacefully together in practice. Our marriage was a continual pendulum swing from one extreme to the other, where we would fluctuate between what I call our 'religious periods', and our 'musician periods'. These periods could last anywhere from a few days to years at a time. The two seemed incompatible, and whenever one took over, it would almost completely eclipse the other.

Whenever we were going through one of our 'religious periods', we would live an austere and 'saintly' life. We would refrain from any kind of intoxicants, even coffee. We would study Sanskrit scriptures, do morning rituals, chant mantras, go on holy pilgrimages, and dance barefoot through the jungles of India. It all seemed quite idyllic, but it was completely detached from any other aspect of life. And while there were many genuinely magical and beautiful moments during those times, overall life felt difficult, restrictive and false for me. There were a plethora of rigid rules and regulations around everything from food preparation to personal hygiene to sex. After the gloss of the new religion wore off for me, I found I couldn't breathe with all these regulations, and I couldn't make sense of why I was actually doing most of it.

In sharp contrast, we would go for long periods, sometimes years, when we would live within a completely bohemian lifestyle as musicians, and have very little to do with religion whatsoever. During these times, we would play gigs anywhere from dumpy Italian restaurants in Texas to large outdoor festivals in front of thousands of people, playing everything from belly dance music to techno-pop to electronic trance. Some of our most extreme performance venues included erotic art galleries, nude poet readings, and wildly hedonistic underground raves in Arizona. In addition to musicians, our close friends and associates included dozens from the gay community, many avant garde artists, DJs of every make and model, a wide selection of ravers, a few prostitutes (who preferred to be called 'escorts'), more belly dancers and 'modern' dancers than I can even remember, a pair of identical twin nude models, lots of dope users, the odd drug dealer here and there, a smattering of schizophrenics, a sprinkling of psychics, and a generally wide array of colourful, arty people and other lost souls who were drifting through life, just like we were. And along with this kind of society came the somewhat mandatory participation in recreational drug use. While not technically 'addicted' to any of this, over time, it became less recreational and more habitual, and we soon found ourselves imbibing virtually anything you could smoke, snort or swallow nearly every evening. Suffice it to say that hallucinogens were certainly highly influential in the making of our best-selling recordings. And while those times could often be exciting, creative and adventurous, for the most part, life felt dark, scary and directionless.

This somewhat schizoid polarity between hedonism and spirituality that characterised our marriage had me swinging between extremes for more than two decades. After spending a period of time on one path or the other, we would invariably find that it took us nowhere. Then, we would simply swing back the other way, and so on, over and over. And all through this swinging, neither of these two sides could be allowed to know each other. I struggled to keep these two worlds separate from each other, so that my 'spiritual' friends would not lose respect for me, and my arty friends would not think I was in some sort of brainwashed cult. My whole identity got pretty confusing, and I wasn't really sure which of these two personae was 'me'— or if indeed either of them was. The fact that people knew me by two completely different names within each of these respective worlds only made my identity crisis that much more acute.

But even amidst the constant pendulum swing of my life, there was one thing that never changed—the shadow of isolation I had carried with me since childhood. For in spite of being around people all the time, no one in the world really knew me. All I ever showed to anyone was a façade of who I thought they wanted me to be, in whatever context I was at the time. Life felt very much as it did in the dream with the motorcycle. I was spending all my time and energy trying to keep up appearances. But these appearances were not in any way connected to what was going on in my real life. Reality was something I showed to no one. I had become a master of disguise, and not a soul knew who was behind the mask.

Meanwhile, behind closed doors, my life was spinning madly out of control.

* * * * *

I lay alone and delirious on the floor of my San Antonio apartment one evening when I was 29 years old.

A few minutes earlier, my husband had flown into a blind rage. I understood and recognised the state he was in. I myself had been gripped by very similar types of rages with my father—that numb feeling of disembodiment; the screams that you know are coming from your mouth, but feel as though they are coming from somewhere else. Yes, this was all too familiar. But this time, the rage took on a life of its own and escalated into an extremity of physical violence I had never before experienced.

After some hand-to-hand struggling, I landed on the floor. My husband, leaning over me, pinned me down and impulsively grabbed the closest object to him—a rubber-soled shoe, my own shoe, in fact. He started swatting me with the shoe, over and over and over, rhythmically, like a machine.

Unable to get away, I covered my head with my arms to protect my face. I was wearing only a thin cotton dress, and it offered me little protection against the relentless slap of the rubber. As he beat me, my husband shouted out with every blow. I remember well the sound of his voice, as it was so full of hatred. He seemed unable to stop swatting, as if possessed, and I was quite stunned at the amount of times I felt that shoe land against my flesh.

In my soul, I knew it was not I he was hitting, but something within himself. But in that moment, my soul was something I could not access.

In my heart, I longed to be picked up and held by the man whom I truly believed loved me. But in that moment, my heart could only feel what seemed like hatred coming from him.

In my body, I felt myself becoming weaker and weaker, and I began to yield to his blows instead of fighting them. For in that moment, I could find within me no more strength to fight.

Eventually my body went completely limp, and I noticed I no longer felt anything at all.

My husband finally tossed the shoe across the room with a shout of exasperation. He walked out of the apartment, slamming the door behind him. He didn't return for several hours—I think. I'm not really sure.

Unable to stand up, I felt myself growing faint, and I crawled to a corner of the bedroom, grateful that our 9-month-old daughter in the next room had somehow stayed asleep through all of this.

Over and over, I asked myself, *Who is this man I call my husband?*

When I got to the corner of the room, I could remain conscious no longer. All I can remember of that moment is the feeling of blacking out right there on the floor. I remember nothing more about that night. I felt nothing until I awoke the next morning when I discovered, to my shock and horror, that my entire body was covered with shoe-shaped bruises—

my back...
  my torso...
    my arms...
      my calves...
       my thighs...
       my hips...

But I didn't call for help.

I didn't even tell anyone it had happened.

Instead, I covered the bulging, black welts of my arms and torso with a long-sleeved sweater, and my equally battered legs and hips with a full-length skirt. I can still see the outfit in my mind, and remember how hot I was when I went out to work the next day. I remember how some of my bruises—especially one on my ribcage and another on my left calf—were so severe I could not help but wince loudly if anything even so much as brushed against them. I remember how difficult it was to move about the next day, and how I tried to pretend as if everything was just fine, even though the slightest bodily movement was so painful it would nearly reduce me to tears. I remember meeting my husband's mother that day, and thinking I had to protect him—that I couldn't allow her to find out what her son had done.

This was not by any means the first incident of abuse I had experienced with my husband. But this was the first time I had been beaten so badly I had to find a way to hide it. And once it had gotten to this level of violence, it set a precedent that would continue for more than two decades behind closed doors. It wasn't always hitting. Far more frequently I was thrown headfirst into walls or hurled over furniture, landing in such a way that I could actually hear my neck crunch. I remember crying to myself many evenings at bedtime because my head had so many bumps on it I couldn't lie down and go to sleep. I remember being strangled in front of our daughter on at least three occasions, utterly convinced I was going to die right there in front of her as I could actually feel my eyes starting to bulge out of their sockets.

But my upbringing had made me an expert in hiding. And covering my bruises, whether physical or emotional, was not so different from what I had done when I was growing up. I covered up my bruises and hid my situation from all of my friends, associates and family, including my parents.

But far more dangerously, I eventually mastered the art of covering it up to myself, until even I did not know what was really going on.

*   *   *   *   *

'So tell me what brought you to come see me today?'

'Well, I have these recurring neck problems. I've had them for years, probably since I was 40 or so. I guess they're related to the fact I used to play violin, maybe? I find that strange though, because I haven't played in more than 20 years.'

'So what happens when you get these neck problems?'

'I get these acute attacks of vertigo. When they're really bad, they get so strong I actually fall over and feel nauseous. It's like the whole world starts spinning around. Sometimes, I find myself toppling over into walls. I can't drive or anything when that happens. Back in the US, I used to go to a chiropractor for this, and he could usually get rid of the symptoms after three or four treatments. But it never goes away for good. The problems just come back after a few months. But now they're starting to worry me. It's worse now.'

'What's worse about them?'

'Well, it may sound odd, but I've been getting this really weird crunching inside my head. I actually hear scraping noises inside my scalp. And then, when the crunching is really loud, my whole head gets tight and it's as if my brain were fluttering. Then I start to hear this really loud,

low-pitched vibration running through my skull. I get migraines from it too. It's really painful, but more than that, it's sort of scary. I've tried everything—yoga, muscle relaxants, acupuncture, massage, but nothing makes it go away for good.'

'Ok,' she says. 'Let me examine you.'

The osteopath, who is also a physiotherapist, spends some time examining my spine, neck and scalp. Then, she looks at me with a somewhat serious face.

Somewhat tentatively, she says something I would never have expected.

'I need to ask you something. But it isn't an easy question to ask,' she says.

'What is it?' I ask.

More directly, she asks, 'Has anyone ever shaken you?'

I am startled by her question, and I feel myself resisting.

'What do you mean?' I ask quietly.

My osteopath repeats the question, this time with far greater emphasis. 'What I mean is, has anyone ever grabbed you by both shoulders and then just shaken you, violently and repeatedly? And not just once, but many times in your life? Like this—' and she moves her fists as if she were shaking someone furiously by the shoulders, to show me in no uncertain terms what she means.

Now I am shocked by her question. I hold my breath, and my resistance puts up a powerful battle. 'Don't tell her,' I hear in my head. 'Tell her "no". Tell her that nothing like that has ever happened to you.'

But I don't say that. I need to know what she seems to know.

'Why are you asking this?' I ask her.

'Because,' she says with some sternness, 'your neck shows evidence of you having sustained multiple whiplash injuries. And I mean multiple. This is not from playing violin. And it can't be from a car accident. I mean, you'd have to have been in one car accident after another, after another—hundreds of car accidents—for this kind of damage to occur. What you have can only have happened from someone repeatedly shaking you multiple times over the years.'

'Oh,' I say quietly, looking down at the floor.

'Oh my God,' I say a moment later, looking into my heart.

'You'd better tell her,' my inner voices say. 'There's no way you're going to cover this one up.'

I tell her my history. I tell her how my head had been thrown into walls. I tell her how I had been hurled over furniture, to land on my head. Yes, multiple times. Two or three times a week for more than two decades. How many times is that? Oh my God. I don't think I can really digest all this. Even by a modest estimate, it has been not dozens, not hundreds, but thousands of times.

'I cannot believe that during all those years I had no idea I was being injured,' I say to her. 'I mean, I knew I was hurt and in pain, but injured? That never even occurred to me. I can't believe this. How can this be?'

'You seem to have a kind of body dysmorphia. I can tell from the way you move. You don't seem to be very aware of being in your body or how you are moving in it. You seem sort of detached from it, in fact.'

'Am I?' I think about this. Something in her explanation makes sense to me.

'What can I do to fix this?' I ask, swallowing my tears.

'You need to build your body awareness. For one thing, you could benefit from having a really intense physical experience. One that reconnects your brain to your body.'

'How do I do that?' I ask.

But she leaves me to figure out the answer to that question.

I go home and cry.

A week later, I go to Spain and let myself fall backwards.

When I return to the osteopath two weeks later, she is amazed at how differently I am carrying myself. She is pleased and acknowledges that I seem much more connected, and says my neck is vastly improved.

Writing this more than one year later, my neck problems have still not returned.

*　*　*　*　*

That morning was the first day I chose to put on my long sleeves and long skirt and to shut the door to the outside world about my abuse. And as I shut out the outside world, my own universe became ever smaller and smaller, in spite of the fact that I had made so much effort to enlarge it.

But the more I covered up the bruises on my skin, the more the bruises went inwards towards my core.

I started to develop illnesses that no doctor could explain or treat. Fibromyalgia, nightmares, panic attacks, arrhythmia, heart palpitations, chest pains and chronic stomach problems were making my life a living hell. The fibromyalgia was the most invasive in my life, being both untreatable and excruciatingly painful. It would prevent me from being able to straighten up from bed in the morning, and I could not lift my right arm without buckling over in pain. Over time, it progressed until I was unable to climb a staircase without crawling on all fours. This went on for a decade, without respite. The rheumatologist told me there was no treatment and that I would just have to 'get used to it.' The heart problems were just as frustrating. The flow of blood to my heart was so erratic that it felt like a garden hose that had been stepped on, causing extreme and chronic pain in my chest and head for several years. I was given a cocktail of beta blockers and other heart medicines that didn't work. My stomach was in constant pain, ultimately ending (as already described) in pancreatitis and gall bladder surgery. Essentially, I felt as though my whole body had gone haywire. By age 45, I felt like I was going on 80, and that I had been given a life sentence to pain, both inside and out.

But mentally, I never truly drew any connection between my emotional world and my physical ailments. Bewildered, over and over I asked myself, *Who is this person I have become?*

* * * * *

When we fall into the dreamless sleep of our own emotional anaesthesia, sometimes the only thing that can wake us from our dormancy is a pain so severe we can neither ignore it nor cover it up any longer.

And for me, that pain was my father's death when I was 46 years old.

My mother had died nine years earlier. And in those nine years when he lived alone, my father had quite radically transformed into a much milder human being. Attributing my mother's death from colon cancer to poor diet, my father suddenly became very health conscious and no longer criticised my vegetarianism. He stopped drinking, made videos of health advice for friends, and grew medicinal herbs in his garden. He started to volunteer for charities and helped other retired people fill in their tax forms. To my delight, my father was now quite keen for us to share our interests, and he loved to hear about my musical projects in great detail. When he was 80 years old, I taught him how to use a computer, which fascinated him as he surfed the Internet and learned how to make his own business cards.

But perhaps the biggest change of all during that time was how affectionate he had become. I cannot count the amount of times my father said, 'I love you' to me in those nine years. And I always said, 'I love you too' in return. Those were the most wonderful years I had ever had with my father.

But around the same time I fell ill in India, my father, then 81 years old, also fell ill back in the US. He was diagnosed with myelodysplasia, a relatively rare and very aggressive blood disorder. Several months of painful blood transfusions helped alleviate some of the symptoms in the early stages, but ultimately the treatments proved unsuccessful in arresting the disease.

Knowing he would probably not live more than another year, my father became overtly concerned with what would happen after he died. Rather than letting go of his worldly affairs, he became more absorbed in them than ever. Every conversation we had revolved around his money and his estate, which drained me every time we spoke. Sometimes he was very affectionate, whilst other times he became obsessively critical and controlling. On those obsessive days, he expressed mistrust in my ability to choose what was best for my own sake, and made many judgemental comments about my future, my lifestyle and, most of all, my husband. He criticised him continually and I found myself wanting to defend my husband to him, which resulted in many arguments. All the things my father had once found objectionable about my life when I was younger seemed to be objectionable to him once again, and communication between us started to break down. Every day became a battle of wills. Daily, I received emails and phone messages with his latest set of complex instructions for how I was to organise my finances. I would reply requesting over and over that we please make room to talk about other things besides money. Time was running out. I wanted to spend time with my father—the one I had gotten to know over those past nine years. He said he wanted to ensure my financial future, but I felt cheated—robbed of our time together—by his priorities.

My father did not appear to understand my concerns, and seemed to interpret my unwillingness to discuss money as a lack of responsibility on my part. Finally coming to the conclusion that I was either incapable of or disinterested in addressing life's more practical matters, he decided to take things into his own hands. One evening he called me to tell me he had changed his will, and that he had made some decisions about how to distribute his estate, which I felt had the potential to put me into a very unpleasant legal arrangement with other family members. While I didn't care at all what he had chosen to do with his money, I pleaded with him to free me of the legal entanglement in which he had put me, but he flatly refused, saying it was because he felt I was basically brainwashed and had no sense of discrimination. He cited my husband and my religion as evidence, using many obscenities to punctuate his points. He expressed his feeling that my believing in God was stupid enough, but to believe in 'my husband's gook religion' only proved I had no common sense, and I could not be trusted to make any practical decisions.

The image of my father coolly snapping off the head of the locust now reappeared vividly in my mind, and it was as if he had now snapped off my own head just as unfeelingly. And with that snap, I realised that this was not at all a new argument we now had on our hands. Rather, this was 'the' argument we had had my entire life. Everything in which I most deeply believed, every value I had ever embraced, from humanity to divinity, were to him mere sentiment and ultimately worthless. I could see clearly that the schism between our outlooks on life had been there for as long as I could remember. But recently I had gotten a taste of a very different father. One who did not judge me. One who listened to my crazy dreams. One who loved to learn new things. And I wanted *that* father back. But *this* father showed no signs of returning that other father to me, and I was furious that he was denying me that father whom I loved. Knowing he was seriously ill, I had been patient with him to that point. But this turn of events pushed me to the limit of my tolerance, and in much the same way as I used to when I was younger, I found myself exploding—

'Is this really how you wish to leave me? This is the legacy you wish to leave behind? These are your final words to me? My last memory of you is to be that you do not trust me? That you have no faith in me? That you think I've made all the wrong choices? Is that really what you want me to feel for the rest of my life? Can't you understand how this is tearing me up inside? I'm not arguing with you about your money. Your money comes at too high a price.

All I ever wanted from you was for you to know me and believe in me. But you don't seem to want to leave me what I really, truly want.'

My words did not seem to create the impact I had hoped they would. My father remained fixed in his decision. The conversation ended in a deadlock, with neither of us willing to relent on our respective positions.

A few days went by with no communication. Then one night at 2 AM, the telephone rang, like a blaring alarm disturbing the sleep of everyone in the house. At the other end of the line was my father. It sounded like he was weeping. He never called at such an hour, and I had never heard my father cry in my entire life, not even when my mother died. He said he wanted me to know that his plans for my future had been made with my best interest at heart. Whilst I was sure he meant this, I could feel he was still unreceptive to hearing my opinions on the matter. And there was also something about the whole set-up of the call at 2 AM that felt strangely uncharacteristic, if not a bit staged, to me. I felt suspicious of him. It was just like when I was a child and I heard his outlandish stories. I had no idea whether I should believe him or not. I had been on the receiving end of his faking similar scenarios in the past. And so, I remained completely indifferent to his words, in spite of his tears.

Then suddenly, sounding piteous, he said, 'I love you, Lynn.'

I had been longing so much to hear these words from him. But at that moment, I was so full of resentment and mistrust, that I regarded this as just another way of manipulating me. So I didn't say 'I love you too', as I usually did. Instead, I just said, 'I'll speak to you later in the week. Good night, Dad.'

The next time I called him, my father had suddenly become cold towards me. Indeed, every time I called him for the next several weeks, he spoke to me as if I were a stranger. He never said, 'I love you,' again to me. Instead he ended each conversation by politely thanking me for my call and then hanging up. I called him twice a week, each time hoping this iciness would melt and we could re-establish that sweet relationship we had enjoyed before he had gotten ill. But his cold demeanour never warmed up. On top of this, he had stopped calling me, and I was the only one who initiated the phone calls. Eventually I felt the need to speak up.

'Look,' I said at the end of one of our calls, 'you never call me anymore. And I am not always sure that you feel like talking when I call. So how about you call me next time? That way I don't have to worry about disturbing you, and you don't have to call unless you're in the mood to talk. Ok?'

'Yes, that's fine,' he said, and then hung up.

I waited for weeks for the phone to ring.

Eventually it did ring. But the voice I heard was not my father's.

* * * * *

'Mom, there's a nurse on the phone,' my daughter told me as I was returning home from work that evening in late September. 'She's calling from the States.'

'A nurse?' I asked.

'Grandpa's dead,' my daughter said.

'Dead?' I repeated.

And for a moment, I just stood dumbstruck at the entrance to our house. Then, shaking, I went inside and picked up the phone. The conversation was surreal.

'Your father is dead.'
'When did he die?'
'Two days ago.'
'Two days ago? And you are calling now?'

There was no response from the nurse.

'Was it sudden?' I continued.

'No, his condition had been deteriorating over the past two weeks.'

'What? You've known for two weeks?'

Again, there was no response. I paused for a moment, and then tried to latch onto whatever glimmer of hope I could find.

'Was he alone when he died?' I asked.
'No, your sister and I were with him pretty much the whole time.'
'Was he in a coma?'
'No, he was conscious the whole time.'
'Was he doped up from medication?'
'No, he was quite lucid right to the end.'

My heart started pounding. I could hardly breathe. I felt like I had been dropped into an alternate universe. This could not be happening.

'So let me get this straight,' I said. 'My father has been dying for the past two weeks, and you have been with him the whole time. He was conscious and completely lucid right to the end.'
'Yes, that's right.'
'And today, two days after he dies—two full days—I receive a call from a complete stranger—not even a family member—who tells me that my father is not dying, but he is already dead, that he did not die suddenly, that he did not die alone, that he was fully aware I was not being contacted, that there would be no chance for me to come see him, no chance to talk to him on the phone, no chance for me to say goodbye...'
'I am just doing what I was asked to do.'
'You were *asked* to do this? By whom? Are you actually telling me my *father* told you not to call me until after he was dead, when it was too late for me to do anything?'
'All I am telling you is that your father died.'
'But why didn't anyone call me *before* he died? Why didn't you call me two weeks ago?'

A pause.

'I'm... I'm sorry for your loss.'

I heard the phone click as she hung up.

My mind at this point had gone completely blank. I felt as though I were in a dream. My brain could not comprehend what had just happened. To shake myself out of this delirium, I decided I needed to do something physical. I went into the kitchen and made dinner for my family. After eating, I cleaned up the dishes, pots and pans. I scrubbed down the counter and tidied everything in the kitchen. Having run out of things to do, I went upstairs with my husband to get ready for bed. Our daughter went off into the lounge to work on the computer. I lay down on the bedding and tried to sleep. Everything I was doing seemed very robotic.

But it was no use. I was unable to rest. After half an hour of lying there, I got up out of bed and walked aimlessly into my daughter's empty bedroom. I didn't turn on the light, but just stood there in the dark for a long time, my mind feeling completely blank. I have no idea how long I stared into space, without moving, without speaking, without being aware of anything. I felt dead.

Slowly, this dark feeling of deadness became increasingly pronounced and my breath became thick and weighty.

I could hear the deadness. It throbbed like a low-pitched pulse of blood pushing its way through the constricted veins of my sleeping brain. Louder and louder I could hear its distant rumblings until it became so loud it scorched right through me like a thunderbolt, setting me aflame. When it hit me, I gasped as I felt an intense physical pain running through my entire body. It was as though someone had thrust a six-foot javelin directly into my gut. It pierced my heart, my stomach and every one of my internal organs. And as I felt it pierce me, I fell onto my knees. I doubled over onto the floor, clutching my stomach with both hands...

...and I wailed and wailed to the sky for my dead father!

I screamed my anguish loudly, crying out to the walls around me—to the vastness that lay both within and without my trembling body—crying louder and louder, and more deeply than I had ever cried before. Oh, such a piteous and powerful sound! Now pierced by the force of the javelin called Grief, all the pity, all the sorrow, all the longing and all the broken-heartedness that I had ever felt in my life was streaming out from my solar plexus, like the waters from a dam that had been burst by the force of a hurricane. Suddenly I was feeling—really feeling. It was a deluge, a tsunami of pain and anguish, of love and sorrow, of connection and separation, in which a single thought was flooding through my mind—

My father is dead. He is gone. The last time he told me he loved me, I did not say 'I love you too'. And now, I will never, ever get that chance!

Hearing my crying, my husband got out of bed. However, he did not come to comfort me in my grief, but rather to express his irritation. Standing silhouetted in the dark doorway of our daughter's room, he scoffed at me disdainfully.

'I don't know why you're so upset he's dead,' he said scornfully. 'We all know he was just a nasty, angry, old bastard who always made your life miserable.'

His words shocked me into silence for a moment.

I stared at him blankly, still huddled on my knees on the floor. *How utterly ironic that he should be saying this to me!* I thought. Two months earlier, my father had pretty much said the same thing about him, and I was defending him to my father. Now my husband's words made me feel like defending my father to him. This had gone on for years and I had always resented the feeling of being stuck in the middle between them. No, not stuck it the middle—*torn in two...*

And suddenly, my entire life crystallised in my awareness. Yes, that was it—I was a person torn in two. As a child, I pretended to be part of the ideal family, while the truth was I lived in a frightening world of isolation. Growing up, I never could distinguish fact from fiction in my father's unnerving portrayals of reality. At the conservatory, I had felt dissected from my authentic voice. At the temple, I had felt physically, culturally and spiritually split in half. Throughout my marriage, I had felt pulled apart by the incongruence between my religious and artistic lives. And lastly, and surely the biggest split of all, I had led a double life by hiding my marital abuse from the world for more than two decades. And now, hearing my husband's eulogy of my father, I felt cut in two once again, this time by the incompatibility between these two men who had been so prominent in my life. And in a single flash, I could clearly see the impact all these splits had had upon me.

And at that very moment, the same moment at which I fully understood that my father was no longer alive, I instinctively knew my marriage was also dead, and beyond any chance of resurrection. And the reason why it had to end was simply this—I had never been truly alive within it in the first place. I could now see I had been dead for more than three decades, long before the marriage had even begun. And the reason why I had been dead is because I had only ever been two halves of a human being, and they were never in the same place at the same time.

But as tragic as this all might sound, this bittersweet blow was the moment of rebirth I had awaited for so long. It was the moment when I began to wake up and feel, to see and hear, to touch and be touched. This was the moment when both sorrow and joy were now somehow possible within a single experience. This was the moment when the numbness of an entire lifetime shattered into a thousand pieces, and I began to regain my sense of being alive.

Many years before, I had felt the voice of a catfish welling up within my throat, and I spoke out for him. Now, I could feel my own voice gurgling up from parts of me I had long forgotten.

And I began to speak.

* * * * *

What? I just don't get it. I'd always thought you were the perfect couple. I just can't believe what you are telling me. If what you are saying is true, I have to say I am really shocked. I mean, I always took you to be an educated woman. What would possibly have compelled you to stay in such a situation for so long? Ha! Not me. I know I wouldn't have. I'd have left years ago—the very first time it happened. I'd have taken him to court. I wouldn't have let him get away with it. Why didn't YOU do that? Why didn't you have him arrested? Why didn't you just leave? What would have been so hard about that? It's not like you were some unskilled woman who had no choice. You could have supported yourself. What was the big deal? Gosh, if I weren't hearing this from your own mouth, I would never have guessed that you of all people would be in this situation. I always thought you were smarter than that. Like I said, I just don't get it—how in the world could an intelligent woman like you stay in an abusive marriage for 22 years?

Oh, yes. I began to speak.

And when I did, people said things like this to me all the time. As I squirmed under this steady stream of unanswerable questions, I became aware that the primary reason I had not left my marriage earlier, and why I had continually covered up all evidence of the abuse, was because I knew I would have to deal with these very kinds of judgements from others. How ironic.

Looking back, it was really small wonder that when I filed for divorce on the grounds of domestic violence, my husband would contest the charges, and not openly admit to the abuse. And really why should he have? I never acknowledged it to myself or to anyone else. We had always pretended everything was perfectly fine. As I discovered when I started to speak openly about it, people had always thought we were the perfect couple. Our public image was sparkling and vibrant. Invalidating that image was something many people found difficult to accept. Moreover, they didn't know what to do with this new story of who we were. The two of us had successfully colluded in creating an alternate version of reality. We had become characters in a play we had written, personae in a very elaborate myth. Neither of us was ever truly present in our marriage.

For these reasons, in the early stages, coming out of hiding frequently felt worse than when I had lived my life as a secret. But within my heart, I knew all of this was the necessary process of healing and rebirth. When your leg goes numb, and you try to stand, you have to go through the pain of pins and needles before you can walk again. This was my period of pins and needles, going from a lifetime of numbness to a new life of awareness. As I became increasingly aware, many things became clear. I could see that the façade I had created for and around myself had kept me trapped within a lonely and fearful place for a very long time. Far from keeping me safe, it had actually made me even more vulnerable, as I had no one to lean into when I needed them. I could also see that, no matter how painful I found the judgements of others to be, the worst critic of all was myself. The sting of other people's words could only touch me if I had already accused myself of these very same 'weaknesses'. There was clearly a lot of self-forgiveness that had to happen now.

But perhaps the most remarkable thing I discovered was the paradox that, now that I had decided to 'come clean' and not pretend anymore to be someone I was not, many people around me actually seemed to *prefer* the lie of who I was to the reality of the truth. After months of emotional torment, I finally sat down and, with great effort, wrote a long letter to my Gurudeva disclosing to him all that had been going on during the two decades he had known us. But for some reason still unbeknownst to me, even though I know with certainty the letter was placed directly into his hands, he chose not to respond to it, nor even to acknowledge receipt of it. For months I waited for a reply until I finally lost hope. As the news of our divorce spread throughout the temple community, the more unscrupulous amongst them made up their own stories about me, saying I must be having an affair on the side and that I was making up these lies about my husband just to cover up my own guilt. Such rumours came through the grapevine of gossip that inevitably found its way back to me. It took all my courage not to respond to them in a storm of public outrage. But what was most upsetting to me at the time was that, after more than 20 years of affiliation with them, not a single person from my spiritual community picked up the phone to call me, or sent me a letter, to ask me how I was. At first, all of this made me furious. I felt resentful, hurt and rejected. I boiled with anger. I made up all sorts of reasons in my mind, including my conviction that the decision to exclude me had been a cultural one, made solely because I was the 'wrong' gender for a temple full of celibate monks.

But over time, I came to understand that anger and resentment would never bring me to a place of peace. I remembered someone had asked me once, 'Would you rather be right or happy?' I had worked very hard at trying to be 'right' most of my life. This time, I wanted happiness. And holding happiness as my goal, with time I could feel what was beneath the surface of both the words and the silence of the people who had turned away from me—it was fear. People were afraid of having to look at something this painful about two of their own. When I was living my life of isolation, I thought I was the only one who was afraid. But now, it appeared many people, perhaps the majority of them, seemed to need the safety net of living in an idyllic but false world, wrapped within a thin veneer of civility. What a lonely world we had all chosen for ourselves. How much of our world was living under the thumb of the fear that said, 'What would the neighbours think?' Instead of feeling angry at the world, I now saw their fear, and felt compassion for the unhappiness within it.

During that time, I lost many people who had previously been a part of my life. You might call it a period of 'cleaning the slate'. I was not only ending my marriage, but also severing my ties to the temple. And, it was also the time for me to walk away from being a musician, which had ceased to bring me joy many years earlier. For a long time I did not even listen to music. How I would fill in the gaping hole I now felt in my relationships, my spiritual growth and my creative expression remained to be seen. But I now knew my only way to inner freedom was to see beyond the narrowness of my own self-imposed limitations, and to let go of the past without clinging to self-judgement.

Of course, I was not immune to setbacks. Old habits tend to die hard. Many times after my divorce, almost without my being aware of it, the perceived judgement of others would sometimes drive me back inwards, to that safe and familiar place where no one could touch me, and that I had known so well my whole life. I stayed alone a lot of the time, staying busy, appearing to be successful and happy. I worked hard and scored achievement after achievement, including a new Master's degree in education. Eventually I became the head of a department at a college and played the role of the 'boss'. Friends expressed amazement at all I had done and how I had rebuilt my life. Now, instead of being one half of the 'perfect couple' I had become 'superwoman'.

But eventually I came to see that I had been recreating precisely the same kind of elaborate stage play that had been present in my marriage, and that I was not much closer to happiness than I had been in the past. I knew appearing to be happy was never going to be the solution to what I truly wanted. It was, in fact, the problem, and it was high time to kick the habit. And just like quitting smoking, or any other addiction, kicking the habit meant letting go of old patterns of behaviour. So, I stopped living in isolation and started reaching out. I stopped covering up my vulnerabilities, and started being honest and open with my friends when I was feeling afraid. I became conscious of whenever I found myself playing a role and let go of needing to look good in the eyes of others. And in doing all of this, I noticed many other things in my life changed as well. My chronic bodily ailments simply vanished. My heart palpitations, chest pressure and anxiety disappeared. My stomach problems stabilised. And my fibromyalgia, that disease which had nearly crippled me, and for which there was supposed to be no cure, evaporated into thin air. My sleep patterns and overall health improved, and people started saying I looked ten or fifteen years younger than my actual age. Through this gradual process of emotional and physical healing, I came to understand the integral links between the body, mind, heart and soul. I learned how to replace all of my resentment and fear with compassion and trust—a trust in the universe that it would catch me in its arms for the higher purpose of allowing something wonderful to take birth within me, and within the world.

And after I had sifted through all the falseness in my life and I finally fell into the arms of that trust, what I found was my own authentic truth, my own authentic voice, and the clear-eyed faces of those who were to become my closest, greatest and most authentic friends thereafter.

I was finally hearing the song of my own Self.

* * * * *

I am caught in the gentle arms of 20 people waiting for me. They stabilise me and then lower me to waist level. They begin to rock me gently. From this place, I can see into their eyes, their hearts and their souls. I am moved to tears and all I can say is 'thank-you' over and over again. I can see the magnificent range of emotions in their angelic faces, just like the bountiful pastel hues that dappled the mountains on the horizon as I fly blindly into their arms.

I fall into not knowing. I fall into not needing to know. I fall into trust. I fall into a sea of wonderful gifts—gifts that are simply here, and were always here, without any effort. All I have to do is let go and let these gifts catch me.

They catch my body.

They catch my heart.

They catch my soul, which has longed so much to be caught.

*　*　*　*　*

More than 40 years after I stopped sailing through the Milky Way with my friends, I returned to Long Island to visit Karen. I hadn't seen Karen or Long Island in 23 years. We were both now in our fifties and our children were grown up. Our parents had all passed away. Karen, who had never moved more than a few miles away from our old neighbourhood, was now living back in her childhood home, as her mother had left it to her in her will.

It was the last week in December, between Christmas and New Year's Eve, and the weather was cold and fresh that day as I made the somewhat distantly familiar journey on the Long Island Railroad to visit my childhood hometown. Watching the names of the towns go by as I rode on the train was itself a surreal experience, but when Karen and I first set eyes on each other at the train station, it was even more surreal. It was like meeting each other's mothers. We both looked so much like them, and it was at first difficult to relate to each other as the childhood friends we remembered. But within a very short time, we rediscovered the playmates that each of us had known so well. We spent the first part of the afternoon walking around the neighbourhood, going to the primary school and the high school, taking note of all the old things I could remember and the new things that had come about since I had left. We reminisced about people who lived in the neighbourhood and how odd it was that, in some way, nothing had changed, but in other ways so much of it was completely different. For me, it was like walking into a time machine, where I had suddenly been transported into a past that had been rapidly fast-forwarded into the present.

Eventually, we walked past the front of my parents' old house. The first thing I noticed were the two green maple trees that sat on the edge of the lawn, near the street. My father had planted these trees more than 50 years earlier, when we had first moved there just after I was born. Our family albums had pictures of them as saplings in the spring of 1955. I could remember that, when I was a child, these trees used to be so thin I could circle their trunks with the fingers of just one of my tiny hands. Now huge and overgrown, these trees, which were exactly the same age as I, could only be embraced by using both arms. They had stretched their roots in all directions, and were so large they had started pulling up the concrete slabs of sidewalk. I remarked to Karen how I remembered we used to roller skate along this sidewalk back then, because it was so nice and smooth, but now it would be impossible. These trees had become a truly formidable presence on the street.

I looked at my old house, now inhabited by people I did not know. Gone were the flowerboxes full of red and pink geraniums and the white enamelled shutters that graced the front windows. They were just plain old windows now. Gone were the lovely privet hedges that lined the property. That area was simply laid to lawn now. Gone were the red maple, the dogwood tree and the yew bushes, with nothing to replace them. Gone was the classic black wrought iron banister that ran up the steps to the front door. All that was left was the chunky, old brick stoop that was starting to show its age. Gone was the lovely brick-red colour of the walls that had once beautifully contrasted the white window shutters. The whole house was wrapped in some sort of mustard-coloured aluminium siding now. The house was in good enough repair, I suppose. But to me, it all felt drab and lifeless.

Something was missing here.

What is missing, I thought, *are my parents.*

I reflected upon how my parents had planted things here on this property that they had wanted to take root. I reflected upon how they had also put roots within me that I carried with me still. I reflected upon how, in spite of the troubled world in which they lived, there was something in their way of life that spoke boldly about being responsible, honourable and contributing to society. It was this 'something'—that one inexplicable thing—that had made this a home for me when I was growing up, in spite of all of the struggles that had

LESSONS FROM THE DAFFODIL

occurred within its four walls. For regardless of their problems, regardless of their 'faults', regardless of their inability to share their feelings either verbally or physically, this little post-war house had been a bold expression of my parents' values. It was the physical representation of their dream—I suppose their 'American Dream'.

When I was young, I used to berate that American Dream as being something ephemeral and meaningless. But that was because all I was able to see of that dream was my parents' anger and frustration with the world. *'For now we see as through a glass, darkly...'*[3] Back then, I only saw through the lens of my own attachments, and could not see the essence of what was really there. But now, through the eyes of compassion, I considered that perhaps all their anger and frustration was merely my parents' way of voicing that real life was very different from the way they had envisioned it within their dream. And in much the same way, my parents' vision of me was equally obscured, because I had my own dreams that were just as elusive to them. All dreams are only ever real to those who dream them. But that does not make them unreal. I could see that now.

Now, standing next to Karen, and walking along the tops of the roots of those two amazing maple trees, I could feel the wonder of the fact that all four of us had witnessed this same world together, from different angles, for more than half a century. I could see that, in spite of leaving this tiny universe when I was very young, I still carried with me all the values my father had planted within the roots of these two trees, even if I chose to express them quite differently from what he had imagined.

As we walked back to Karen's house, I glanced up this familiar row of Cape Cod style houses, and saw that this somewhat unexceptional suburban street was not just a street, but rather a set of dreams—the dreams of our parents, and of our own dreams as children as well. And while I mourned for the fact that my parents' lovely home was no longer the beautiful shrine to the American Dream it had once been, I also celebrated the fact that I, along with my oldest friend, Karen, could stand there and remember how lovely it had once looked.

*   *   *   *   *

Karen and I sat in her living room. It was remarkable how she had transformed this house since her own parents had died. The house was covered with Christmas decorations in every room. Even the bathroom had Christmas towels and a jingle bell on the door. There was, of course, the traditional tree in the living room, but everywhere you looked, every door, every shelf, every window, every wall had a Christmas picture, a ribbon, a bell, a Nativity scene, an angel, a light, a bit of tinsel, a candle, a candy cane, a reindeer, a snowman, or some other ornament placed ever so carefully and thoughtfully. There was no angle forgotten, and the whole house was a warm wash of gold, white, red and green.

Karen turned on the lights of her Christmas tree. Then she lit a scented candle called 'Christmas Cookie', and we began to talk about our childhood as the sun started to set in the pale, white winter sky.

For the first time, I spoke to Karen about what had actually gone on within the four walls of my parents' house, and how I felt when I was growing up. I told her all about my father's stories and how scary things were for me back then. She finally understood why I had been so quick to leave home. She said she had no idea these things had been going on all those years.

Karen then revealed to me some things about which I had never known. She told me that for years her father had quite regularly beaten both her mother and herself. She described how she would hide inside her bedroom wardrobe with the door shut, terrified that he would find her and beat her with a belt. I remember how slight and delicate Karen had been as a child, and the thought of this made me shudder. Both of our fathers drank a lot, but it had affected Karen's father more than mine. Eventually he succumbed to alcohol-related illnesses, and her mother died of Alzheimer's disease, her mental illness already evident when we were children, although we didn't understand what it was back then.

We looked at each other in disbelief. Neither of us had had any idea all these things had been going on in the other's home. Surely, we both knew there had been arguments. After all, in those days, none of the homes had air conditioning and we all kept our windows wide open in the warm weather. So, pretty much on a nightly basis, we would hear shouting coming from at least one of the neighbours' houses. But shouting became something we learned to ignore. We were taught to stay quiet about it and not to bring it up in polite conversation. As a result, no one would ever think to ask another neighbour if they were in need of help, as it would humiliate them.

How alone we had both felt back then. It was clear now why we had felt so alone.

The 'code' of our parents' generation had been not to speak to anyone of what went on behind closed doors. But now, facing each other, we could feel this code no longer had any power over us. In fact, the very act of sitting there and talking so freely with each other was something we could never have done when our parents were alive, and there was a certain amount of liberation in the simple honesty that was now between us. No longer afraid, no longer pretending, I felt our hearts soften, and our voices mellow, as we spoke about our parents from a very different perspective. They were human beings to us now, not just our parents. We talked about their fears, their struggles, their triumphs, their idiosyncrasies. We spoke with gentleness and compassion. We spoke with humour and lightness. The weight of the past could no longer keep us earthbound.

Karen said, 'You know when I used to come over to your house and we'd play on the swings? Well lots of times, I'd come over because I actually wanted to fly away—fly away from my home, my parents, my whole life, really. And I always imagined I really could fly away—just fly away on those swings.'

The instant Karen said the words 'fly away', I knew I had to write this story.

And in truth, on my backyard swings, Karen and I *could* fly anywhere we wanted, and be anyone we wanted to be. I still find it funny how when we played 'make-believe' on those swings, we were actually being ourselves, and that it was in the 'real' world where we were pretending to be people we were not. I could only imagine how much our parents might also have been wishing they too could fly away, and how alone *they* all must have felt back then.

Karen and I looked at each other, seeing the reflection of our mothers' eyes within each other's faces. We found we now could allow that reflection to flow through us, without resistance.

By the light of the Christmas tree, sitting with my beloved childhood playmate, I could feel our hearts take flight in the delight of the present, freed from the shackles of the past.

* * * * *

They call it 'The Fall of Trust'.

It entails falling backwards from a platform, blindly, into the arms of a team of trusted friends. It doesn't look so hard at first, but at the point of surrender, you realise how scary it is to let go, after a lifetime of holding on.

They are all great gifts, these friends.

So, blindly and trustingly, I let go and fall into those gifts.

I am held. I am safe.

I am valued. I am loved.

I fall into these people, but also into the trees, the mountains, the planet and the sky.

They are all holding me and rocking me.

This moment in time is holding me and rocking me.

And amongst those gifts, am I as well.

And I, too, am holding me and rocking me.

* * * * *

After our reminiscences, Karen bid me goodnight, and I settled into the big overstuffed bed she had prepared for me in her finished basement. As I let myself sink into the immaculately prepared white bedding, I felt safe and cherished in this place, and I drifted off with ease into the kind of blissful slumber one has on a cold winter's night.

And then I had the most exquisite dream.

It is wintertime, and I am walking along the street of my childhood home around four o'clock in the afternoon. As I walk, I notice all the houses are decorated for Christmas. Being vaguely aware that I am dreaming, this seems appropriate for this time of year. But in the dream, the decorations look just as they had back in the early 1960s. Every house is decked out in multicoloured lights. Every house has a wreath on the front door. Tidy little spruce trees and yew shrubs line the front of every house, and they are all covered with warm, glowing lights of blue, green, red, amber and white. But what is most beautiful— most striking—is the blanket of pristine white snow that lies on the lawns, the trees and the rooftops, glistening in the pale winter sun in the late afternoon, as the sky begins to change in hue from day to dusk. I look around me, and see that no one is out anywhere on the streets. I walk alone, making fresh footprints in the newly fallen snow, an untouched memoir that has an unspoken sense of quiet acceptance. There is something charming about this scene.

Then suddenly, I am transported about a mile away to the neighbouring town, and find myself standing in a queue to board a train in the middle of a car park of the public library. I stand there, along with three or four other people, on a platform you might stand on when waiting to board a children's miniature train in a holiday park. 'This whole scene makes little sense,' I think. 'There was never a train platform that ran through the centre of the library car park.' I become very curious to find out whether or not a train will actually arrive here.

After a short time, a train does arrive. But it is no children's train. Instead, it is an old 19th century train, complete with a smoke stack and very ornate fittings. The wheels have golden spokes and there are clusters of gilt florets dotted along the glossy, black finish of the carriages. The outside of the train is strewn with Christmas garlands and evergreen branches, and the top of the carriages have a layer of pure white snow that has somehow managed to be undisturbed by the motion of the train. It is as if the train had simply materialised here from some unseen dimension, without having to move. Such a stunning train!

The train sits at the platform, huffing and puffing very gently, waiting for its passengers to board. There are no doors to open, and I only have to step onto the train to find myself inside. As I enter, I am immediately drawn in by its tastefully gilded fittings against the highly polished mahogany walls, and its rows of deep green leather bench-style seats, studded with brass tacking along the edges. 'This train is truly a work of art,' I think to myself.

I enter and sit down on one of the bench seats, facing opposite the direction of travel. I can see the library now outside my large sightseer's window. I am only vaguely aware of the handful of travellers on the train, but they have seated themselves in other carriages, so I am really on my own here.

As I look out the window, I see the train is starting to move. The sky now takes on the indigo quality of a dusky late afternoon in December. There is something lovely about this, and it brings to memory a sensation of the warmth I used to feel after a day of ice skating on the local pond, on one of the rare days that it was frozen solid enough for skating, and we would come indoors to warm our toes in dry woolly socks, and sip copious mugs of hot chocolate and whipped cream.

I sit relishing this feeling while the train chugs away, and I watch as the scene begins to transform. The indigo dusk dissolves into the blackness of night and the lights from the town are now visible. Then, most remarkably, the train starts to rise from the ground—first just a few feet, but then higher and higher. Then, ever so easily, the train starts to fly, all the while chug, chug, chugging, its old-fashioned steam-driven locomotive pulling us into the December sky.

The old-time whistle blows and echoes through the snowy landscape. We are now high enough off the ground to make out entire neighbourhoods, but still low enough to be able to see the features of the buildings.

Soon, the train flies above my childhood neighbourhood.

It is midnight as I look down upon the tiny town below me. The sky is black with a silver-white full moon hanging like a Christmas tree angel atop the holiday landscape. The entire town is sound asleep and multicoloured Christmas lights are still ablaze on every house. There is a full, rich blanket of powdery virgin snow in all directions. It sits undisturbed on the rooftops, the bare tree branches, the landscape. Snow is continuing to fall ever so gently.

I notice everything has become completely silent—including the train—and the only sound I hear comes from the soft and barely audible popping sound of snowflakes upon the plane of already fallen snow.

'This is', I think to myself, 'what is meant by 'Silent Night'.

As I watch this beautiful and captivating expanse of quiet and stillness, I become aware that much is happening beneath the surface. The bulbs of the spring flowers are gathering their energy to take birth after the snow melts away. The animals slumber in dreams as they hibernate through this period, taking energy into their bodies so they will be strong and full of wisdom when Earth calls them to re-emerge into the light of day. The roots of the great trees store their life force, patiently standing vigil until it is time to release the first buds of spring. There is nourishment here too, as the winter squirrels eat from the store of nuts they had buried throughout the summer months.

This is the place of being in which becoming can take place—a place where transitions occur, and possibilities are spun out in simplicity, and without struggle. It is where new life and new beginnings are kept safe and warm and allowed to be caressed by the elements until destiny at last calls upon them to act.

As I take in this uplifting panorama, I become acutely aware that I am sitting backwards as the train flies above the town. Yes, I am looking back, seeing what had been before, and reflecting upon the past even as I move forwards in this train. And as I gaze upon this scene, the train suddenly takes a turn north, and it starts to rise further and further into the moonlit sky. It pulls away from the little town, until the Christmas lights become a sea of coloured dots, like confetti on a sparkling snowy backdrop.

We rise higher and higher, until I know with certainty we are not coming back.

The scene dissolves before my eyes and I wake up.

As I woke, I knew I had finally flown away from my childhood. I had finally let go. I had let go of my father. I had let go of all the pain, fear, judgement and blame of the past, both towards him and towards myself, which I had held onto for more than 40 years. It all slipped away, easily and effortlessly, and I fell delicately into the power of the love I felt for him, and had always felt for him, and that I knew he felt for me. And as I fell into that love, I was caught by an inexplicably fresh, newborn love of Self I had never known before.

The next morning, I left Karen's home, and the hometown of my youth. But this time, I left with the sense that I was no longer trying to escape the quarter-mile universe, but I had finally flown gracefully and elegantly up and away into the sky of possibilities, with the memory of all that was good about the past etched forever upon my heart.

*   *   *   *   *

'How in the world could an intelligent woman like you stay in an abusive marriage for 22 years?'

For a long time, I had no ready answer to this question when people asked me. But I finally found the answer at my grandson's second birthday party.

My husband and I had not even spoken in the six years since our divorce. At first, this was mutual; but over time, it was largely due to my own stubborn unwillingness to speak to him. I had rationalised many things to myself. I had rationalised that I had nothing to say to a man who would not admit to the abuse that had occurred during our marriage. I had rationalised that I had no wish to have a relationship with someone who would not speak the truth. I had rationalised that we had both moved on, especially as he had remarried a year or so after we split up.

I made up countless 'good' reasons to justify my decision not to speak to my former husband. And because of this, my daughter, now grown up, expended a lot of time and energy to ensure he and I never crossed paths. But ever since I had returned from New York, I felt myself going through a gradual process of release. I had released my parents, which had the curious effect of my allowing them to enter and to flow through my personality, long after they had departed from this world. I released all of my past religious experiences, and slowly came to find my spirit awakening in a way that illuminated even the darkest corners of my heart. I released my resentment towards music, and rediscovered an even greater pathway to my personal expression through writing, which I had abandoned many years before. And as I became lighter and lighter, I found I could also listen to music again, with greater appreciation than I had ever known in the past.

But most of all, I released my need to be miserable, and I grasped with both hands the great golden ring of happiness as my birthright, knowing now it was the birthright of every living soul in this world. And to bring that message forward, I changed careers completely, leaving the world of education behind, and I became a life coach, a public speaker and (most of all) a writer, so I could help others to find the same joy I was now feeling. Life, at long last, had purpose and meaning.

But there was one blip on the radar that still needed my attention—I needed to release my marriage, once and for all.

Over the years, I had come to understand that whatever you avoid is the very thing that controls you most. I had come to understand that the more energy you spend avoiding something, the more you carry it with you, and the more tightly you are clinging to it. I did not fully know what exactly it was that had its grip on me about the marriage, but I knew intuitively I would never be fully free until I stopped avoiding the man who had been my husband for more than 20 years, the man who will always be the father of my daughter, and who was now also the grandfather of my grandson. And so, I told my daughter to go ahead and let us meet on my grandson's second birthday. I was not sure what I was going to find there, but everything within me told me that meeting my ex-husband was the 'right' thing to do, and that it would heal my heart.

As I entered my daughter's house and saw her sitting with her son and her father, I found it somewhat jarring to take in this man sitting across from me, who was now more than twice the age he had been when we first met. I clearly remembered the day when an immature 25-year-old girl had first laid eyes on that handsome 27-year-old man, and now saw the span of life that had passed since that time, and how it had both aged our bodies and seasoned our beings.

I sat down on the sofa and, much to my amazement, found that he and I were able to speak like old friends who had not seen each other for many years. We caught up on what we were doing, who we had heard from and how life had changed. The conversation felt natural and easy. I was both pleased and surprised, if not also a bit confused and awkward.

In the course of our conversation, I mentioned that I was finishing a book. Much to my surprise, he asked me what it was about, and I described a little bit about *The Garden of the Soul.* In the back of my mind as we spoke, I thought about how just that morning, I had been struggling through the third rewrite of this story 'Fly Away', feeling that something was still missing in it. I didn't tell him about this story, but he listened with interest as I told him about the overall concept of the book.

Then, quite unexpectedly, he said, 'I know I was the one who stopped you from writing.'

These words stunned me. I was not stunned because he said them, but because my own personal transformation over the years had helped me dispel the false beliefs we had constructed around our relationship in the past. Yes, it was true I had stopped writing after we had come together. I had impulsively thrown out my portfolio of poems one night in reaction to his criticism of them, swearing never to write again. But to say he stopped me was just another myth I had created, and obviously one that he had come to believe as well. When I threw out my poems, I convinced myself that I had done it as an act of love—a tangible sign of my own willingness to give up anything for my husband, and to gain his acceptance. But I now understood this was anything but an act of love; it was, in fact, an act of war.

Indeed, that one act had enabled me to carry around the 'prize' of being able to blame my husband for my own innate feelings of voicelessness. For more than 20 years, I carried that blame around with me like a dead weight tied around my neck, and I found every opportunity to use it like a weapon against my husband whenever I felt small or unheard. And over time, I tossed out other parts of myself too, giving myself more and more weapons against him. But rather than making me feel stronger, as I acquired more weapons, I became increasingly small and voiceless because the weapon of blame could only be strengthened via my own self-destruction. Blame grew like a cancer within my heart, and I am positive that it manifested as all those physical illnesses I had during that time. Blame became a way of life—or, rather, a way of 'walking death'.

Blaming my husband was also the way to justify my own feelings of isolation. But in truth, my isolation had nothing whatsoever to do with him. I had already been living in a box long before we met.

In the past, I had longed to hear my husband acknowledge his role in my stopping writing. But now, six years after we had divorced, when I heard him say, 'I know I was the one who stopped you from writing,' I could see in an instant that this was not true. He hadn't stopped me from writing. I had cut off that part of myself in an act of anger and self-violence. My irreversible act of throwing out my poems and closing down my voice was no different from my father's impulsive act of snapping off the head of the locust. And just like the headless locust, I had sailed wildly and dizzyingly through my life for many years, blind, directionless, and cut off from my own heart—the source of that voice.

Then, even more to my surprise, my ex-husband asked me whether I would let him *read* the book when it was finished. Nervously, and rather unconvincingly, I said yes, but my inner voice panicked with that same old fear of anticipated judgement to which I had been accustomed for so long. *How could I let him read this?* I thought.

But then, my heart spoke to me and asked, *Listen! What is this moment telling you?* And I could recognise there was something here that was meant to be included in the story 'Fly Away'. I did not yet know what it was, but I knew the story would not be complete without this moment. There was some vital learning to be found in this moment. So I began to listen to the moments that were happening with great attention, so as to hear what was there.

Later that afternoon, my son-in-law's father and younger brother arrived, and the seven of us celebrated my grandson's birthday with cake and the giving of presents. The biggest present that day was a slide and swing set my daughter and son-in-law had bought to put in the backyard of their modest semi-detached home in Hertfordshire. Together, all of us spent a lovely spring afternoon in the garden assembling the play set.

My grandson was old enough to know what to do with a slide and swing, and as soon as we had finished tightening every nut and bolt, he gleefully started climbing up and down the slide, and swinging his stuffed animals on the swing.

As I watched my grandson play, I could not help but reflect upon the blissful life I had had with Karen on my own swings half a century earlier, and how much joy those swings had brought us. In my heart, I sent an inner wish for my grandson to have that same joy and freedom, unencumbered by any of the unspoken shackles I had experienced. I wished for him to sail to unknown universes, to feel the rush of the air against his cheeks, to hear the buzz of the bumblebee in his ear, to let go of the chains that keep us earthbound and fly to wherever his imagination wished to take him...

And within that precious moment, I looked around the garden and I felt a sense of something I had not felt in a very long time—

Family.

Here was my daughter, her fiancé and son.

Here were two grandfathers and a young uncle.

And here was me, 'Nana'—the grandmother.

No, we are not the nuclear family of the 1950s or 60s. We are not the American Dream (nor are we even in America anymore). We are something very different. Both sets of grandparents are divorced. The young parents were not even married yet (they married the following November). There is no stay-at-home-mom in this family. All of the adults go to work during the week, and the child stays with a childminder. Surely this family is a completely different entity from what I had known as a child. But nonetheless, this is, without a doubt, a family—*my* family. I had been missing the feeling of family for years, especially since my father had died, and now I suddenly saw it, felt it and was part of it.

What a wonderful surprise, I thought.

And what was probably most surprising for me was that, in my heart of hearts, I knew my ex-husband was also a vital part of my family. And I felt this was all as it should be.

At the end of the afternoon, I prepared to leave. I came into the lounge and found my daughter's father sitting there alone. There was an awkward moment where I thought, *Hmm...what's the 'right' thing to do here?* Then I remembered some advice I always give my daughter when dealing with relationships, and I told myself, *It is never wrong to make the first move.*

So, taking my own advice, I held out my arms, inviting my ex-husband to a goodbye hug.

Immediately, he leapt out of his chair and embraced me with warm affection. He held me close, touching my cheek and my hair gently, saying how glad he was to see I was happy and how good it felt that we could at last be friends, 'If that is what we are now?' he asked tentatively.

I could find no words to say in response to this unexpected display of softness.

And then, he said the words I had waited for years, decades, to hear.

'I'm sorry for all I did to you.'

It was as if the weight of the world had suddenly been removed from my shoulders.

But—

It was not because of what he said. Mere words could never have created the euphoria my soul now felt. What lifted the weight was the fact that I realised I had *already* let go of the need to blame, both him and myself, for anything and everything from the past. Blame did not exist. It was an illusion I had created, played out by the roles I had authored in the convincing drama of my own life. But now, no longer *seeing as through the glass, darkly, but rather face-to-face,*[4] I no longer needed that illusion to make sense of who I was. And just like the motorcycle in my dream, the old story simply slipped away, without effort, ready for the next story to begin. And as I felt the illusion release me, I felt a lightness of being I had never known before, propelling my heart to fly higher and higher.

This precious moment came so unexpectedly I simply did not know how to react. So, I just held him for a few short moments and heard myself saying—

'There's no need... no need...'

And truth be told, there was no need. I had let go of the need. The need for blame, shame, guilt, pain and anger—all that I had clung to for 28 years, and maybe for all of my life prior to that—now dissolved effortlessly without so much as a whimper. I finally felt just as I had when I found myself floating down alongside that great tree of my dream, reaching out for one limb after another as they bent gracefully to my touch, sensing a rush of anticipation and joy as I finally landed softly in that wheat-coloured field of homecoming that had, to that point, only existed within the hazy world of my unconscious wanderings.

I went home and sobbed for two solid days.

And within those tears, which felt beautiful as they streamed from my eyes, I finally found the simple answer to the question of why I had stayed in our marriage for so long—

We had loved each other.

Yes, our marriage had been generally turbulent, often violent and frequently unhappy. And then, it reached the point where it simply had to end. But none of that invalidated the truth of our affection for each other, even if seemingly imperfect. In truth, we had loved as best we knew how at the time. And this was as much as either of us could possibly have done. When I could see this truth, I realised I could just as easily say the same about my relationship with my father. With my tears, I held to my heart all the good that both of these men had brought into my life. And then—

Listen! What is this moment telling you?

Fly away!

All these years I had been trying to fly away—fly away from my problems. But that's not flying. All I was doing was simply swinging back and forth like a pendulum, going nowhere. Happiness, love, freedom, expressiveness, fulfilment and delight—none of these can be found until you actually do learn how to fly.

And, funnily enough, I had known how to fly all along. The bumblebee had taught me when I was playing on the swings in my backyard when I was 7 years old—

'The only way to fly is to let go!'

Let go of fear and judgement.

Let go of resentment and blame.

Let go of pretending and isolation.

Let go and do not fear where you will land.

And simply trust that when you fall back to Earth, someone will be there to catch you.

*   *   *   *   *

Gently, the team lower my legs, and place my feet back on the ground, one at a time. I stand upright on my own now. I wriggle my toes as I reconnect with the Earth beneath me. I am elated and feel a euphoric rush fill my head and lungs. My eyes take in the captivating view of the gorgeous Spanish woodlands. I inhale the aroma of the scent of the Earth. I shiver slightly at the touch of the cool December Mediterranean air against my skin. Out of the corner of my eye, I can see Manuel smiling. I grab my journal and go to sit beneath a magnificent pine tree and write these words...

For in this moment
   there is joy
And in the next
   there is still more...

       When we learn to fall
         we begin to fly
       For we fall into
         the arms of God.

Wow, I think, now that is really the ultimate *rush!*

*   *   *   *   *

'Fly away!' said Karen.

I shut my eyes and let go, trusting I will be carried safely.

My lungs become filled with the air that is rushing against my cheeks.

And I fly into the sweet embrace of my own life.

*   *   *   *   *

Revisiting the Daffodils

I raced to the woods that morning to make sure I found the Daffodils before they left.

Such transitory Flowers, these Daffodils, I thought, the damp morning air making my lungs ache from breathing so hard whilst running. *They last such a very short time, but they herald in the arrival of all the other flowers. And such deceptive Flowers, too! They laugh and giggle and play, but really I'm starting to believe they are the most powerful Flowers I have met so far!*

At last I turned the familiar bend and saw them huddled and whispering amongst themselves within the shady spruce grove. Overjoyed, I cried out, 'Yes! The Daffodils are still here!'

Hearing my cry, the Daffodils turned to see me running towards them, and their sunny voices called out to me shouting, 'Hello! Hello! Over here! Come over here!'

I arrived at their hiding place and stopped, gasping to catch my breath from all that running.

'You look funny!' they laughed. 'Your face is all red and your nose is running!'

I was home.

I sat down amongst the Daffodils, who clamoured around me, as if to warm me with the big, yellow blanket of their petals. Here I was, once again in their delightful company. Now again, I could feel my breath slowing down more and more until it eventually moved with the pulse of the Earth itself.

I told them the story 'Fly Away'. I told them all about the swings, the bumblebee and the locust. I told them about all the people, places and things in the story. I told them about my childhood games, about my flights to the Milky Way, about my dreams, my fears and my tears.

Then the Daffodils asked—

'Most playful, joyful, and inspirational friend! Oh soul of our imagination! What have you learned about the Principle of Becoming?'

I sat and shut my eyes, so as to feel the Principle enter me, until the learning became clear.

'I have learned the difference between "make-believe" and "pretending",' I said.

'Oh! Please tell us what it is!' they begged.

'Well,' I started slowly, 'to make believe is to create new possibilities, but to pretend is to deny what is there.'

The Daffodils seemed pleased. 'Ooh, that *is* interesting,' they twittered. 'What else can you tell us?'

I took a moment to get a picture in my mind of how I looked as a child when I played 'make-believe'. In my mind's eye, I became that magic parrot named Polly aboard my spaceship to the Milky Way. Then, I reflected upon all the other roles I had played in life by 'pretending'—the entertainer, the perfect couple, superwoman, the boss at the college—all those roles.

Then, I had an answer for the Daffodils.

'I have learned,' I replied, 'that within my childhood make-believe was the seed of all I was meant to become—all I could ever have become. I can see that I was already becoming someone who was meant to explore new places, and to navigate the journey, and to take others along with me on that flight. I can see from my make-believe that my life was meant for magic, for wonder, for creation. I can see that I was never meant to live in a quarter-mile universe, or in any other universe that has four walls.

'But,' I continued, 'I can also see how mistaken I was about what I needed in order to become that person. I used to believe I would find her if I went to lots of different places and experienced lots of different things. Oh, yes, all of that was fun and it enlarged my greater understanding of life, but really, I now know the real journey for me was to begin when I allowed myself to fly freely upon the wings of my own imagination, unencumbered by all the 'pretend' parts of me, and to be the navigator within that limitless world where no walls exist. This is who I was becoming all along. This is the only person I could ever have become.

'And,' I continued, 'I can see that whenever I was pretending in life, I was not being the navigator. I was not fully on my life's journey. I was simply going back and forth between one point and another—just like when I was on the swing. I'd believe I was going somewhere, but really I was simply lost without a map. But now that I understand the difference between make-believe and pretending, I have become the navigator of my life once again. I can see where I am and where I am going, and I am able to change directions, to get back to who I am whenever I get lost. I have learned the secret of Becoming.'

The Daffodils ruffled their little skirts and smiled approvingly.

'A secret? Oh, tell us the secret too!' they chimed.

'The secret of Becoming is rebirth,' I continued, almost instantly.

'I have learned there cannot be any rebirth without death.

'I have learned there cannot be death without letting go of the past.

'I have learned it is only in letting go that we actually can Become.

'It is only in Becoming that we can grow.

'It is only in growth that we can explore, expand, imagine, inspire, invent and create new worlds—countless worlds, unlimited worlds!

'It is in Becoming that we find creation itself.

'And 'letting go' is the key to that creation. It is a great paradox. I used to think we would get smaller or become less by letting go of our grip on things; but rather, the more we let go, the greater we become. Understanding this secret fills me with a joyfulness I could not find before.'

I lay amongst the Daffodils for a few moments, allowing the cool moist air to fill my lungs. As gently as a spring rain, the final lessons of my learning finally formed words upon my lips.

'The great secret I have learned is that letting go is really very simple. For years, life was always a struggle—like trying to lift a big rock up a hill. The gravity of my own life always weighed me down. I would get up the hill one inch at a time, but the top never seemed within my vision, and nothing ever really changed. I felt as though my life had no purpose and that my existence made little impact upon the world.

'But now,' I continued, 'I have let go of that weight completely. I have set the rock down on the ground once and for all. I no longer insist on dragging it around everywhere I go. Now, instead, I pick up tiny pebbles, light, smooth and pleasant to the touch. I drop them into the waters of my own spirit and see the ripples rippling outwards. And as I release them, I can see that this freshness, this lightness of my being, does indeed have a purpose, and does indeed create an impact, as the ripples tickle all that they touch, and change the world ever so slightly and delicately with everything I bring to it. My universe expands ever outwards, in a never-ending dance between ripple and water. The patterns are mesmerising and ever-changing. I can create newer and newer possibilities simply by dropping a pebble into the world through the consciousness of my actions, which starts the ripples of change and transformation in all directions.

'When I simply let it go, and I let it all become. I cannot imagine anything more simple, yet more powerful, than this.'

The Daffodils twittered in approval.

I sat down for a moment, taking in all that I had just said. A bigger picture of my life became clearer to me.

'For decades I roamed through life not allowing the natural course of my life to unfold,' I told the Daffodils. 'I tried to be the person I thought everyone else wanted me to be, and so I never became anyone—not for me, not for others. All the 'me's' of my life were false images, like shadows or paper dolls, just pretending to be me. When I let go of anger, grief, resentment, fear, blame and judgement, towards both others and myself, the true 'me' was finally able to be born.

'After decades of fearing and resisting that letting go, when I finally did let go, I found it was as simple as putting down that heavy rock and replacing it with those magic pebbles. And from this single, simple realisation, my entire life has been reborn.'

The Daffodils sighed in unison. 'Aaahh!' they sang.

'So, if the secret of the Principle of Becoming is to let go' said the Daffodils, 'what is the *power* of this Principle?'

'The power?' I asked, pausing to consider the enquiry.

'Why, the power of the Principle of Becoming—is that it is always present!' I cried in great surprise.

'The power is that we are *always* becoming. It is an illusion that things remain the same. The power within becoming is that it is unlimited, infinite and eternal. There is no limit to what is becoming. I look out upon the rolling hills and see the sky ever-changing, the wind, the air, the colours, the sounds—all of it ever-changing, ever-becoming. And within it all, I know that I too am ever-becoming. In every moment, creation is becoming. To cling to anything, regardless of whether we perceive it to be good or bad, is futile. There is no point in time or space when we are not becoming. And in this knowledge, I find great peace, for I know that no matter what I see or think or feel in this moment, there is always more and more to experience, to know and to become.

'The true power of the Principle of Becoming, then, is *hope*. It is the knowledge that infinity is all around us. It is already within our bodies, our minds and our hearts. We have no need to go chasing after it. Becoming is already here. We have only to let go and let it unfold.'

Sitting upon the soft black earth, I drew my knees towards my chest, encircling them with my arms. And gazing softly at the horizon as it became a celebration of colour, I watched the sun begin to make its descent in the western sky.

'The funny thing is,' I said after a few minutes, 'for much of my life I thought "becoming" had something to do with the future. For a very long time I believed I was miserable in life and I sat waiting for the ever-elusive "someday" to come to me when happiness would arrive. But this is simply because I had embraced a view of time where I thought I had to wait to "become" happy.

'Within all those moments when I felt miserable, I could not see the Principle of Becoming surrounding me at every moment. I could not see my own evolution, my own growth, my own expansiveness within those moments. I felt myself shutting down, going in, collapsing and shrinking.

'But now, I can see that within every moment lies the seed of the next, and the next, and the next after that. I can see that at every moment, we are becoming, and in every moment is another opportunity to become again and again. It is simply a matter of seeing it in front of us. Becoming is never-ending. Within each moment lies yet another chance to begin again— and another and another and another.

'We begin to fly when we allow ourselves to fall into that unlimited, all-encompassing and ever-expanding universe of possibilities that is at our fingertips at any point in time. There is no need to wait to become. Becoming does not arrive one day. Becoming is here at all times and in all places. This is the thrill, the sheer ecstasy, and the power of the Principle of Becoming.'

We all sat together silently for a moment, watching the sun turn from gold to crimson.

'Now I understand,' I said slowly, 'why, in spite of my feeling like life was very painful during those times I just described to you, all of those stories actually comprise the most joyful story of my life. For they are the tale of my birth of Self. True understanding of the Principle of Becoming is the key to incessant and never-ending joy.'

'Yes,' the Daffodils chimed. *'For in this moment there is joy. And in the next there is still more,'* they sang. And they continued to hum merrily for several moments.

The Daffodils smiled. In all directions I saw their cheery faces, and I could not resist the urge to stand up and spin around and around and around, my arms wide open and my face looking up to the dusky sky, until I got so dizzy I simply fell upon the ground, to the musical laughter of my flowery friends.

'We told you there was much you already knew!' they giggled in unison.

'So now,' they asked, 'what will you do next?'

I stood up amidst that sea of bright yellow bliss, and I felt my heart open up with love for these wonderful, sunny Daffodils.

Then, I gave them my sincere promise.

'I will walk daily through the Garden of my own Soul.

'I will nurture it and tend to the weeds that spring up within its flowerbeds.

'I will learn more and more about the Principle of Becoming from the simple stories of my own life.

'And,' I concluded, 'I will tell all I meet about the joy they will find when they do the same for themselves.'

*   *   *   *   *

SECTION FOUR:
LESSONS FROM THE LILY

THE PRINCIPLE OF BEING

CHARACTERISTICS AND ATTRIBUTES:
serenity, peace, tranquillity, satisfaction,
wisdom, patience, smiling, compassion,
understanding, reflection, wholeness, intuition,
maturity, bliss , self-awareness, spirituality,
continuity, acceptance, non-attachment,
connection to all that is around you,
awareness of all that is

GUIDES:
river, bridges, graffiti, ammonites,
ducks, swans, geese, driftwood,
unknown urban artists, a stranger in the park,
a stranger at a bus stop, faces on the underground,
ancient castle ruins

SONG of THE Lily: ARCHANGEL

In the dark recess
of the ancient cathedral
down winding pathways
    and ever
        downwards

Within a marble-pillared cavern
I happened upon
    a wondrous lake
its placid surface
    as yet untouched
and undiscovered
    pristine waters

—so crystalline
    —so pure.

The earth embraced
    its liquidity
with jewelled
    chandelier-like arms
It kissed its sheen
    with blazing light

—so brilliant
    —so consonant

i swooned to see
    the image of
    that mirror and that light

intertwine

—so delicately
    —so naturally

then melt!
   in synchronicity

—one glorifying
   —one clarifying the other
in the unbridled joy of recognition.

Who knows how such a chance encounter came to be?

My breath

  simply

   stopped.

Life filled me for the very first time.

*   *   *   *   *

The Lily — The Principle of Being

I t was in the dead of winter, that night. For some strange reason, I couldn't sleep, feeling restless and adrift. I tossed and turned for hours until something inside me said, *Wake up!* and I bolted upright in my bed, as if someone had shaken me awake.

I sat there blinking as my eyes gradually adjusted to the darkness, and then looked around the room. After a few moments, I could see quite clearly, making out forms amidst the shadows, although colour was not yet visible in the dark. Soon, my eyes saw the room awash with a faintly blue-white hue coming from outside. Curious to find out what was creating this haunting light, I got out of bed and went to the window to look.

As I pushed aside the white voile curtains of my bedroom window, I saw a bright platinum-coloured full moon hanging in a vast, empty sky. My Garden was filled with its sombre, reflective light in all directions. This seemed a barren-looking landscape in this cold season, as the flowers of summer, which had now retreated to the underworld, were all fast asleep beneath the earth, waiting for the spring to return. As I gazed upon this scene, I noted how the rest of the world also slumbered whilst I stood there, sleepless and wondering what had called me to awaken on that cold, clear winter night.

I had a strange urge to open the window, in spite of the cold. I felt a frosty blast of arctic air enter my lungs as I undid the latch.

How still and spacious it all is, I thought, breathing in the cold night air. *My Garden looks like a magic Garden tonight.*

Suddenly, I felt an odd tickling upon my earlobes, as though a mystical voice were whispering something to me without words. Vaguely, I began to make out the sound of someone singing, as it echoed from some distance across the frozen landscape. Excitedly, I wrapped a purple woollen shawl around my shoulders, slipped my fuzzy pink slippers onto my feet, and went out into the Garden to find the source of that voice.

I walked through the Garden as if in a dream, following the trail of the mysterious chant. Slowly, it became more and more audible, until I could hear quite clearly a soft, melodious voice that sang alone in the cold moonlit night. Following the lure of this voice, I walked along the serpentine pathways until I came to a hidden courtyard of glistening marble walls about six feet high, ornamented by a row of delicately carved rosewood trellises running around the top. Soon, a mesmerising scent filled the air. I turned towards that scent and I could finally see her pure white figure, illuminated by the reflective light of the full white moon, beaming through the latticed patterns against the barren earth.

It was the Lily—singing wondrously to her lover, the Moon.

I crouched down behind one of the walls, and watched and listened to the Lily, as she softly sang her most enchanting melodies, letting the chilly silver rays of the Moon bathe her in ecstasy all the while. Her lilting tones resonated and rebounded in all directions across the white walls of the marble courtyard. I felt moved to tears as I listened, not because her singing made me sad, but because it was simply so exquisite. The music of her opalescent voice was like the primordial vibration of the entire universe.

I could not dare to come out of the shadows to speak to the Lily that night. Instead, I chose to sit and gaze at her from a distance, while listening to her midnight litany. Throughout the night, I remained entranced by the serenity of her streamlined form, her pure white petals and her powerful, inner strength. When I returned home just before dawn, I sensed some sort of significant shift had occurred within me, but I couldn't quite define what it was.

The next night, I returned. And the next after that. Again and again I returned for several evenings. Hearing the midnight concert of the graceful white Lily had now become a nightly ritual, as I found in her the source of my inner peace. She was so serene and tranquil it was impossible to worry about anything when I was around her. If ever I felt agitated or confused, an hour or so in the proximity of this exquisite flower would bring me to a place of spiritual quietude that made me feel fully aware of both my own existence, and of the totality of existence itself.

By the twelfth night, the Moon had waned significantly, and I wondered whether I would still be able to find the courtyard of the Lily in the darkening light. At midnight, I donned my shawl and my slippers as usual. I went out into the Garden, hoping the aroma and the music of the Lily would show me the way forward, in spite of the fact that I had no moonlight to illuminate the circuitous pathways. But on this particular night, I could neither hear any singing, nor smell the sweet scent of the Lily. Having no means of guidance at all, I soon became lost in the darkness. Turning this way and that, I could not find my direction through the Garden, and began to feel a sense of panic coming over me.

'Where am I supposed to go?' I cried out in a loud voice. 'I'm lost!'

'Hush, now. You cannot get lost in your own Garden!' the Lily spoke to me in her mild, calming voice.

I turned and saw her standing, tranquil and composed, illuminated by a single sliver of a moonbeam, her strong white petals reaching upwards like a hand outstretched to heaven, as if holding the whole world within their soft embrace.

Surely, I thought, *the petals of this Lily are able to contain all that is, all that was, and all that will ever be.*

'You are completely safe,' she assured me. 'This is the exact centre of your Garden. You can see anyplace, and go to anyplace, from here.'

Standing next to her, and hearing her speak to me directly, I felt the deep and sobering presence of the Lily. Even in the darkness of the waning Moon, and standing upon the barrenness of the sleeping Earth, she shone brilliantly like a single pearl inside a secret treasure chest. Her calmness and reassuring nature drew me closer and closer, until I was sitting close enough to touch her with my fingertips.

The Lily bent her sweet head to find the touch of my cold hand, and I could feel the flow of loving acceptance emanating from her. Her presence was so powerful I could not take my eyes from her, and I felt no need to do anything, say anything, or know anything. Here, it was simply enough to sit silently and to listen to the subtle music of our essence. And as I did, I realised I recognised this song of the Lily—for it was the music of my own heart.

We listened to that unstruck music of existence throughout the night, without a word. And all the while, I knew I was safe. I was being held firmly within the graceful, unwavering, bow-shaped smile of the lovely Lily.

This Lily was very different from the other Flowers. There was something within her nature that reminded me of all of the other three, but she was unique amongst them. She alone was the flower who stood in the very centre of the Garden; she was the one around whom all the others grew and flourished. She was quite right—from here, I could indeed see all directions clearly. From here, I could see the path to anyplace I wanted to go. From here, the distance to any point was the same. From here, everything was equally visible, audible and knowable. This was not a place where I needed reference points and legends on a map. This was the place of absolute Being.

I returned to the Lily night after night, even when the Moon was in its darkest garments. I found I was able to find the Lily more and more easily as the nights went by, by intuition alone.

The Lily was always blissfully sweet. She seemed never to need anything, and was always satisfied with whatever the Sun, the Earth, the Air and the Rain saw fit to provide her. Although as regal as a queen, she chose to sit in a solitary, barren plot of earth where she could easily breathe in the world around her.

Many nights, the Lily and I would sit together without saying a word for hours at a time, feeling perfectly happy in each other's presence. And then, as the night drew to a close, we would watch the sun come up over the eastern horizon. The way the light shone through her snow-white petals was quite striking, setting her aglow as if a golden halo were emanating from her body. I always felt as though Time itself slowed down whenever I spent time with the Lily—as if everything were moving just slowly enough to examine it, to see it clearly, and to understand it.

And as Time slowed down, I slowed down with it, until I was also moving slowly enough to examine myself, see myself and understand myself. I began to wonder how I fit within the totality of everything else I could see from this central point of my Garden. The hunger for wisdom was starting to awaken inside me, and I felt the need to know more about the mysterious power of the Lily.

So, one evening in the dark fortnight, when the Moon was barely more than a slice of light in the sky, I decided it was time to ask her to teach me. Humbly, I tiptoed as I approached her, while she was chanting her evening prayers. Seeing me, the Lily smiled modestly, casting her eyes ever so slightly downwards, as if to express a hint of shyness to mask her fondness for me. Consumed with genuine affection, I could not help but divert my eyes as well, and we sat like two ancient friends who no longer required words to convey the profound feelings they had for one another. In silence, we allowed our hearts to sing in harmony for hours, which mystically transformed into aeons that were both never-ending and never-beginning. The music of our hearts stretched out into the universe until it seemed to go on forever.

Then, because she knew I had something on my mind, the Lily broke the silence and asked softly, 'What can I do for you, oh friend, whom I hold as dear as my own Self?'

I could feel my entire body smiling. It smiled so earnestly I could feel it start to beam outwards from the light of my eyes. And as that light shone upon the powerful form of the Lily, I felt myself become fully aware of the simple sensation of being alive, and of the ebb and flow of the cyclic nature of Time itself. It was as if I could stand above the universe and be witness to its wonder and its mystery, its joys and its sorrows, feeling fully present and essential within that glorious and infinite tapestry before me.

Here, I am complete, I thought to myself.

Allowing the fullness of my Soul to fill me up, I resisted the urge to fall into a dreamlike trance and I somehow found the words I wished to say to her.

I knew the Lily had much to teach me, so I asked her—

'Most compassionate and peaceful Lily! Oh Soul of my Soul! Please tell me—what can I learn from you?'

The lovely Lily raised her head and gazed softly and directly into my eyes, showing me the light of her own essence.

She now stood straighter than ever, her sturdy petals fully outstretched to the sky above. It hardly seemed possible, but the colour of her petals appeared to become whiter than white, almost translucent, like mother of pearl or the colour of the full Moon. Then she began to chant a melody I had not heard her sing before, one that was so beautiful I felt as though I had fallen into an ocean of nectar.

After she concluded her hymn, the Lily spoke to me with great feeling.

'From me,' she replied softly, 'you can learn the Principle of Being,'

'What is the Principle of Being?' I asked her. 'Does it mean that I must do nothing? Does it mean I must have nothing? Does it mean I am nothing?'

The Lily smiled with calm patience, as if to say, 'We have all the time in the world to work on this together.' The waning Moon, barely visible now, sat low on the horizon giving the barest glimmer of light. Like a flashing jewel in this deepening darkness, the Lily now began to reveal her knowledge.

'The Principle of Being is serenity, peace and tranquillity.

'It is wisdom, understanding and intuition.

'It is patience, satisfaction and continuity.

'It is smiling, acceptance and compassion.

'It is maturity and wholeness.

'It is reflection, self-awareness and spirituality.

'It is non-attachment to all that comes and goes.

'It is connection to all that is around and within.

'It is awareness of all that is.

'It is life without moments.

'It is Immutable Existence.

'The Principle of Being is seeing the wholeness in the smallest of the small.

'It is simultaneously seeing forwards, backwards and where you are without motion.

'It is hearing the music within the silence.

'It is the ability to walk everywhere, both within and without.

'In short,' she concluded, 'the Principle of Being is Flow.'

The stillness and quietude of the Lily shook me like a cataclysm. This sounded like an awful lot to learn! I looked down at the ground for several moments, feeling overwhelmed by my own insignificance. Without finding the courage to look up, and consumed by meekness, I finally replied to her.

'But beautiful teacher, how can I come to know all that you know?' I asked in a soft, sorrowful voice. 'My life is always starting and stopping. What do I know about flow? I am always in a rush. How can I possibly learn how to live a life without moments? I am so small. I cannot possibly ever be enough. How can I learn all of this?'

'Oh, but there is much you already know!' she said simply.

The straightforwardness of the Lily calmed me. Her directness made me sit up and become much more aware of my heart, which now stirred with the desire to taste the wisdom she seemed to believe I already possessed.

'Me? What could I possibly already know? Where have I learned it?' I asked.

The Lily sighed delightfully.

'Your Garden is so full of lovely Flowers,' she said. 'And you have already learned so much. Just take a leisurely walk and sit within your own Garden. Let it reveal to you what is already there. You know the way by now.'

She was right, of course. I had already learned the lessons from the Garden that the Rose, the Iris and the Daffodils had taught me. I knew everything I could possibly wish to learn was to be found within the Garden of my own Soul.

'Oh most compassionate Lily,' I asked, 'where in my Garden shall I look to find the Principle of Being?'

The Lily straightened up her powerful figure as if to say, 'There is nothing to fear' and, more serenely than ever, she said, *'Be confident, my forever friend—*

In all directions are your Guides
in fleeting moments far and wide.
The River and the endless Time
will show you all you wish to find.

I did not at all understand what the Lily meant, but I had by now learned that when Flowers speak, something miraculous is about to happen.

Then, the Lily went silent, and gently folded her petals, as if folded in prayer, to speak no more. As she folded them, the bright crimson dust from her centre fell like kumkum powder upon the earthen floor. The slender sliver of the winter Moon kissed this sacred spot and scattered the dust away into the night.

The next night, when I went to look for her, she was gone. Try as I might, I could not find the Lily. I stood on the exact centre of the Garden, but she was not there.

I returned to my bedroom and shut the window against the dead of winter.

That night, I dreamt the fragrant red dust from the Lily had spread to every corner of my Garden. As the winter frost melted, and the springtime broke forth from the earth, the honeybees came to worship this sacred dust, and kissed it gently with their hungry tongues.

Still dreaming, I heard again a familiar sweet song on a Full Moon night—but this time it was sung by, not one, but a choir of pearly voices. In my dream, I looked out from my window and saw a brilliant flash of white, like a galaxy of stars that had fallen from the heavens, gleaming in the shadows. Thousands upon thousands of Lilies twinkled in the moonlit night of my dream, as they sang directly to my soul. Their songs were so mystical I simply had to go outside to sit amidst their glorious hymns once again. For several hours I listened to their sweet singing, as our eyes exchanged affectionate glances. I learned their melodies, and soon we sang together the all-embracing and enlightened songs of the Lily—the songs of Being.

Then, something again called to me, saying, *Wake up!* and I awoke.

I sat upright and looked around the room. And as my eyes gradually adjusted to the coming of the early morning light, I could see and remember clearly many incidents in my life that had been full of the wonderful things about which the Lily had spoken. Just as I had learned from the other Flowers, I could indeed recall many incidents from my life that had been lessons from the Lily, but I hadn't recognised them as such.

I could see how years of comparison and measurement against the rest of the world had finally yielded to acceptance and non-attachment. I could see how timelessness and continuity were present in my life, even when others were dashing around in an endless feedback loop. I could see the underlying knowledge that everything simply 'is', even though it is also in a continual state of flux. I could recall time after time when stillness filled me and touched every part of me, even amidst a swirling sea of change.

It was all there—all that the Lily had described.

The Lily's teachings were indeed, just as she had said, all to be found within the Garden of my own Soul, within the simple stories of my own life. And as I reflected upon these stories, I understood more and more how the Principle of Being is sometimes as inaudible as a whisper, or as elusive as a phantom, but is ever omnipresent and unchanging. But mostly, I realised how the stories of my own life had taught me to find peace within the knowledge that all one needs to do in life, is simply be.

And so, I felt the desire to write some of these stories down within these pages...

*   *   *   *   *

MESSAGE ON THE BRIDGE

W here do we start the story of one's life?

My daughter is a grown woman now. She is herself a writer, and this is the very question she posed at the beginning of one of her own works. It's a good question, I think. Charles Dickens chose to begin the story of *David Copperfield* with the words, 'I am born.' That seems like a logical enough way to start the story of one's life. But what marks the point of one's birth? How many beginnings have we had within our present lifetime, and how many endings? Is life merely a starting and an ending point with a chronology of events in between, or is it a pattern woven into a fabric of personality that is intrinsic and eternal? When I think like this, I imagine an intricately woven tapestry. We might ask the question, 'Which one of these threads makes this design so beautiful?' But even though your eyes might be drawn to that pretty magenta strand that brightens up the dark midnight-coloured background of the tapestry of your life, the fact is that if you remove any one of these pathways of yarn, the whole fabric will unravel, the picture woven into it will disappear, and the tapestry will simply disintegrate. When I think like this, I ask myself, *How can we place greater meaning upon any single event over another in our lives?* If I do that, I am not seeing the whole picture. If I do that, it means I prefer some of the threads to the others. It means I am playing favourites with the stories of my life, and my life unravels and loses its integrity. The beauty of it vanishes into a mist of irrelevance.

But the impartial mind knows that each of the threads is equally beautiful. Each of them brings contrast and depth to the rest. Birth and death, pain and pleasure, joy and sorrow are all simply different ends of the same string, a gentle dance of shadows born from light. Tennyson once said, 'I am a part of all that I have met.'[5] Indeed, this is true. And there is no way to separate one part from the rest once they have crossed each other's paths. They become inextricably absorbed into one another, like paints that have been thoughtfully mixed together by the artist before being applied to the canvas.

All of it. That is what life is—all of it.

We are artefacts emanating from the mind of the Supreme.

We are each a masterpiece with a soul.

So where *do* I begin this story?

* * * * *

It is like a river of humanity, and I am swept up by its current.

It is nearly 7 PM on a Wednesday evening. I step onto the long passageway of the escalator exiting the London Underground in Victoria Station during the rush home from work. I, like so many thousands of other commuters going up the 'up' escalator, stare vacantly into the sea of faces of everyone who is coming down the 'down' escalator. 'But today is different,' I think to myself. 'Today is the day I will bump into someone I know.' Obsessively, I scan the crowd trying to find a face I recognise. I imagine I will see a friend coming down the 'down' escalator, and that I will call out to him or her. We will both be surprised and delighted that we have unexpectedly crossed paths. We try to make arrangements to meet, but we continue to move further and further away from each other. My imaginary conversation ends with me shouting out, 'I'll call you!' because, the fact is, the other person is going down whilst I am going up. Eventually, we can no longer see or hear each other. The destination of my friend lies in a different direction from mine. Our connection is fleeting and impermanent. I feel sad and lonely to see my friend go.

My reverie comes to an abrupt halt. I have reached the top of the escalator. I did not actually see a single familiar face amidst the thousands and thousands of people I passed on my journey today.

As I realise this, the feeling of loneliness is even more pronounced than it was in my fantasy.

I step off the escalator and continue walking onwards in the relentless flow of people now making their way to the ticket barriers.

*   *   *   *   *

When I first moved to London in September 1999, I was struck by three things.

Firstly, I was astounded by the amount of litter. I couldn't believe it when I saw people casually dropping candy wrappers, paper cups and cigarette packs onto the street and train platforms as if it were normal. Having just arrived from the States, I was not at all accustomed to this. People in the US didn't just drop litter as a matter of practice (I am old enough to remember the 'Keep America Beautiful' campaign against litter that started in the 1960s). This strange behaviour seemed completely incongruous with my memories of my visit to England in the early 1970s, and with my pre-conceived notions about the refined nature of the English culture. But then, someone pointed out to me that the reason people were dropping litter in the streets was because the Council had removed all the litterbins in the city earlier in the decade, in response to terrorist bombings during the days of the IRA. Every Londoner knew dustbins were the favoured drop points for time-delayed bombs. So dustbins suddenly became rare sights on the city streets and train stations. I found it interesting how a whole culture could change so quickly when someone comes into the space and threatens it.

That was nearly a decade ago. Since that time, the IRA have not made the headlines as frequently, and the managers of the British Rail stations came up with a solution to the platform litter in the form of clear plastic bin liners hanging from plastic rings. This way, it was thought, a would-be terrorist would not be able to stash a bomb without someone noticing. Of course, no one could have anticipated that a new wave of terrorists would emerge, this time from a different continent, and that they would circumvent this tactic by sitting on trains and busses with backpacks full of explosives strapped to their own bodies. For many months after the 2005 London suicide bombings, you could sense the nervousness on the London transport system, whenever someone carrying any sort of bag boarded the train, tube or bus. But human beings adapt to just about everything with time. For even though the nightly news sometimes would have us believe terrorism is more imminent than ever these days, many Londoners I see now seem almost blasé about it. But at least litter is no longer an issue.

The second thing I found quite remarkable when I first moved to London was the amount of people who smoked cigarettes. Again, in the US there had been many aggressive anti-smoking campaigns over the years, and many laws prohibiting smoking in public places. I knew hardly anyone in my generation who smoked, and very few of the younger people I knew in the US smoked either. When I first moved to Britain, it seemed as if smoking was the norm rather than the exception, and I had to get used to going into smoky environments, especially when first inaugurated into the UK pub culture. When I began teaching at the college, I found it very striking how freely and openly even 16-year-old students would smoke during breaks between classes, and how 'normal' it all seemed to them, compared to American kids who would still be hiding their cigarettes from parents and teachers at that age. Since that time, however, the government has implemented many anti-smoking strategies, including a ban on smoking in pubs and restaurants, and smoking doesn't seem to be nearly as prominent in the UK as it was a decade ago.

But the last thing that really struck me when I first moved to London was the graffiti.

Now, you might have thought I would have been used to it, because I originally came from New York and, as everyone knows, New York City has got to be the graffiti capital of the world. I mean, these days you can walk down Fifth Avenue and pay $3000 for a framed litho of Keith Haring's graffiti-turned-art. Furthermore, in 1999, I had just arrived from Phoenix, Arizona, and the Chicano gang culture there was rapidly transforming the walls and billboards in the south and central parts of the city into distinctly Latino graffiti canvases.

But London graffiti is a breed unto itself. It is not necessarily the most creative or even the most interesting—it is, however, the most overwhelmingly prolific I have ever seen. The sheer magnitude of the graffiti I saw on my first train journey into London Victoria completely astounded me. There was not a visible inch of wall along the rail line that was not tagged with one of hundreds of names like 'Panik' or 'Toxic' or 'Mime'. Hundreds and hundreds of names—so many that, try as I might to remember them, I cannot. And where there are hundreds of names, there must equally be hundreds of individuals somewhere in this vast, imposing city who selected these names as their own. In reading the types of names they selected for themselves, I cannot help but feel the overriding dysfunctional nature of the relationship between the authors and their modern environment.

These are not merely 'tags'—they are statements.

They are not merely statements—they are primal screams.

'I am Panik,' one author shouts. He is saying, 'Watch out! I am going to shake you up!'

'I am Toxic,' shouts another. He is saying, 'I am here and you'd better not mess with me.'

Another says, 'I am Mime. I have no voice in this impersonal world, so I am going to make you listen to me.'

Their names empower them—they who feel powerless. Their names allow them to rise above these feelings of powerlessness and to shout their discontent and frustration to the rest of society. But in some way, this could also be said of the terrorist. One party communicates with paint, the other with pipe bombs.

These days I live in East Anglia, and so, whenever I come into London on the train, I watch the names unfold as I ride through the north part of the city. These names have become as much a part of the urban landscape as the Tower Bridge or the

London Eye. I know I am getting near London when I see the names.

* * * * *

When I first moved to Bedford in June 2005, I was struck by three things.

The first was that there were lots of dustbins and the city was clean. No one here gave much thought to the threat of terrorist attacks.

The second was that even more 16-year-olds smoked than in London.

The third was that there was a noticeable lack of graffiti.

This is not to say Bedford is 100% graffiti-free. Nor does it mean you will not see any graffiti as your train pulls into the station. But still, compared to London, most walls are walls, not canvases.

You can imagine my surprise, then, when one day I was walking to work and saw some graffiti on the bridge.

* * * * *

Bedford is a pretty little town. I immediately wanted to live there when I was offered a job at the college. There, I did not need to make a 4-hour commute to work every day as I had in London. There, I could walk to work every day, sipping my coffee and taking time to clear my head before the day started, as I strolled along the banks of its beautiful river.

It is beyond question that the crowning glory of Bedford is the Great Ouse, the lovely river that winds its way across the town, dissecting it horizontally into north and south banks. During the Victorian era, the Embankment was constructed, and today this portion of the river is lined with rows of stately maple, horse chestnut and weeping willow trees, and embraced by elegant and colourful gardens, always meticulously groomed. Year-round, the river itself is always full of regal, white swans, along with flocks of grazing geese and families of mallards.

Almost daily, you will see small houseboats and canal barges sauntering lazily along its waters, or teams of rowers racing up and downstream. The Ouse is a well-loved river in Bedford, and at any given time, on any given day, townspeople of all ages linger along its banks, whether walking, bicycling, picnicking, jogging, or simply sitting on the grass or park benches, as they watch the river flow. At the beginning of every Christmas season, there is a spectacular pyrotechnical pageant on the Embankment, and every alternate summer, there is the River Festival, where tens of thousands of people come to enjoy the wonderful energy of the River Great Ouse. Over the years, I have come to cherish this ancient river like any other Bedfordian would, and I delight in seeing the seasons come and go, evolve and dissolve, both within its waters and upon its banks.

At either end of the Embankment there are two bridges for motorised traffic, with a long stretch of river in between them that cannot be crossed by car. Along this stretch, there are two pedestrian bridges. To the east is a modern bridge built in the late 20th century called the Butterfly Bridge. It is an interesting modern structure comprised of many white strands of cable, giving it the appearance of outspread wings, hence its name. When you walk on it, it tends to bounce a bit, and children love to jump up and down on it when they cross it. Further west is a much more formidable and much older Victorian footbridge, built in the 1880s, made of iron and painted in traditional 19th century fashion in white and green enamel. This very pretty structure is referred to as The Suspension Bridge, as it arches gently across the river, like a rainbow stretching from one bank to the other. When I used to work at the college, I would walk across this bridge on my way to work nearly every morning. I would often stop at its summit, to take in the view of the river in either direction. To the east, I could see the path of the river as it moved away from town towards the outlying villages. To the west, I could see the church steeple in the town centre poking its spire behind rows of treetops. Whenever I see this view I feel a strong sense of delight over the privilege of living in this sweet, little town, and being able to walk along the riverbank on a daily basis.

So of course, when this idyllic scene was disrupted one early October morning by the sight of graffiti on this bridge, it seemed incongruous, if not irritating.

It was just another daily walk to work. I was crossing the bridge from the north bank, and as I neared the summit, I noticed there was something scrawled across the black asphalt pavement. It was poorly scribbled in black spray paint. It had only two words, written in block capital letters. It read:

'I AM'

My initial reaction was anger.

I heard myself thinking something to the effect of, *Damn! I can't believe some jerk wrote on this lovely bridge. What purpose does that serve? What's the matter with people these days? Don't they have any sense of pride?*

Looking back on it, I suppose you could say I reacted with the typical social outrage you would expect of the average middle-aged person who sees graffiti in a public place. My thoughts were almost an obligatory blitz of disapproval that someone of my generation 'must' express against the modern world, so as to assure yourself you are a 'good', law-abiding citizen. It was almost as if this kind of muttered disapproval had the power in and of itself to help keep society from falling to pieces. I had become the voice of morality.

The next day, I went to cross the bridge again as usual. It had rained the night before, and as I neared the summit, I found myself curious to know whether the graffiti had been washed away from the rain.

After all, I thought to myself, *that graffiti was rather 'unprofessional'. It's nothing like the 'serious' London graffiti. Whoever wrote it probably used cheap paint.*

But the rain had not washed it away and the message on the bridge was still there. I felt myself becoming increasingly critical.

Ha! He calls himself a graffiti artist? I said to myself. *What's the point of this graffiti? It isn't even written at the highest point of the bridge. Why bother to do graffiti if you can't even paint it on the right place?*

The next day, when I crossed the bridge, I noticed the lettering was not in the centre of the walkway.

Look at that, I thought. *The words are not even centred. It looks lopsided. It really irritates me that people show such a lack of care. He wants to be an artist? Why can't he do it right?*

As days went by, I saw this tenacious graffiti again and again. And every day, I found something else to criticise about its lack of artistic merit.

The words are just scribbled on the pavement... there is no artistic skill in the script itself... there are no outlines to the letters... there is no crispness or definition to it... the words are just a semi-black blur.

After couple of weeks had gone by, I found myself criticising the paint the author had chosen to use.

Not exactly an effective statement! I thought. *You can hardly see the black paint against the black asphalt. What's the point of graffiti if it's so hard to read? I think the fact that this paint has lasted this long is sheer luck. I really wonder how much longer this rough, non-descript scribble is going to last. Gee, if you are going to bother being a graffiti artist at all, why don't you use something more permanent?*

Then, after a full month of walking across this graffiti every day, I finally found myself asking the questions that simply had to be asked—

What the heck is this person trying to say anyway?
What does he mean, 'I AM'?

It was a mystery.

The next day, as I crossed the bridge, I repeated the words to myself—'I AM.'

I am...I am what? I asked myself.

I stopped dead in my tracks.

I AM, I repeated to myself.

I am—something? Then what?

I am—someone? Then who?

Can I quantify what I am?

Wait a minute... do I need to? I asked myself.

I laughed to myself when I said this.

How ironic, I thought. *How many times have I said how much it bugs me that everybody is always measuring themselves against someone or something else? I've always said I hate that kind of thinking. I am a student, I am a teacher, I am a musician, I am a woman, I am a wife, I am divorced, I am young, I am old, I am a mother, I am a daughter, I make X amount of money a year, I am this tall, I weigh this much, blah, blah, blah...All these different 'I AM's', and not one of them tells us who we really are. It's the very thing that drove me nuts in the music world, at the temple, everywhere...*

I wonder what this graffiti person was thinking...

*   *   *   *   *

The month of November had brought some chilly, damp weather. One morning, as a gentle rain fell from a pale, grey sky, I walked to work as usual, listening to the light pattering of the raindrops against my umbrella. As I approached the bridge, the enigmatic words 'I AM' flooded my mind. I started to cross the bridge and noticed that the black asphalt footway was darker than usual because of the rainfall. When I reached the top of the bridge, I paused and gazed westwards to admire the misty English landscape for a few minutes, and to contemplate the words I had now begun to think about on a daily basis.

Look at this, I thought. *How fragile and frightened people are. How much they cover it up with immeasurably complex measurements. They measure themselves by their families, their religion, their points of view. In the half a century I have walked upon this planet, all of these things have changed in my own life, as they do in anyone's life. My grandparents and parents are all gone. My child is grown up and has a child of her own. I have had several partners, but am with none at present. My religion has changed many times over the years, and right now I have no formal religious practice. My occupation and interests have changed even more frequently. I have changed my perspective of the world seamlessly and continuously from childhood to youth to adolescence to adulthood to middle-age—and nothing seems to indicate that such fluidity of change will ever stop. But still here I am.*

I cast my gaze downwards towards my feet, and looked at the poorly scribbled words that had been written by some unknown person nearly two months before. The slightly faded black letters were hardly discernible against the dark, wet asphalt.

I AM? I thought.

Yes, just 'I am'—that's all. That is the sum of it. It is like walking along the river and seeing the water flow. The river is changing from moment to moment, but there is still only one river.

*　*　*　*　*

Autumn merged into winter. Each morning, the sun came up later and later, and some mornings it was still slightly dark when I started for work. The days were cold now, and I walked to work quite briskly most days. But one morning not long before Christmas, I came to the bridge and decided to stand at the summit for just a little while, just as the sun was starting to creep over the horizon. I looked towards the awakening town, its streetlights still illuminated, and noticed the bare-armed branches of the chestnut and maple trees that lined the Embankment. Their tall, twisted and sinewy forms, just barely lit by the emerging sun, appeared like black silhouettes against the richness of the indigo December sky.

I began to reflect upon the coming season. Winter is a time of taking account of all that has come before. It is a time for examining things as they really are. It is not the time for passionate drive and growth, but for peaceful renewal and regeneration. Winter is the only time we can see the actual form of the trees, as they are devoid of foliage. They have passed their season for growth and activity, and over the autumn months have been letting go of all they had produced throughout the steamy days of summer. What purpose would it serve if the trees were to decide to cling to their leaves or their fruits past their season? They would only rot upon their branches and cause them to utilise all of their energy to maintain them in a season inhospitable to their sustenance. Instead, wisely, the trees allow these fruits and leaves to drop away, with no more fuss than a slight pop as they fall to the ground. In the autumn of their lives, the products of their passions are just as lovely when they become a golden and russet carpet upon the forest floor, as they once were when they served as a canopy of green sheltering us from the blazing sun.

Now, in the winter of their lives, the trees let it all fly graciously away in the frosty winds, and thus all that is left is their true, naked selves, rather than the products of their actions. If the trees were not so unattached, there could be no regeneration, and no revelation of their true form. We might look at such a tree and think it is old and black and gnarled and twisted, but who amongst us, when gazing upon that bareness, cannot see the true beauty and elegance, the true strength and splendour of the trees? None of us would ever call such a tree 'ugly.'

But we humans seldom reach this level of self-acceptance. Far too many of us seem incapable of acknowledging the self-beauty that lies within our raw form—the form of our 'being-ness'. Rather, we foolishly choose to see value only within the fruits of our own summertime—our status, our money, our youth, our physical beauty—in spite of the fact that these fruits are destined to blow away in the winds of time, just like the leaves of the mighty chestnut trees.

In their bare nakedness, the trees are saying, 'I AM', I thought, as I stood on the bridge.

I pondered my own 'am-ness.' Exactly how aware of it was I?

How much do I really have a sense of myself? Here I am walking to work every day. Why? Is it just to earn a living and pay the bills? Why do I work so hard at my job? Is it because I need to 'measure up' to something—to be 'something'? I worked hard to get to here. But what exactly is 'here'? Is 'here' the label I currently call myself? If so, which label is it? Is it my job title, my education or my marital status? These have changed so many times over the years. And how many dozens of other labels have I had? By how many different names have I been introduced? How many jobs, how many friends, how many places of residence, how many colleges, religious practices, musical groups...

How many times have I worked hard for one of these labels, only to turn direction and work just as hard to seize yet another? Why? Do I feel a need for all these labels at some level? Or am I totally incapable of thinking of myself without these labels? How much do I really know who I am?

I found myself becoming increasingly philosophical.

Well, if Truth is true, it must be true at all times and in all places, I thought. *If it is true some of the time, and in only some places, it cannot be Truth. Not real Truth. All of those things we measure ourselves against cannot be the real Truth, because they come and go with time. They change at every moment. The only thing that stays the same, the only thing that is really true, is the statement, 'I AM'.*

The message on the bridge had me firmly within its grip.

So now the question is—who am I without anyone or anything else?

*   *   *   *   *

Spring was coming.

I continued to cross the bridge every morning. But now, being so familiar with the route, I found the need to look at other things. So, I began to watch the other people who routinely crossed the bridge at the same time of day. To my surprise, I noticed no one else seemed to pay any attention whatsoever to the graffiti scribbled on the pathway. People simply stepped over the words or sometimes even directly on top of them, without ever bothering to look down and read them. With time, I too began to notice them less and less, and sometimes I walked right by them, forgetting to look at them, and only realising this when I had reached the other side of the bridge. And in spite of my occasional cerebral musings, most of the time my primary thought was simply that I must get to work on time. And once I had arrived at my workplace, the message on the bridge faded almost completely from my memory, much as the words themselves were beginning to fade day by day on the black asphalt surface of the bridge.

If people could become blasé about terrorists, it seemed an easy thing to imagine I would eventually become just as blasé about a few scribbled letters on a footbridge. Still, the idea disturbed me.

Are we all simply walking around like zombies, without questioning what life is all about? I wondered. *Do any of us know who we actually are? Are we all wondering whether anyone else knows who we are? Does anyone bother thinking about what is going on around them?*

Or is everybody thinking about these things, but just not speaking about them? Is every single person who crosses that bridge reading the words of the graffiti, thinking about them, but not daring to say anything about them? Is this lone, unknown graffiti artist who scribbled a message on a footbridge in Bedford the only person bold enough to speak out loud and make a statement that no one else dares to express?

*　*　*　*　*

The ides of March had now passed, and a sea of multicoloured tulips was just beginning to burst into a spectacle of colour in the flowerbeds that lined the Embankment. One day, I walked to the top of the bridge and paused for a few moments, just a few inches from the now familiar and quite faded words.

Breathing in the spring, I could sense a change stirring within me. It was time for a new beginning, a new perspective.

Today I stand here watching the River Great Ouse as it flows towards the east. Tomorrow, I might turn and look to the west.

Today I am looking at what is now my home. But this was not my home so very long ago.

Today, I am standing here reflecting upon words written a few months ago. Tomorrow they may disappear.

These words were written by someone I do not know. In all probability, I will never meet this person.

All of this is present.

And at every moment, all of this is changing.

How can I ever touch this moment? How can I ever know it?

But changing or not—it is still the same river.

And changing or not—I am still this person I call myself.

For years I have hunted for Truth, trying to find that which is true at all times and in all places. And now, in this moment, I see Truth everywhere I look. Truth is that which does not change with time. It is that which stays when the seasons change. It is that which is seen when all the leaves of summer are blown to the four winds, and all that remains are the bare bones of our essence. It is that which remains year in and year out, and speaks aloud the only two words that never change with time and place—

'I AM'

I am—and that is enough.

*   *   *   *   *

By April I had come to look forward to seeing the graffiti on the bridge as if it were an old friend. I found myself theorising that it was probably written by a young person, and perhaps even someone who, in society's eyes, was less 'well off' than many other youngsters. I marvelled at the idea that someone so young and vulnerable could have written such a wise and powerful message that spoke directly to my own heart, and had impacted me so profoundly.

By May, I had learned to delight in the naïve lopsidedness of the words, and the fact that they were so devoid of 'art'. I had developed a quiet affection for their clumsiness, much as you would feel when watching a baby stumbling as it takes its first steps. I had come to love its uplifting statement, which to me seemed completely opposite in intent to the aggressive, albeit much slicker, more skilful and more colourful, postings of the urban 'taggers' of London.

And then, one day in June, when I crossed the bridge, the message was gone.

It hadn't simply faded away. It had disappeared completely overnight. I looked around the Embankment and saw many workers from the Council tending the grounds. No doubt someone had reported the graffiti and the Council had cleaned it up. A very thorough job, too. I could see no trace of the words at all. It was as if they had never been there.

In a passing thought, I mused with some sarcasm, *So does that mean the message is now, 'I WAS'?* and laughed slightly to myself.

But no, the message hadn't changed. The words were still inside me and I carried them within me. It didn't matter whether they were visible on the bridge or not.

And this is also true of people, I thought.

My grandparents and my parents are all dead. They have left my line of earthly vision. But still I cannot say they 'were'. I see them every day when I look in the mirror. I hear them in my own voice whenever I speak. They 'are'.

My daughter is a grown-up woman with a child of her own. My grandson will know my parents and grandparents every time he talks to me. And they will know him as well, every time I talk to him.

And while I will probably never meet the author of the message on the bridge, I will always know him (or her).

And now, all who read these words, typed upon my laptop, will also come to know the author of the message on the bridge.

Things appear to change from moment to moment, but there is still only one river.

* * * * *

The following autumn, I still walked to work every day. But things had changed. I had a new boss and my once 'new' job didn't have the same appeal as it had had nearly two years before. The little things I didn't like, but I had tolerated when I first took the job, now seemed to consume my every waking moment, and my sleep as well. Desperately, I wanted to find that 'am-ness' I had once found in my morning meditations. Almost compulsively, whenever I neared the top of the bridge, I looked for any trace of the words that once had been there, but I could find none. I missed seeing those words.

Throughout the winter, I continued to walk to work mechanically, like a robot, five days a week. Every time I crossed the bridge, I felt an ever-increasing sense of emptiness, as though my own 'is-ness' were flowing further and further downstream and away from me through the white water rapids of Time. I could not find myself. Work was no longer satisfying. I found no pleasure or delight in anything I was doing. I wasn't sure of the 'I AM' at all anymore. I kept asking *Who am I?* but I couldn't find the answer.

Then one day, on an otherwise completely insignificant Tuesday afternoon in the month of February, I sent an email to my boss that ended with a single word—

'WHY?'

I turned off my computer at the uncharacteristically early hour of 4 PM, and simply walked out the door of my office. I didn't know at the time that I was never to return.

* * * * *

Shaking from acute stress, I went to the doctor, crying uncontrollably. He told me that clearly, I needed a holiday, and told me to go away somewhere remote for a while where no one could contact me. That suited me just fine.

So, I escaped for a few days to Lyme Regis in Dorset in the southwest of England to 'find myself', once again. It was a very cold, wet week. I stayed in a friendly but somewhat frumpy little B&B that was on a tiny lane near the sea. I woke each morning to the plaintive sound of seagulls, and spent my days indulging in Dorset cream teas and walking along the beach and the Southwest Coastal Trail. One morning I went on a fossil hunt to find ammonites. Ammonite fossils are quite prolific in that part of England, hence the name 'Jurassic Coast' by which it is commonly referred. I remember the feeling of awe I felt when I first held one of the 200-million-year-old fossils in my hand. The knowledge that I was holding the remains of a creature that had lived so long ago was something I could hardly fathom. What was the likelihood it would fall into my hands on a random walk along the beach in the 21st century? There are some spectacular displays of ammonites along the beach in Lyme; the remains of some of them, in a place called 'The Ammonite Graveyard', are several feet in diameter. As I stood amongst this fossil cemetery, surrounded by the remains of living entities so mysterious they felt like aliens from another planet to me, I found myself wishing I could ask them, *Who are you?* I wondered what they could tell me had they been able to speak.

At night, I read and wrote in my journal. I went out to dinner every evening at a restaurant down the street. I was feeling rather listless on my own. I wasn't sure what I was going to do when I returned home to Bedford.

One day, feeling somewhat down in the dumps from all of this (the constant rain didn't help), I walked alone along the river walk to the point where the River Lym flows into the sea. At this point, there are fortress-like stone walls protecting the town from the tide, and you will find a massive anchor and a row of obsolete cannons that nowadays serve no purpose other than to entertain the tourists. Wandering a bit aimlessly, in somewhat of a self-indulgent funk, I eventually came to the end of the fortress. Having nowhere to go from this point but down, I took some steps to the lower landing. When I got there, I looked upon the ground of the small walkway that stretched from where I stood across a small sea inlet.

To my surprise, I again saw some graffiti—again scribbled in plain black letters. As I had learned to pay attention to random graffiti, I decided to find out what kind of message the universe was sending me that day.

I couldn't help but laugh out loud at my own mental weightiness when reading the words of yet another anonymous author, who was delivering a new cosmic message, as if from beyond.

It read:

'GRAVITY CAN'T GET YOU HIGH.'

Ok, I thought, *time to lighten up!*

* * * * *

Blue, blue, blue—
That was the colour of the sky that stunning morning in May. Bluer than blue could be, with breathless little cotton puffs of clouds dotting it, as if placed there simply for the sake of looking beautiful. The weather was perfect—neither too hot nor too cold. So I grabbed my journal and decided to go sit along the south bank of the River Great Ouse—perhaps to write, definitely to watch, and hopefully just to be.

As I sat, I could see about 30 black-headed geese grazing intently on the lawn only a few paces from me. As they grazed, they honked at each other intermittently. I could hear high-pitched calls responded to with low-pitched grunts. It was a pretty funny-sounding chorus, and geese are pretty funny creatures. Sort of comical, really. They get so intent when they graze. They're always a bit frantic, or at least that's how it seems to me. They yank up grass almost non-stop, as if trying to shove as much into their gut as possible, as fast as possible. They remind me of people playing 'Supermarket Sweep'—that TV show where, in order to win the game, you have to fill up your basket with the most groceries. But in the case of the geese, the 'shopping' cart they are trying to fill up is their big belly, as they get fatter and fatter. They eat the grass so fast I don't know how they even have time to chew (hmm...do geese chew?) or swallow the grass. It's more like they inhale it.

Eat, eat, eat. Eating machines, really, these geese. From my park bench, I could actually hear the crunching sound of the grass being wrenched from the earth and munched by this gaggle of geese. It's quite a sound. They were like an army of grazers and no one was going to stop them. And if anyone does get in their way, they'd better watch out! I've seen many a gander take a pretty nasty nip at a passing dog, if he deemed the dog was getting too close and too curious for comfort. The geese even turn on each other every now and then when competing for the same patch of grass. More than once I saw one goose nip at another's tail, as if saying, 'Get off my turf. I'm eating here. Scram, Goosy!' Then the other goose (whose feathers got nipped) would jump and waddle off quickly to another patch of grass and continue to pull up the soft green shoots, as if nothing had happened.

Watching all this brought many questions to my mind. As geese seem to do everything in groups, I found myself wondering how they know when it is time to stop eating. Who gets to decide? Do they wait until the biggest, fattest goose is satisfied and they all stop eating at once? What happens to the poor skinny goose who hasn't yet had enough to eat?

I told myself to stop asking all these questions about geese, and I returned to allowing myself just to sit and watch life around me.

Beyond the geese lay the river, the lifeblood of all activity in this place. The level of the river was still quite high that morning, after nearly a solid week of rain. But it was no longer bulging or brown as it had been during the recent storms. The silt had now settled down into the riverbed, and the surface of the water was shimmering in the sunlight. The aftermath of the rain was drifting downstream in the form of a small floating island of debris that had fallen from a tree from some point unknown. I watched as two green-headed mallards hitched a ride on top of it, pecking at it to find something tasty to eat. This activity caught the attention of a few of the swans, who came over to investigate. But the debris continued to float, drifting more and more downstream, passing under and past the old Victorian bridge, pulled by the current of the ever-moving river. The swans lost interest in it, as they had no desire to follow the course of this raft of branches and leaves and plastic carrier bags that had gotten caught on it. Soon, the ducks lost interest too. The mallards hopped off the floating island and the swans continued their placid journey upstream, unconcerned. I watched the floating island drift out of my line of vision and took note of the eastward flow of the River Ouse. I found myself wondering what the river looked like further downstream. The ducks had jumped off the floating island, but my mind continued to drift along with it, for several moments after it was out of my sight.

My attention returned to the present moment as I noticed that upon the river, in all directions, were dozens of the signatory white swans of Bedfordshire. I have always been in awe of these creatures. I watched them as they glided effortlessly along the current, following the natural flow of the river. I found myself even more fascinated by how equally effortless their motions were when they wished to swim upstream against the current. The swans simply fluffed out their large, white parachute-like wings to catch the wind, using them like the sails of a boat, and flopping their webbed feet like the rudders of the boat to steer them this way and that. Like this, they were able to sail easily and rapidly wherever they wished to go, seemingly without any effort whatsoever. It was a wonderful sight to watch. They seemed so peaceful, confident and poised. They also seemed like they were having fun out there. It was apparent to me that the swans had learned the trick of the path of least resistance in life. Their happiness was not the result of hard work like the geese. They had learned how to use the energy of everything available to them in any given moment—the flow of the water, the wind, and the wonderful resources of their own bodies. For them, swimming upstream was easy because they were always working with what the universe was giving them, instead of fighting against it.

All this made me think back to my days in India, where I had met so many elderly sages who were considered enlightened souls. In India, such a person is called a *paramahamsa*—a great swan. Back then, I was never really clear on why this word was used to describe the enlightened soul. I had always assumed it had to do with the purity and elegance and beauty of the swan. And while this is undoubtedly part of the reason, looking at the swans that day helped me to understand more about what enlightenment actually is, and I began to realise that true *paramahamsas* are those rare people who are always poised and full of happiness because they know how to utilise all that the universe provides them—just like the swans. Life is effortless for them because they know how to flow with grace and ease no matter what the current.

I found the swans' movements an appropriate metaphor for how I felt that day in late May. For the first time in my life, I was allowing the universe to carry me along, and I was moving rapidly through life without the struggle I had felt for more than half a century. I could feel a clarity of Being emerging within my heart and mind. All I needed to do now was watch and listen to what the universe was saying.

And, in that moment, what I felt the universe was telling me was to invite others into this wonderful, exceptional, natural moment in time and space. So I took out my mobile phone (not a very 'natural' thing to do, in this 'natural moment') and sent a text message to every person I knew in Bedford. It said:

'To all my Bedfordian friends—
The weather is FANTASTIC 2day.

Hope u r getting outside and basking in it.'

I went through my mobile's address book and sent this to at least 20 people. Within a minute, one woman texted me back and said,

'I wish!'

Well, at least she was honest.

One other person immediately called me to say 'hi' and that he was indeed going out into the beautiful day. He invited me to meet up with him and his wife later that evening. That was nice.

But of the 18 other people, not one replied.

I found this to be pretty unbelievable.

I started to make up all kinds of reasons why I received no replies. I started to imagine all of them hunkered down in their offices. I imagined them reading the text and scowling at it, inwardly criticising me for sitting out here by the river at 10:30 AM on a 'work day'. I imagined them with their heads hunkered down with pinpointed focus, just like the geese grazing on the lawn. Work, work, work. Working machines, really, these people. *Who does she think she is? She should be working!* they were probably thinking.

But the fact is, I was working. I was writing the story you are now reading. I write. That *is* my work (well, part of it anyway). I have chosen this path. So, I was actually at my job—in my office, so to speak. For so many years I had drifted along the current of my life, and ignored my real vocation. Now, in choosing the life of a writer, it was part of my job to be there on the river that day, tapping into all that inspiration. How else could I write?

We choose our work, but many people forget that. We imagine we have no choice to choose otherwise. But really we have chosen. When we have chosen to be 'choiceless', we tend to rationalise and defend our choicelessness by saying that working day in and day out at a job that does not make us happy is the 'right' and 'normal' and 'responsible' thing to do.

We persist at it for years, always unfulfilled, but insist there is no other way. Then, if we live long enough, we get to retire.

Never again, I think to myself.

It's just like being a goose, I thought. *Work, work, work, until the biggest, fattest goose tells them they can stop. Then they can go on holiday or retire. How many people do I know who postpone their own happiness for most of their lives, thinking holidays and retirement will finally allow them to enjoy the fruits of their labour? Why has everyone accepted such a post-dated cheque for happiness? What happens if they die before they ever reach that point? What's the point of living like a goose?*

Somewhat disgruntled, I tossed my mobile phone back into my handbag, convinced I was not going to receive any more responses to my text. My mind continued to muse over all the different ways I could compare human beings to water fowl.

I started thinking about the ducks. When the floating island of branches, leaves and rubbish was drifting downstream, the ducks were concerned with it at first, but then they let it go, knowing that if they stayed with it, it would take them far from their homes. They knew it was not in their best interest to stay with the floating island, even if it was full of wonderful things to eat. Staying close to home was more important to them. They could always find something else to eat near home. Then, they jumped off and swam upstream, against the flow of the river. That was their choice. Swimming upstream was actually better than allowing the current to take them off course. The ducks took the action they felt would serve them best.

But in my experience, we humans are not always so logical. I see it all the time. We hop onto a floating island drifting in a direction that will take us way off course from ourselves. But unlike the ducks, we sometimes will stay on this island of debris, and allow it to take us so far downstream that the journey back to ourselves seems too difficult even to consider. That's when we find ourselves in the wrong life. That's when the 'I AM' seems so far away from us, that we cannot get a sense of who we actually are. Not being able to come into contact with our own essence, we become engrossed in the debris itself—all the 'stuff' that comes in and out of our lives through the natural flow of time and circumstance. What is this 'stuff'? It's all the things we say we 'have to do' in order to be 'right' or 'responsible' or 'normal' in the world. We become so dependent upon the stuff that we completely lose sight of the reality of who we are. We have come to accept this debris as our reality, as we passively allow it to take us wherever it will take us—farther and farther away from our true selves.

But in reality, the debris is useless.

I only know all this because that is how I used to live. So many times throughout my life, I had hopped onboard one 'floating island' or another, looking for the answers to my life. I had left my parents' home, hoping to find salvation in music in Boston. When that didn't work, I sought to find myself through studies, travel, relationships and still more music. Over the decades, I continued to seek to find myself through my marriage, through motherhood, through religion, through my teaching, through more and more musical endeavours, and finally through climbing the ladder of 'success' in the professional world of education. But while all of these things taught me and gave me so many precious things, things without which I would never have reached this point, and things for which I am forever grateful, the ultimate Truth finally hit me when I read the words 'I AM' on the bridge:

Hello? Are you listening?
If you want to 'find yourself',
stop looking outside yourself for the answers.
Thank you!

It was then that I simply stopped everything I was doing. Everything. I suppose you might say I hit a 'mid-life crisis'. But that's not really what it was. I believe it was 'a calling'. The message on the bridge had called me to stop pretending to be happy, and to go and get happiness, once and for all. Instead of continuing to work so hard to climb the ladder of success with no happiness to show for it, I simply walked away from my career. Instead of living life by rules that did not bring me happiness, I let go of all my outdated fears and beliefs, and embraced uncertainty with zeal.

I heard the call and had finally responded. And when we respond to the call, the universe has a tendency to send us messengers to guide us along the way. About a week after I walked out on my job, a woman I had met at a bus stop said to me, 'You ought to be a counsellor. You are so easy to talk to.' I didn't think I wanted to be a counsellor, but sensing this was yet another one of those cryptic messages from the universe I seemed to be getting lately, I thought I'd look into it. I bought a few books on counselling from the bookstore and took them home. I opened the first one and on the first page the author spoke about emerging fields of 'talking therapies' and mentioned the term 'life coaching'. I had only vaguely heard about coaching, and decided to look it up on the Internet. When I read what it was, I instantly recognised 'me' in the description. I put the counselling books away on my bookshelf, never to read them. Instead, I located a coaching training organisation that attracted me and signed up for a short introductory course in London.

When I went to take the course, the very first question they asked us was, 'What is your dream?' I still remember how I answered the question. I said, 'My dream is to finally live a life where my inner world and my outer world match up!' The person I was speaking with said to me, 'Well, it sounds like your dream is a spiritual one.' I said, 'Yes! Yes! That's right. My dream is spiritual. I am here to find out who I am, and why I was put on this Earth. That's why I came here today.'

By the end of the weekend, I heard myself saying I would not be going back to the office. At the time, I thought that was just an offhand comment, but the truth is, I didn't go back. I continued my training and embarked on a whole new career at the age of 52. The woman on the bus became my first client. My life was transformed. I had, after more than half a century, finally aligned my outer and inner worlds. I was, and still am, blissfully happy. I still find it hard to believe.

Instead of staying on the floating island of debris, I had begun to swim within the cooling river of my own life. It is the river that contains our sustenance, not the debris. It is from life that we will find life, not from dead, disconnected matter. It is in life that we will find meaning and become aware of what it means to be alive.

When I sent my text message, every person had the choice to take a moment to enjoy this wonderful day—or not. They had the choice to live within the world, or to live outside of it looking in. Instead of choosing to step into the world, we might choose to stay outside, and say longingly, 'I wish!' Or perhaps we don't even get that far. Perhaps we say, with some irritation, if not also a hint of enviousness, 'Who do you think you are to be out there? Get back indoors.'

I had chosen to enjoy that wonderful day.

Hmm. Ducks are pretty smart, I thought to myself.

*   *   *   *   *

After spending the better part of an hour writing those words, I shut my journal and decided it was time to make a move to get some errands done. I got up from my seat on the park bench and started walking along the winding pathways that weave along the riverbank. The beautiful day was still captivating my thoughts and awareness, and I found myself smiling, breathing and nearly singing. My heart became full with joy at that moment, and I thought it such a pity that I could not bring one of my friends, or at least someone else— anyone else—into this scene with me, so we may enjoy it together.

As I headed for a small wooden footbridge that leads to the other side of town, I took a fork on the path and saw a man, who seemed to be in his mid-forties, sitting on another park bench. He had his arm draped over the back of the bench and there was a bicycle standing a few feet from him. The man was dressed in jeans and a simple white vest. He was doing nothing except looking out silently at the river.

'The weather is fantastic today!' I said to him as I passed by.

The man looked at me and smiled politely. 'Yeah, it's about time we had a nice day.'

I stopped walking. I had just been wishing I could share this day with another human soul, and here he was. We started talking about the heavy rains of the past week and how nice it was to be able to sit outside after a week indoors. At first it was just your typical polite 'Let's talk about the weather' conversation at which the British are so adept. But then I started to sense there was something that lay beneath this man's words that willed me to stay and speak with him, and not just dash off to do my shopping. He started to talk about being bored, about how life was always the same day in and day out.

He said, 'I feel like a robot.'

'What a coincidence,' I said. 'That's just what I said only a few months ago.'

As we were now involved in a conversation, I introduced myself to the man and asked him his name. For this story, I'll call him Pete.

I asked Pete what he meant when he said, 'I feel like a robot.'

Pete told me the only reason why he was out in the park that day was because he had 'nothing to do'. He said he was out of work and had been so for many months. He told me a little bit about his past jobs, and a bit about the circumstances that had led to his unemployment.

'And now I've got nothing to do all day,' he said.

Pete then asked me what I did for a living. I told him I was a life coach. I had only started my new career a few months earlier, and I proudly handed him one of my shiny new business cards. Pete had never heard of life coaching, and he asked me what a life coach did. Being a new coach, I fumbled a bit as I attempted to tell him a little bit about it, but I knew the best way for him to understand what I did was to 'be' a coach. I also got the feeling Pete was looking for something, asking for something.

'So how are you like a robot, then?' I asked him.

At first, Pete seemed to struggle to find the right words to explain what he meant. But then, he said, 'I feel like a robot because I do the same thing every day. I get up, I go down to the betting shop to put a couple of quid on the horses, and then go home to watch daytime TV. I eat dinner and go to bed. The next day, it's the same thing all over again. I keep trying to think of something else to do, but that's all there IS to do. That's why I feel like a robot.'

'So, do you mean it feels like you are just like a machine—doing things mechanically without any feeling? Without any choice?' I asked.

'Yes. That's it,' he said. 'That's exactly what I mean. I've got no choice. I'm completely stuck. There's nothing else I can do, but get up, go to the betting shop and watch TV. I wish I could do something different.'

'You came out here today, didn't you?' I replied.

'Yeah, but that's nothing,' he said.

'Did you do it yesterday?' I asked.

'No,' he said, 'yesterday it was raining in buckets.'

'Yes, but you could have come out into the rain, and you chose not to,' I said teasingly.

'Yeah, I'da got soaked,' he replied.

'So you did have a choice,' I said.

'Hmm...I guess,' said Pete, a little hesitantly.

'And today you chose to come out to the river,' I said.

'Yeah. Nice weather today,' he concurred.

'And I see you chose to ride your bike here today,' I said.

'Yes,' Pete said, looking over at his bicycle. 'It's a good little bike, that.'

'It's a nice bike. It must be nice to ride. The point is, you could have chosen to walk to the river today, but you didn't,' I said.

'Yes, that's true. I kinda see what you mean,' Pete said, doubtfully.

'But,' he added, 'all that stuff—it ain't nothin'. I mean, it's not 'something'. Not *really*...is it? I mean, you say I'm choosing, but the stuff I'm choosing isn't really anything?'

'What do you think?' I asked him.

'No, what do *you* think?' he asked back, his grin just wide enough that I could see he had several teeth missing on either side of his mouth.

I smiled back at him. 'Ok, since you asked, here's what I think. You have a choice. And you've been choosing all along. You chose to come out today, you chose to ride your bike, you chose to come to this river and to sit on this bench. And then, you chose to talk to me.'

'But, that doesn't count. You came up and talked to me first,' Pete said.

'Of course it counts!' I said waving my hands emphatically in the air. 'Do you know how many people I said 'hello' to in the park this morning? You are the only one who actually 'chose' to talk back to me!'

'Really?' he asked. 'I'm the only one?' And he looked around at the other people in the park.

'You may think what you are doing is nothing,' I said, 'but it's something. It's something to me. It's something you chose to do. Other people aren't choosing to do it. So, it's got to be something if others aren't choosing it.'

Pete laughed and looked at me a bit quizzically. At least this conversation was definitely something different, something he hadn't heard the day before, or the day before that. At least he wasn't being a robot right now.

'Go on. Tell me more,' he said.

'Ok,' I continued. 'Do you see that bench over there by the river? Well, about an hour ago, I was sitting on that bench thinking, *What a fantastic day!* So, do you know what I did? I took out my mobile phone and I texted at least 20 people I know in Bedford telling them I hoped they were outdoors today enjoying this incredibly beautiful day.'

'Yeah?' Pete said. 'So what happened?'

'So what happened is—nothing!'

Pete laughed.

'What do you mean 'nothing'?' he asked.

'I mean nobody even replied. Well, actually one person did call, and he was enjoying himself outdoors. He invited me to a gig tonight.'

'That's cool,' Pete said.

'Then another person just texted the words "I wish!"'

Pete laughed again.

'But not one other person replied, not even to say "Hello". Imagine. Eighteen other people and not one reply. It was amazing.'

Pete thought for a moment without saying anything.

'So, what does that make you think?' I asked him.

Pete raised his eyebrows. 'Well, I don't know what it makes me think. What does it make YOU think?'

'It makes me think they are all trapped in their offices and jealous of you and me!' I said.

Pete really laughed now, his half-toothless grin even more apparent.

Then, with a tinge of disbelief mixed with wistful imaginings, Pete asked timidly, 'Do you really think they are jealous of you and me?'

'Of course they're jealous of you and me,' I said, waving my arms now, and not just my hands. 'Look at the wonderful conversation we are having in this fabulous weather. What a gorgeous day we are enjoying. And all those people have chosen to stay indoors under fluorescent lights, staring at their computer screens. They may not even choose to come outside for lunch. Who wouldn't want to be us right now?'

'Yeah,' Pete said, taking a moment to look out across the river. 'Yeah, who wouldn't want to be us right now?'

But then, after a moment, he shook his head, rejecting the idea.

'No. That's not true,' he disagreed. 'I'm not here by choice. I'm out of work. I've got nothin' else to do. It's different for a person like you.'

'What do you mean 'it's different for a person like me'?' I asked. 'How is it different? How am I different?'

'Well, I mean, you've got all sorts of qualifications and stuff,' he said.

I found myself blinking and making a weird face.

'Huh? Why have you assumed that I have 'all sorts of qualifications'? I haven't told you anything about myself.'

'No, but you can do all sorts of stuff,' he said. 'You must have qualifications to be able to do that stuff you do. And besides, I can tell by the way you talk and all.'

'I am sure you can do all sorts of stuff, too,' I said.

'Naw, I can't do stuff,' he said.

'I bet you can. Tell me about something you love to do.' I said.

'Something I love to do?' Pete thought for a moment. Then his eyes lit up. 'I love to make my daughter laugh,' he said.

'Great. Tell me about it,' I said.

Pete smiled at me a bit shyly; his voice and whole body language softened.

'Well...' he began, 'the other day, my daughter—she's six—I was talking to her on the phone and she was cryin' about somethin' that happened in school that day.'

'Yes?' I prompted.

'Well,' Pete continued, 'I wanted to get her to stop cryin'. So I started sayin' stuff that made her laugh and all.'

'And?'

'And?' Pete thought for a moment. 'And, well...and then she stopped cryin' is what happened.'

'So what you're saying is that you're really good at making your daughter laugh,' I said.

'Yeah,' he said. 'Yeah, I guess I am really good at that,' Pete said, grinning from ear to ear. The broad toothless gaps in his smile now made him look quite sweet and innocent.

'And what you are also really good at, is knowing how to make your daughter stop feeling sad,' I said.

Pete thought for a second. 'Well, I hadn't really looked at it that way before, but yeah, I guess that's true too. I mean, I started telling her how good she was, how nice she was, how pretty she was—and smart too. She's real smart. I told her all that. Then she started feelin' real good and she sorta forgot all about bein' sad and all.'

'So what you are really good at, is being able to feel when someone is sad, and knowing how to make them feel better,' I said.

Pete looked at me, but didn't say anything.

'And,' I continued, 'what you are also really good at is being kind to people, and in giving them support without even being asked,' I said to him.

'Well, maybe I am...' he said slowly. 'But I don't think my daughter's mother would agree with that!' He laughed sardonically.

Pete looked down at the ground, as if embarrassed, and said, 'And then there was this woman at work one time. I don't think she would agree with that either.'

Pete then told me about an incident that happened at his last job where something he had said to a female co-worker had been deemed inappropriate. He told me how she had issued a complaint that ended up getting him fired on the grounds of sexual harassment. He told me sincerely that in his heart he really hadn't meant it the way she had taken it. But even though he felt he wasn't really at fault, and that the woman had misunderstood his intentions, he quite honestly admitted that perhaps it was all his own mistake in judgement, and that he should never have said what he did.

He told me about how difficult it was for him to say this to me, and how ashamed he felt. He could not look me in the eyes. It was obvious he was holding himself prisoner within his own feelings of guilt.

I told him how brave he was to tell all this to me, a total stranger in the park.

'Anyway, that's what got me where I am right now,' Pete said, looking out across the river. 'Because of my mistake, I lost my job. And I ain't been able to pull myself together ever since. So now I'm just stuck in a rut, with nothin' to do. And I just can't think of what there is I could do. I ain't good at nothin'. Nothin' at all.'

'But we just saw that you are good at lots of stuff. You are good at making people feel good,' I said.

'But that ain't nothin',' he said. 'That's just the same as everybody else.'

'I don't agree,' I countered. 'Have I made you feel better today?'

'Yeah, sure you have,' Pete said.

'And how many other people in the park have done that for you today?' I asked.

'Nobody,' Pete said.

'So there you go,' I said. 'Making people feel better isn't something everyone else can do. Or if they know how to do it, they don't always bother to do it. But you're the kind of person who, when someone needs some cheering up, you just go ahead and cheer them up. You don't even need to be asked. Isn't that true?'

Pete thought for a moment.

'Yeah,' he said, thoughtfully. 'Yeah, actually, that is true.' He sat up straighter on the park bench, his eyebrows furrowed as if trying to process a new idea.

'So, what kinds of interesting things could you do where you make people feel better?' I asked him. 'I mean, it has to be something you don't do every day, and something you don't think is boring.'

'Hmm...' Pete thought. Then he shot me a mischievous glance.

'Well, I could go out for a drink with you,' he said.

'Yeah, nice try,' I said. 'And what if I don't want to go? Then you're back to square one. Try to think of something else.'

'Ok, well, it was worth a shot,' he said. 'Hmm...what could I do? Oh, I just don't know,' Pete sighed, shrinking back on his bench.

Then, he brightened back up a bit and sat upright again.

'Well,' he continued, 'there was this one time, a long time ago, when I volunteered for a charity. I helped people and it made them feel better. It was only for a single day, but it was sorta nice. I guess I could go see if there was somethin' else I could do at a charity somewhere.'

'Well, there you go,' I said. 'That's something different.'

'Yeah, that's definitely somethin' different,' he agreed.

'And you found it interesting?' I asked.

'Oh yeah,' he said enthusiastically. 'I really enjoyed it.'

'So volunteering is something different you might find interesting, where you could use your talent for making people feel better. That's one thing you could choose to do if you wanted. What else can you think of?'

Pete thought again. This time it was obvious his imagination was getting fired up.

'Well,' he said with animation, 'sometimes when I ride my bicycle, I pass by this museum that has all this local history stuff inside. I keep thinkin' it would be really interesting to stop in and have a look some time.'

'Hey, now that's a lot different from watching daytime TV,' I said. 'You could certainly choose to do that tomorrow if you wanted.'

'Yeah, I could, couldn't I?' he said.

But then Pete suddenly sat back with a scowl.

'But all that stuff's nothin',' he complained. 'It's not *really* somethin', is it? I mean, it's not like a job or somethin'. It's just stuff. Not *real* stuff.'

'Pete,' I said, 'you said you are tired of living like a robot. You said you are bored. You said the big problem for you right now is that things are the same day in and day out. Right now you just thought of two things you *could* do tomorrow morning that would be different. You said you would find them interesting. You might even be able to use your talents.

'So, what if you woke up tomorrow morning and decided you had something special to do, and you did just one of these things, even for a little while? What would your life feel like?'

'Yeah, it would be different. Not like a robot anymore, but...' Pete trailed off for a moment, and then countered, 'But then what? After I do those two things, what's next? Then, I'm right back to the same old rut.'

'How do you know that?' I countered back, seeing in my mind's eye all the seemingly random coincidences that had occurred over the past two years, which had changed my life and had ultimately brought me to meet a man named Pete while walking along the river one day. 'How do you know that in one of these places something even more interesting won't pop up? How do you know you won't meet someone who can lead you to something completely new? How do you know you won't find your next step right there in one of those places? Maybe you'll find a lead for a job there. Maybe you'll bump into a stranger who could help you. Maybe you'll make a new friend there. Maybe you'll learn something that will take you in a direction you had never imagined. The possibilities are endless. You simply don't know what will happen if you make a choice today to try something new.'

Pete squinted his eyes as he mulled over my words, and pictured the possibilities for himself.

'Yeah. Yeah, that's right,' he said with conviction. 'How do I know that won't happen? Lotsa things could happen.'

As he said this, I felt myself unconsciously exhaling a deep breath, and I felt as though the island of debris upon the river had broken into tiny little pieces, and the gurgling waters were again flowing freely without hindrance.

I looked at Pete and began to speak more softly, looking directly at him.

'Pete, I said, 'all you have to do is to choose one thing to make your life different. Choose one thing, and something else will happen, it is guaranteed. It may be a very small thing, but that small thing can turn into another small thing, and another again. And before you know it, after all the small things have happened, one day you realise that things are really different.

'And today,' I concluded, 'that one small thing you did was to choose to ride your bike to the river, sit on this bench, and talk in friendship with a stranger, who happens to believe your life is important.'

Now Pete also exhaled. With a hopeful look on his face, he watched the river in silence for a few moments.

Then, more softly, I added a postscript.

'You say you want to stop living life as a robot. So I've got a challenge for you, Pete,' I said.

Pete looked at me. 'Go on then,' he said, smiling warmly.

'I want you to think of one thing—just one small thing every day this week that is different from what you did the day before. It doesn't matter how small it is. It can be as simple as riding your bike to a new part of town. All you have to do is ask yourself, *What can I do today that is something different?*'

'You mean, all I gotta do is think of somethin' to do?' he asked. 'Somethin' different? That's all?'

'Yup,' I said. 'But here's the catch—you think of it and then, you've gotta *do* it, whatever it is.'

'Ok,' he said. 'I get it.'

'And you know what,' I continued, 'when you have done one thing every day for a week, send me a text. You'll find the number on my business card. Then, I'll meet you in town at a pub of your choice and you can buy me a drink while you tell me all about your adventures.'

'Really?' he asked. 'You'd do that?'

'Sure,' I said. 'But I'm serious here. This isn't a date and I'm not going to meet you if you haven't done anything. I'll only meet up with you to celebrate that you found something to do every day this week. Is that a deal?'

'Yeah!' he said. 'Sure, it's a deal.'

We shook hands on it and I finally went on my way, leaving Pete smiling, still sitting on the bench along the river. I wondered what would happen next.

About two hours later, I received a text from Pete. He wrote, 'Hiya Lynn. Still can't think of nothin. What r u doin 2nite? How about a drink?'

I sighed. I didn't reply to him. This was not the deal we had made.

He did not contact me again.

I have walked along the Embankment of the River Great Ouse many times in the months since that morning in May. Never did I see Pete sitting there again. Once or twice I wondered whether I should text him to find out what had happened, but then I decided against it. It was a single moment in time, where two people came into each other's lives, and left just as quickly—like the raft of leaves that floated upon the river after the summer rains; like the words of the graffiti that had now been scrubbed away on the old bridge.

And just like the message on the bridge, I could not help but reflect to what degree the confluence of our chance meeting had set each of us on a slightly different course in life thereafter. We had each become yet another thread woven permanently into the tapestry of one another's lives. We had each become that singular recognisable face in the throngs of people travelling up and down the escalator, where we shout, 'I'll call you!' and disappear out of sight.

*   *   *   *   *

I hadn't realised until I arrived at the river that it was Remembrance Sunday.

It was a very cold November morning. I sat drinking a cappuccino at a riverside bistro, as I watched streams of families in their Sunday best parading up and down the Embankment. Many old men were dressed in military uniforms replete with war medals. Some of them walked in small groups together, while others walked with their ladies in tow, all flamboyantly decked out with those inimitably British hats (that look to me more like birds' nests) that middle-class ladies wear on such occasions. A pair of kilted bagpipers also walked down the street, and it occurred to me I had probably missed some sort of commemorative service. I left the bistro to stroll along the riverbank, and saw rows of poppy wreaths gathered upon the War Memorial in the centre of the Embankment gardens. Grandparents, parents and children were out, simply for the opportunity to spend time together on a Sunday. Up and down the river, on the north bank and the south, generations of Bedfordians were out walking along the River Great Ouse on this bright, and very cold, November morning.

As I walked along the Embankment, I watched the chestnut trees as they delicately dropped their long, russet-coloured, spear-shaped leaves onto the ground, to rest alongside the crispy, flake-like leaves that had already fallen from the maples, creating a soft carpet that rustled and crackled as I scuffed along through it. Like a child, I found it impossible to resist the urge to kick them all about as I walked, just to hear the music they made, to smell the dampness from the earth, and to watch the bright white sunlight catch their earthy colours as they scattered around my toes.

How easily trees live with the passage of time, I thought. *They are the great Time Lords, the grandfathers, the elders, the gurus of time. They understand the rhythmic dance of the seasons. And when it is the season for letting go, they simply allow their leaves to fall, unattached to them, elegantly baring themselves to the elements with serenity and grace.*

And I thought of all I had let go of over the past few years.

I sauntered slowly in the direction of the town centre, and got the urge to visit Castle Mound, as I hadn't been there for over a year. This is the site of the once-formidable Bedford Castle, where an apparently very long and gruesome battle ended with the castle's destruction in the 13th century. Today, there is nothing left of the original castle except for a very tiny and insignificant-looking patch of grey bricks. I went up to the top of the mound and read the historical placards that had been set into the earth there, and suddenly found it very ironic that on this day, Remembrance Sunday, when everyone was busy remembering the veterans of various wars of the 20th century, all of which had been fought in distant territories, I saw not a single person here on Castle Mound, at the very scene of an actual battle that had taken place in Bedford town.

From atop the mound, I watched dozens of people walking below, all adorned with bright red poppies on their lapels signifying their remembrance of veterans of various wars. I reflected upon how both my grandfather and father were veterans of World War I and II, respectively, and how this day was as much for them as anyone else. I thought about how, although they left this world long ago, I could still remember them both quite well. I thought about how my daughter had never met my grandfather, and how my grandson will never meet either of them. I thought about how the passage of time blurs our memory and how people eventually forget those who came before. The mound upon which I stood was itself the site of a lengthy and grizzly medieval battle, where the blood of hundreds of English men, women and children had once, no doubt, soaked the very soil that lay beneath my feet. But in spite of being Remembrance Sunday, not a living soul had thought to come to remember those who lost their lives on this spot some 800 years earlier. But it is not surprising. No one alive can remember anyone who died here centuries ago.

Time passes. Many of us lose sight of our connection with the past. We cannot see how the past travels along with us, and how our lives are continually being shaped by it, whether consciously or not. But life is a delicate dance in which we are continuously adapting to the passage of time, each of us flowing graciously from one generation to the next. Like the river, our route is constantly shifting. Like the tree, there is a time when the seasons come and go. And, just like the trees who allow their leaves to fall in harmony with the seasons, simply by letting go of what once was, each of us allows the next in line to flourish and to grow.

As I stood atop this ancient battleground, I realised my unique vantage point at that moment. I was in my fifties, and could see life both backwards and forwards from this place in time and space. I could see two generations behind me and two ahead of me with equal clarity, like two ends of the same endless river. I could see my mother's face in my face, and my father's face in my daughter's. Time stretched equally in all directions. How many other faces, both past and future, could I see within my own? There was no way of estimating. I felt as though I could hold it all within my arms. There was not a moment I could not feel, could not contain, or could not breathe. Within that moment, I felt every moment. I could feel the energy of thousands of years of people who had, at one point in time or another, looked down upon the River Great Ouse from this tiny plot of earth. So too, I could feel the heartbeat of all who were yet to come, long after I left this Earth, this singular point in time and space.

Time is merely a reflection within a mirror that we choose to turn either this way or that.

As I looked down the winding path of the River Great Ouse I could see the old Suspension Bridge where, just a year earlier, I had read some poorly scribbled words that had changed my life forever. For in planting within me those enigmatic words, 'I AM', a person I will never know provoked me, mocked me and challenged me to change my life, until I finally let go of the past, so I could step into the timelessness of that person I had always been, but had never turned around to see. And within that timelessness came also the expansiveness of knowing there were no real barriers between myself and anyone around me, and that to say 'I AM' is no different from saying, 'THAT THOU ART.'

I had arrived. I was home. I was me. And life was filling me for the very first time.

*   *   *   *   *

It is like a river of humanity, and I am swept up by its current.

It is nearly 7 PM on a Sunday evening. I am travelling on the Circle Line from London Paddington to St Pancras International after returning from a short holiday in Devon. There are thousands of people in the London Underground and I am lucky to get a seat. Obsessively, like so many thousands of other passengers travelling with me on this journey, I scan the crowd trying to find a face I recognise.

'Today will surely be different,' I think to myself. 'Today is the day I will bump into someone I know.'

I look about me and notice men, women, children and infants.

I see black skin, white skin, brown skin and all shades in between.

I see young and old, heterosexuals and homosexuals, conservatives and liberals.

I hear northern accents, southern accents, Jamaican accents, American and Canadian accents.

I hear English, French, Polish, Russian, Spanish, Chinese, Hindi, Arabic and African languages I cannot identify.

I see loud people, quiet people, happy people, tired people, angry people, drunken people, nervous people and laughing people.

I see lots and lots of people.

With curiosity I see them all—their eyes, their hands, their smiles, their clothes, their jewellery, their hair.

And as I see them, I wonder—

'What is this one thinking?

'What is that one feeling?

'What is the joy this one has seen?

'What is the sorrow that one has known?

'What is the delight?

'What is the wonder?

'What is the secret?

'What is the desire?

'Who has this person loved?

'Who has loved this person?'

Like a gushing river, the train rushes through the channel of the London Underground. As I sit, I am aware that we are all on the same journey together.

And I realise that, today, I finally do know everyone on this train.

*   *   *   *   *

We travel on this river we call Time
  like leaves adrift within its flow
We dip and swirl through every rill

—our journey through eternity

We touch
    we feel
        we understand
            we move onwards

Unsure of what we wish to find
    but that we must, our hearts do know
We leave so others may become
    —and so they too may come to be.

Ever flowing
    ever growing
        ever changeless
            ever onwards to the sea

We see ahead, we see behind
    a light within us starts to glow
A wisdom borne of seeing All
    —and knowing we are ever we

Nothing is ever nothing
    In anything is everything
You change me forever in all you do
    In all I am, you are there too

*   *   *   *   *

Revisiting the Lily

That night, I think I slept more deeply that I had ever slept before.

But it was a most unusual sleep, for throughout the night, I walked continuously through an endless flow of dreams. Or perhaps they were not dreams? I cannot really say for sure.

I lay upon my bed. The window opened and the net curtains flapped in the chilly night wind. I felt myself rise from my bed and stand in the centre of the room, dressed only in a thin white cotton nightgown that reached nearly to the floor. All at once, the walls dissolved and I found myself standing upon a vast expanse of tiny diamonds, covering the earth like snow. I could not resist playing with them with my bare feet. They tickled my soles, feeling even softer than the white sands of the beaches of the Caribbean. I looked down at my toes and noticed how the facets of these diamonds sparkled and glistened in a dance of limitless colour—

> *violet, plum, peach and lemon*
> > *sunshine yellow and sky blue*
> *fuchsia, turquoise, amber, coral*
> > *silver, copper and chartreuse*
> *indigo, burgundy, aubergine*
> > *apple red and tangerine*
> *butterscotch and aquamarine*
> > *emerald, moss and bottle green*
> *bright white, crystal-white, pearl-white, moon-white*
> > *all of them dancing in the night.*

Then these diamonds started to vibrate. They began to move in circular and triangular patterns. Soon they were swirling all around my feet. They became a kaleidoscope around me, shifting continuously. Beautiful patterns assembled, one after the other, as I watched an intricate interplay of shapes and colours formed by the dance of the tiny crystals. Each time I saw a pattern, I became mesmerised by it, and found myself enthralled by its beauty. But no sooner than I saw the pattern, it immediately dissolved to form yet a new one.

'No, wait!' I cried out. 'Can't you stop just for a moment? That one was so beautiful! I don't want it to disappear! Bring it back! Please?'

But the crystals kept on moving. Again and again I saw new shapes, new sizes and new hues take form and disappear, always to reveal yet another shape, another size, another hue.

At first, I felt a sense of loss each time one of my favourites left my vision. But then, I found myself becoming curious. As the moments progressed, I became more and more excited to find out what unknown pattern would be next, and next after that. Soon I began to delight in all the patterns that appeared, without preference for one or the other.

But then, something even more remarkable happened.

My vision softened completely. The lines around the patterns softened. The boundaries between the moments softened.

Soon, within a single moment...
within a moment...
within a moment...
I stopped seeing the patterns altogether.

I saw only the beingness of continuous unfolding. Everything was one continuous flow, one continuous stream that was constantly changing, but that was nevertheless always the same.

'How remarkable! There *are* no patterns.' I mused aloud.

'Good evening,' she said simply.

I looked up from my toes and saw the Lily standing before me in the centre of my Garden, just as she had been on the night we first met. But that night her appearance was unlike anything she had shown me in the past. Her form had transfigured into a stellar pattern. Her petals stretched outwards in all directions, emanating a radiance that shone like the moonlight. The beams of that radiance hit the walls, and then reflected and folded back upon themselves, forming an intricate mandala all around the Lily, as she stood upright in the exact centre of all that was. Soon, the beams of light wove about, into increasingly complex designs, until the entire courtyard became one massive mandala, etched upon the diamond sands beneath my feet.

It was dazzling.

I started to hear the tones of a gentle mantra rising melodiously, as the crystal sands began to chant aloud...

'Give-Receive-Become-Be...'

Such a stunning flower, this Lily, I thought to myself. *She is the blissful and ever-present centre that holds within its soft embrace the turbulent seas of change.*

'You look just like the Moon,' the Lily said with great affection. 'You are dressed entirely in white. Your face is luminous and your eyes are bright. Please, come sit with me tonight.'

Somehow, within my dream, I took my seat in such a way that the Lily and I were both sitting exactly upon that same spot in the centre of the Garden. It was as if logic no longer ruled the universe, and we no longer needed to consider the boundaries of time and space. We could be in the same space together.

Enveloped by her silky stillness, I heard her ask me, 'Tell me, my old friend, what brings you here tonight?'

I told her about the message on the bridge. I told her about the 'I AM'. I told her about the floating island, and about the ducks, the geese and the swans. I told her all about the people I had met, and the places and things I had seen. And, of course, I told her about the river.

Then the Lily spoke lovingly.

'Most compassionate and peaceful friend! Oh Soul of my Soul! These are wonderful stories, and I am so curious to understand more deeply from them. So, please tell me—what have you learned about the Principle of Being?'

I gazed into her centre, which was now also my own centre, so as to feel the Principle enter me.

Finally the learning became clear.

'I have learned about attachment and non-attachment,' I said.

The Lily smiled. 'I can see this wisdom clearly in your face,' she observed. 'What can you tell me about attachment and non-attachment?'

'Quite simply this,' I replied, 'attachment is what prevents us from seeing the Truth. It is only through non-attachment that we can know anything as it truly is.'

'This sounds interesting. Explain more,' she requested.

I took a moment to dive into the ocean of understanding that appeared now before me, and allowed the satisfaction of the Truth I found within those waters to flood my body, heart and mind.

Then, the words simply flowed from my lips.

'For years and years, I sought Truth. I told myself that if I could find Truth, it would bring beauty and meaning and purpose to my life. And during my quest, I always told myself, *If Truth is true, it must be true at all times, in all places.* I told myself that Truth could not be complex or something only the intelligent could understand. I told myself Truth could not be the property of a select group of people. Truth had to be something that was always there, always available, always knowable. But the irony was, I relentlessly kept seeking Truth in different places, people and ideas that continuously came and went throughout my life. So of course, nothing would ever pass the litmus test of my guiding belief. I kept telling myself, *No, not this, not that.* Nothing I found was true at all times in all places. It was only true some of the time, in some places. I only ever found relative truth, relative beauty, relative meaning and relative purpose in my life. Something was always missing. The more I learned, the less I knew.'

'And now?' she asked.

'And now, I have found that it was my attachment that was getting in the way of my finding that Truth, that beauty, that meaning and that purpose.'

'Tell me more,' the Lily prompted.

'Ok, I'll try to put it into words,' I said. And I took a moment to think of how to explain what I had come to understand intuitively.

'Well, it's like this. Just a few moments ago, when I looked at the kaleidoscope made by those tiny diamonds, I was at first completely bedazzled by the beautiful patterns. But the patterns were ever-changing, ever-moving, ever-transforming. Soon, I realised there actually were no patterns because there was not a moment where they stayed the same. The pattern was only an idea I had locked into my mind's eye. Once I had locked it, I didn't want it to change. But in truth, the pattern never really existed. Or if it did exist, it was for no more than a fleeting moment. The more I think about it, the less I can define it. I cannot even measure the fraction of the second of a second in which the pattern existed.

'But when I let go of the need to hold on to the idea of a pattern, the true beauty of what I saw was in the continuous melding and twisting and newness I saw at every moment. Once I released the need to see the patterns, I could see the wholeness of what was actually there. I could understand it. I could appreciate it and be in awe of it. There was no end to it, no beginning. It was limitless. It was only my attachment to the form that had made it appear to be limited.

'And that is also exactly what I learned along the river,' I said. 'The river itself was ever-changing. The seasons were ever-changing. People and things came into my life and out of my life. People and things came in and out of the river's life. There is no now or then, or here or there. There is no this or that. Reality is both everything and nothing, all at once, depending on how you choose to look at it. The river is always changing, yet always the same river.

'I stood upon that bridge and saw my own life. I saw I was all that I had ever been, and still that I was none of it. I was both the totality of all I had ever known and experienced, and also something else that was always the same beyond all of this apparent change. This is Being. Being is that place where we are not measured against anything else. We simply are. So we are both everything and nothing, depending upon how we choose to see ourselves. And while so much of my life, I saw myself as nothing, I now have seen that all things are contained within everything else. I have seen that all moments are contained within every other moment. I have seen I can hold everything, feel everything, and see everything with equal attention within my heart. When we hold all things to be equal, there can be no such thing as better or worse, and there can be no judgements. And when we do not judge, we can maintain a state of equipoise in all situations. We take delight in all that comes our way. When we do not judge, we are unattached. It is only through non-attachment that we can see the whole picture, and not just the tiny picture we tell ourselves is best. This is how I learned that it is only through non-attachment that we can know anything as it truly is.'

The moon-white radiance of the Lily now increased in intensity, and I could hear the colours humming in all directions.

'I can indeed hear Truth resounding within your heart,' she said. 'I sense there is also a wonderful secret there, and I wish to know it. What can you tell me about the great *secret* you have discovered about the Principle of Being?'

The Lily was as one with me now, as the words flowed without effort.

'I have learned the secret of unconditional love!' I cried.

'How wonderful!' she exclaimed. 'Please tell me this secret.'

'Well, again, it all has to do with attachment and non-attachment. Most people seem to believe that by being attached to something you have greater connection. But actually it is just the opposite. When we are attached, we are less connected, and when we are detached, we become more connected. I learned this from watching the ducks on the river. At first they jumped aboard the floating island, looking for food. That is when they were attached. But then, they hopped off as it continued to flow downstream. Furthermore, if they had tried to keep the floating island for themselves, they would have had to expend a lot of energy fighting against the flow of the river. But by being detached from what was flowing in and out of their lives, they were able to stay connected to the life force of the river itself. They were able to maintain connection to their own essence.

'And this is also and especially true when the object of our attention is someone we believe we love. When we are attached to others, we might try to hold on to them, to keep them, to direct them, and to persuade them to follow the same course as we wish to go. But when we do this, we become disconnected from both their essence and our own. We cannot connect to another living being when what we love about them is merely what we wish them to be, and not what they really are. When we are disconnected from their essence, we cannot know them.

'We cannot love that which we do not know, and we cannot know that which we cannot see fully. When we learn how to see—fully see—our loved ones, the world, our own selves, without attachment, we finally learn to love. But love is not static. Like the river or the kaleidoscope, it is a place of limitless possibilities. Love is boundless. There can be no predicting what comes next. It brings uncertainty, which most people fear. Most people wish to control their futures, their relationships and the world around them. Uncertainty is like a monster to them. But to one who is unattached, uncertainty is the ultimate beauty because it means all things are equally possible and equally valuable. It is only through non-attachment that we can see this. When we are unattached, and we embrace the uncertainty as the ultimate beauty, we love everything equally because there is no trace of judgement or control within our hearts. And when there is no trace of judgement or control, we learn how to love all things, all beings, all times and all places— unconditionally.

'And this, dear Lily, is the point when everything became beautiful, meaningful and full of purpose in my life. This was the point that I knew I had been shown Truth. And Truth is unconditional love.

The Lily smiled at me approvingly. Our eyes held each other for a brief moment, and then I concluded with an afterthought.

'You know, long ago I used to believe non-attachment was a bitter tonic. But now, I realise non-attachment is the sweetest nectar. I feel happy all the time. And do you know why I feel happy all the time?' I asked her.

'Tell me!' she begged.

'It is because through non-attachment I have also ceased to judge myself, to limit myself or to force myself to become that which I was never meant to be. I have released my fears of being judged, and released my need to limit or control the boundaries of my own life, or to have to live up to some external measuring stick of achievement. And in doing so, I have come face to face with my own essence, my own Being. Through non-attachment I allow myself to flow along my natural path—the path of least resistance to the Self—the path I was meant to take, and the only path I could ever have taken.

'When I release myself from the bondage self-judgement, fear and my own attachments, and embrace the beauty and unlimitedness of the unknown, I step at once into the reality of my own Soul. I step into that great unfathomable 'I AM'. I step into my essence. All at once, I am connected to my Self. And in connecting to that Self, I am also connected to all around me. For essence is essence. There are no boundaries. I know without needing to know. I hear without the need for words. I see without the need for forms. And this, dear Lily, is the sweetest thing.'

Sitting in the centre of my Garden, I felt the rays of the Lily now emanating from my own body.

Then, I heard her voice, although she was not speaking, 'So, finally, dear friend, please tell me, what is the true *power* of the Principle of Being?'

The power? I asked myself. And I stopped for a moment to feel the power fill me.

'Why, the power of Being—is that it sets us free to *Become!*' I cried in great surprise.

'From the Daffodil I learned that judgements are the chains that had kept me stuck in one place for a very long time. Since then, I have set myself free from this bondage by letting go of judgement altogether. And now, through the Principle of Being, I am no longer holding on to an image of myself that is false or forced. It has set me free to Become that person who I truly am. When I simply embrace the Principle of Being, there are no 'things'. There is only everything and the eternal flow of that everything. And within that flow are unlimited permutations of possibilities where beauty is boundless, joy is boundless, abundance is boundless. The tiny things I had imagined myself to be were but a fragmented and minimised view of who I actually am—just snapshots of something that never had any reality on its own—just like the patterns of the kaleidoscope.

'Who we actually are, is endless—both changeless and ever-changing.

'Ultimately, the greatest power of the Principle of Being is not just in how it sets us free to Become our true selves. It is also how it sets us free to Become true *together*. It enables us to see that we are all the same as one another, whilst completely unique at the same time.

'Oh, dear Lily, 'Being' is the place where endless, wonderful paradoxes dance and rest and delight within each other. It is the confluence of both continuity and change, of both oneness and difference. It is our essence, our wealth, our beauty and our power. All of this is our Being.'

'*You change me forever, in all you do. In all I am, you are there too,*' sang the Lily.

And the sea of diamonds chanted it in response to her, their colours bending and twisting and waxing and waning and swelling and relaxing around the centre, until finally the waves quieted to a tranquil green ripple.

Then after some time, the Lily spoke again.

'I told you there was much you already knew!' she said simply. I leaned my head against her soft white petals, taking in her powder-like scent.

'So now,' she asked, 'what will you do next?'

I sat in the centre of the mandala and listened to the mantra that surrounded me. I took the essence of the Lily into me, and allowed my spirit to flow into hers. There was no distance, no difference between us. Whatever was not, simply dissolved. All that was there was the awareness of all that was.

To the east, I could see the gentle rosy hues of the coming daybreak as they peeked through the lattice of the rosewood trellis. Before I allowed the morning light to shake the slumber from my eyes, and to waken from this wondrous dream, I gave the Lily my most sincere promise.

'I will walk daily through the Garden of my own Soul.

'I will nurture it and tend to the weeds that spring up within its flowerbeds.

'I will learn more and more about the Principle of Being from the simple stories of my own life.

'And,' I concluded, 'I will tell all I meet about the Peace they will find when they do the same.'

* * * * *

Epilogue:
Meeting the Gardener

SONG OF THE GARDENER: HOW TO BE A MASTERPIECE

Use your brain
    as the instrument of your heart

Let it play
    the melodies that reside there

It is not the composer—
    only the strings

It is not the player—
    only the bow

You are the composer—
    your heart is the music

Listen to its music
    and compose the symphony
    that is You

So that others may hear it
    run your fingers along the strings of your mind
    tuned by the fine senses of your own imagination

Set them in motion
    with the bow of your actions

Let the strings vibrate
    the resonance swell

So all may delight
    in this music—

This music of the heart—
    This music that sings from within you

This music that IS
    You

But beware the vanity of the mind—
    and never let the fiddle
    believe himself to be the fiddler!

                   *   *   *   *   *

MEETING THE GARDENER

W inter is rapidly approaching. The pale yellow sun looks almost white against the clear blue sky.

I don my duffle coat and woolly muffler to make my way into the open air. The Earth, like any good mother, has begun to tuck in her little ones for the coming slumber, wrapping them up snugly with her soothing scent and warm, rich blanket of black soil, and I watch the squirrels as they run madly burying the acorns that the oak trees have dropped for them to gather. The last of the oak leaves are scattering into the four winds, like tiny little particles of life of the trees that bore them, and they sail upon the chilly updraft to destinations far beyond the trees' reckoning.

The flowers are gone—from my view, anyway. They are still somewhere out there. Somewhere else where the seasons are upside down from mine. Life never ceases. It only appears to come and go.

I find a peacefulness here in this Garden, which I have spent so long cultivating—a peace arising from the knowledge that, until this moment, I had long lived with the feeling that I was somewhere between here and there, but that in this place, in my Garden, I can dwell easily and effortlessly within the preciousness of Here and Now.

While strolling through the lanes and reflecting upon the seasons past, I heard a rustling amongst the fallen leaves. Believing it to be yet another squirrel burrowing through the earth in search of buried treasure, I did not pay it much heed at first. But then, I heard a voice coming from the rustle.

'My goodness, look at all these leaves!' said the voice. 'There must have been a lot of flowers here last season!'

I turned and saw a tiny little man, playing with a pile of russet-coloured leaves, tossing them into the air.

'Who are you?' I asked.

The little man stood up and brushed the leaves from his clothing. He wore a royal blue cloak, trimmed in crimson and gold. Upon his feet he wore a pair of satin brocade slippers embroidered with pictures of peacocks in multicoloured threads. He had an emerald-studded crown of gold upon his head. And most amazingly, he stood no more than a foot or so in height.

'I am the King of the East,' he said.

Knowing well who this King was, I bowed from the waist to show respect. *He may indeed be only one foot tall,* I thought, *but he is nevertheless a King.*

'Welcome to my Garden, Very Good King,' I said warmly.

'Ah! Yes, thank you for your welcome. But how do you know I am a 'very good king'?' he asked. 'You have only just met me.'

I told the King about the Four Flowers. I told him how they had all spoken to me about him—how they had first come to him homeless and ignorant of who they were or what they were; how he had given them direction and protection; how he had listened to their intuition and nurtured their growth; how he had helped them to find meaning and purpose; how they had flourished and become vibrant, sensuous, beautiful and full of joy.

I told him how highly the Flowers had praised his wisdom, and how he had been wise enough to command them to become what they truly were, and the only thing that was ever within their nature to be—Flowers, and only Flowers.

'And also, dear King,' I added, 'these Flowers did the same for me. Through them, I have found the path of least resistance to my Self. No longer do I battle against my own nature. In a word, these Flowers have taught me how to blossom.'

'Yes,' said the King, making a comfortable seat for himself atop a large mushroom beneath the oak tree, 'I have also learned this lesson of the path of least resistance from the Flowers. And I failed many times before I learned it fully!' He laughed heartily, at his own expense.

As the King was now seated, I took this as an invitation to sit as well. I made a seat for myself upon a carpet of crispy leaves, facing him. I settled in, sitting cross-legged, feeling eager to hear more.

'Please do go on,' I requested.

The King began his story. 'Well, I was not always a 'very good king'. A long time ago, when I first met the Flowers, I tried to turn them into something they were not. I thought only of my role as a King. I believed there were certain things a King should do and not do. But I didn't really understand what it meant to be a King. I thought a King must always be in charge of absolute right and wrong. I tried to force the Flowers to live by laws I believed were 'befitting' someone under my command. I could not see that I was killing these Flowers.

'It was only when I simply started listening to what they were saying to me, without needing to understand it, that I felt the wisdom of the Flowers. I learned how to listen to the music of their life force, the rhythm of their dance. Only then, when I learned how to hear these things, they began to flourish.

'But I also flourished with them. My heart became green and rich with the scent of the Earth. The raindrops not only fed the Flowers, they fed me as well. They washed my Soul with gentle kisses and I became ecstatic as I felt their tongues sliver over me. I laid myself bare for the Rains, and to receive their tears of joyful nourishment. I soaked them in and drank deeply from these life-giving drops of moisture. And as I drank them, I felt ever-increasingly full of Life.

'Soon, the waters spread to every corner of my Garden. The seedlings of the little Flowers, lying deep within the earth, tasted the waters and shouted in gleeful anticipation. Their shouts burst through the soil, making way for them to reach for the Sun. They took from me, their Gardener, that which I loved to give, that which has been laid bare, laid full, laid rich within the freshness, the moistness, the greenness of my own heart.

'And—they became Flowers.

'They became who they are. I didn't have to try to make them become Flowers. This happened naturally. All I had to do was till the soil of the Garden to let them become what they were meant to become.

'Yes, I am the Gardener of these Flowers. I have raised them. I have tended to their needs. I have cultivated and protected them. And lovingly, they have smiled at me. They have delighted my eyes and teased my nose.

'And perhaps my smiling eyes have delighted them as well.' And he sat and mused over this thought for a short moment.

'So, you see, these Flowers are indeed very generous. They are so full of love and compassion for me that they only told you about my wisdom, and did not tell you about the ignorance I have had to overcome. They did not tell you about all the years I lived in a barren land bereft of colour, scent and life. They only told you about my Garden—the beautiful and wondrous Garden of my Soul.'

The King cast his eyes downwards. For one fleeting moment, there was a look of sadness in his face, and he looked as if he might even cry. But instead, right before my eyes, I saw this sadness rapidly lift and turn into gratitude. The Iris had filled his heart in an instant, and his face bloomed with the Principle of Receiving.

The King looked up, his eyes brimming with an electric buzz I could feel even from where I sat.

'I am the wealthiest King in all the world,' he said, a tear in his eye. His face was now beaming with affection, and I could now feel the Rose also radiating from his heart. All the sadness was gone. The Iris and the Rose were blooming visibly within him.

And then, I saw his self-judgement wash away, as the Daffodil brightened his face with humour and delight as he said, 'I did the very best I could at the time. I was a different person then. And I have let go of all of that. I have no regrets. All of that was necessary to help me become the person I was always meant to be— the Very Good King.'

Then, a beautiful stillness came over him, as I saw the Lily fill his awareness with a brilliant white light.

'And now,' he said, 'I simply am who I am. And that, as it so happens... is... well... very good!' he slapped his knee and laughed out loud.

He was so jovial I could not help but laugh with him.

'What an amazing transformation!' I said to him. 'I find it wonderful to see you, to watch you, as the Flowers bloom upon your face. It is a beautiful sight.'

'Yes,' said the King. 'And they bloom upon your face as well. And that is also a beautiful sight.'

'Really?' I asked. 'I am afraid I am not very skilled yet at seeing the Flowers within myself. I can still sometimes lose touch with them.'

'So let me be your mirror, then,' said the King. 'I will show you the Flowers within you. I will reflect to you the Garden of your own Soul.'

I looked at him quizzically. I felt a bit nervous, but my curiosity was stronger than my resistance.

'Yes, let me see you,' he said, placing the thumbs of his miniature hands under my chin. 'That's right. I will see you. Then you can see yourself, too.'

The Very Good King leaned back on his mushroom throne and looked into my face. I could feel his deep, warm eyes looking directly into my heart. At first I felt uncomfortable, and could not bring myself to look directly at him, so I diverted my eyes every few seconds. I felt a lump form in my throat, my emotions very near to the surface. I noticed at first that I was not breathing, and that I felt a tenseness welling up within my chest. So I released the air from my lungs and let it flow naturally, until I was simply breathing in and breathing out. Finally, when all of the obstacles had been cleared away, I faced the King with open eyes, and open arms, allowing him to see directly into the core of me.

The King dove deeply into my essence, and spoke to me.

'Let me tell you the story I see within your eyes. The story begins with the Flowers themselves.

'As I watched the Flowers in my Garden grow, I learned they were extremely provocative. You might even call them promiscuous! They simply cannot help but flirt shamelessly with the honeybees, who would love to drink deeply from them. The honeybees would go mad for the Flowers and could not resist them. Intoxicated and dizzied from love and drink, the bees would hasten to make honey so they could drink this sweet liquor ever more and more.

'Next, the butterflies would hear the noisy buzz of the drunken honeybees, and fly upon the wind to reach my Garden. I would watch the blue and pink and yellow and polka-dotted creatures as they shouted excitedly at the sight of the Flowers and dived deep within them to sip their nectar. I could hear the sound of them licking their lips in delight. Very soon, they too would become inebriated and fall into a blissful slumber, and simply float by my window in a dreamlike state on gentle breezes.

'For years, I watched these drunken little flutter-bys carry the nectar of the Flowers into your Garden. The bees, mad for the dazzling colour of the butterflies, followed them like suitors. They played together. They played in the Garden of your creation. You felt them, but you didn't know who they were. The bees and the butterflies searched high and low for Flowers in your Garden—Flowers that had come from the Earth, been nourished by the Rains, and been embraced by the Sun and the gentle Breezes...

'But for a very long time, they saw no Flowers, and they sighed in disappointment—

Alas! Alas! No flow'rs today.
The Gardener is on holiday!
We honeybees will fly away
and try again some other day.

I cast my eyes downwards. For one fleeting moment, I felt the painfulness of regret well up in my throat. I felt as if I might start to fade into a dark shadow within myself.

But the Very Good King lifted my chin with his tiny thumbs and I again looked into the mirror of his kindly eyes. And within one single glance, all the shadows within me lifted and I saw only light.

'But now the bees are buzzing,' he continued. 'You can hear them. You can see them.

'And now, you can see within my eyes who you really are.

'You are the Rose—
    You are the music and the musician,
    the poetry and the poet,
    the rhythm and the drummer,
    the heartbeat and the heart.

'You are the Iris—
    You are the magic and the magician,
    the dream and the dreamer,
    the senses and the sensuous,
    the awestruck and the awe itself.

'You are the Daffodil—
    You are the creation and the creator,
    the discovery and the voyager,
    the joy and the joyful one,
    the inspiration and the inspired.

'You are the Lily—
    You are the wisdom and the wise one,
    the tranquillity and the peaceful one,
    the satisfaction and the fully satisfied,
    the serenity and the serene.

'You are the Flowers.
'You are the Garden.
'You—are the Gardener, my love.'

The gaze from the soft, grey eyes of the Very Good King now spread and spread around the Garden, until its greyness became a vast, unspoilt lake of silver waters, in which I could see my reflection with crystal clarity.

'And—I am also you, dear King!' I cried out in great surprise.

'There is no more need for a mirror,' I said with a calmness I had never known before.

I took his tiny hands in my own and said, 'Everything I need is already here—right in my own Garden.'

And in one irresistible act of total abandon and delicious surrender, I dove headlong into the silver-clear pool of my reflection and stepped into the person I always was, and was always meant to be.

*   *   *   *   *

The sun is low on the horizon now, and I am sitting on the veranda overlooking my Garden, which spreads as far as the eye can see. With a lightness of spirit no longer bound by the laws of gravity, I listen to the song of the Earth as it makes its way across the Galaxy. Within that music, I hear all that lives, breathes and desires.

I hear the worlds. I hear myself. I hear you, too.

I become Life itself.

Life is so simple, as to be nearly incomprehensible.

Life fills me, and fills me more and more.

And I become so full, that I have no choice but to share my Life with you.

*   *   *   *   *

Acknowledgments

M ost people envisage the writer's path as a lonely one, and that the magic that flows from the writer's pen (or laptop) comes from months of hard work in isolation. And while that is true in a certain sense, there is no act of creation that comes as a result of the efforts of a single human being. As so much of this book contains stories either about special people in my life, or inspired by people who have come and gone along the way, I must take a few moments to mention them, because without their presence in my life, this book would never have been written.

First and foremost I wish to thank all the personal friends, family members and mentors, both alive and deceased, and whether mentioned by name or not, who appear as the primary characters of this book. These people are Albert, Anthony, Chloe, Eric, Gurudeva, Henry, Karen-Marie, Jane, Manuel, Margaret, Marco, Patricia, Ralph, my amazingly talented daughter, Vrinda, and a man I met along the River Great Ouse whom I refer to as 'Pete'. Each of you has been an undeniable key player in the creation of my own 'hero's tale'.

Secondly, I wish to thank at least a few of the people who, simply through random conversations we have had, triggered the seed ideas for some of these stories and poems. These people are Dominic, Dorothy, Karen-Marie, John, Juliet, Mikhail, Seb, and several unknown graffiti artists in London, Bedford and Dorset. All of you have been the unknown source of my inspiration.

I also dearly wish to give extra special thanks to my book coach, Antony Parry, who expertly coached me to develop my creative process in moving from a 'lone writer' to a bona fide author, as well as to Susan Norton who most sensitively coached me through the process of fully embracing my own voice as I began this project. Without the help, guidance and belief I received from both of you, I doubt I would have had the courage and focus to take on this project and see it to its completion.

It is absolutely essential that I thank my wonderful Co-Active Leadership tribe 'The Badgers' (all 20 of you!), as well as our incredible mentors Patrick Ryan and Mary Butler. Each of you was a magical key that unlocked the door to that previously elusive fearlessness I needed to enable me to express myself fully and powerfully in the final draft. You are more than family to me and I know without a doubt this book would not have unfolded in the way I truly wanted without your love, support and encouragement.

Others have been vital to the artistic, financial and technical processes of the book. I wish to thank my dear friends Angela, Christine, Linda, Ranjana and Stephanie for allowing me to 'test drive' these stories by reading aloud to you for many months. I also extend my deepest gratitude to Alan, Derek, Fran, Gail, Lina, Patrick and Simon, as all of you did the extremely important work of being my beta readers for the final draft. My deepest gratitude goes also to Lina, Ranjana, Susan and Sushma, who, without being asked, offered to help with some of the financial needs for the creation of this project. Of course I simply must thank my artists Christine Brown and Kristina Berglund. Without your beautiful and inspired artwork, this book would be a completely different entity. Many thanks also go to Jessica Keet for faithfully preserving my voice in her sensitive and highly-skilled copy editing, to the folks at Arima Publishing for their care and professionalism, and to my fabulous Promotion Manager, Teresa Morrow, without whose dedication the launch of this book could never have happened.

And lastly, and most of all, I wish to thank the music, the composers, the river, the ducks, the geese, the swans, the mockingbird, the bumblebee, the locust, the crow, the fish, the flowers, and all the other entities on this planet who have taught the lessons revealed to me throughout my life, and especially during the writing of *The Garden of the Soul*. You are forever my beloved guides, and I owe all I know to your generosity and wisdom.

–LS

Notes

1. Page 152.: Bhagavad Gita, chapter 10, verse 8.

2. Page 181. Brown, Frederic, 1955. Poem "*Imagine*". Appearing in *The Best of Frederic Brown,* edited by Robert Bloch, Nelson Doubleday, Garden City, New York, 1976.

3. Page 286. Alluding to New Testament, I Corinthians 13:12. "For now we see as through a glass darkly; but then face to face: now I know in part; but then shall I know even as also I am known."

4. Page 299. *Ibid.*

5. Page 325. Tennyson, Alfred Lord. Ca. 1834. Poem "Ulysses". Verse 3, line 1.

About Author Lynn Serafinn

Born in Brooklyn, New York in 1955, and now residing in the United Kingdom, author Lynn Serafinn is a Personal Transformation Coach, teacher, motivational speaker and talk radio show host. Owing to her long and diverse professional history in the music industry—from symphony violinist, to opera singer, to east-west fusion artist, to a number-1 electronic dance artist in the 90s—Lynn's writing is lyrical, rhythmic, colourful, highly visual and undeniably metaphoric. She was the ghost writer and editor on several published books on Vedic spirituality and philosophy, and is the author of the eBook *The Path of Least Resistance to the Self*. **The Garden of the Soul** is her first full-length book.

Lynn was educated at New England Conservatory of Music, University of Texas at Austin and University of Phoenix, and holds a B.Mus. in music history and an MAED in adult education and distance learning. Awarded the National Defence Foreign Language Fellowship in 1980-81, Lynn journeyed to Calcutta where she began her long-term study of Indian music and religion. A fully qualified teacher, she taught music and music technology for many years, and was the recipient of the Microsoft UK Innovative Teacher of the Year Award in 2005. She holds a CPCC through the Coaches Training Institute and is a graduate of the Co-Active Leadership Programme. Now living on her own in Bedford, England, Lynn is the Founder/Leader of the Global Wellness Circle, a thriving community-based holistic education project spread throughout the United Kingdom. She has a grown daughter, who is also a writer, and a young grandson.

Book Blogsite: www.give-receive-become-be.com
Social Network: http://gardenofthesoul.ning.com
Talk Radio: www.blogtalkradio.com/Lynn-Serafinn
Create-a-Life Coaching: www.create-a-life.co.uk
Global Wellness Circle: www.global-wellness-circle.com

Printed in the United Kingdom by
Lightning Source UK Ltd., Milton Keynes
138217UK00001B/32/P